GETTING YOUR WAY

GETTING YOUR WAY

STRATEGIC DILEMMAS IN THE REAL WORLD

JAMES M. JASPER

The University of Chicago Press
Chicago and London

JAMES M. JASPER is the editor of *Contexts* magazine.

The University of Chicago Press, Chicago 60637
The University of Chicago Press, Ltd., London
© 2006 by The University of Chicago
All rights reserved. Published 2006
Printed in the United States of America

15 14 13 12 11 10 09 08 07 06   1 2 3 4 5

ISBN-13: 978-0-226-39475-6 (cloth)
ISBN-10: 0-226-39475-1 (cloth)

Library of Congress Cataloging-in-Publication Data

Jasper, James M., 1957–
    Getting your way : strategic dilemmas in the real world / James M. Jasper.
        p. cm.
    Includes bibliographical references and index.
    ISBN 0-226-39475-1 (cloth : alk. paper)
    1. Social interaction.   2. Strategy (Philosophy).   3. Motivation (Psychology).
4. Problem solving.   5. Persuasion (Psychology).   6. Choice (Psychology)   7. Life
skills.   I. Title.

HM1111.J37 2006
303.3'42—dc22

                                                                    2005034148

For Ed Amenta and Jeff Goodwin

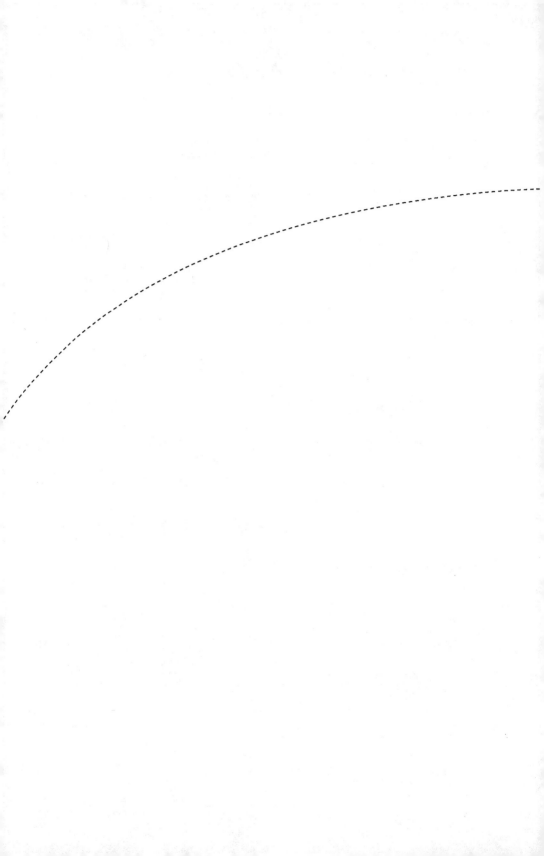

CONTENTS

DILEMMAS

PREFACE

Strategic action is anything but the careful calculations of game theory. It is moved as much by love and hate, anger and indignation, inspiration and tradition as by costs and benefits. It is embedded in culture and institutions. It is a social pursuit, not a mathematical calculation. It is fun, nerve-wracking, and exhausting.

The social sciences have mostly turned this exciting area of human life over to game theorists, whose elaborate equations have made strategy almost synonymous with game theory. And after decades of elaboration, game theory's mathematical power is unassailable. But does it tell us what we really want to know? Game theorists have had to make so many simplifying assumptions—about goals, choices, players, and arenas—that we really cannot recognize the humans who are supposed to be at the core of their models. Game theory is no longer a *social* science at all.

My goal is to craft some theory about strategy from the ground up, starting with my own empirical research and familiarity with how humans act in the real world rather than in journal articles and laboratory experiments. I have studied states and policymaking, moral protest and social movements, immigration and the effects of geographic mobility, the ways in which humans think about nature and other species, and our nostalgic uses of the past as a means for criticizing the present. In all these cases I have paid attention to how individuals feel and think about the world around them. I care about people's "subjective" point of view. To me, the human mind is relevant to social science. This subjective emphasis is one of the things I hope is distinctive about *Getting Your Way: Strategic Dilemmas in the Real World.*

Sociologists and anthropologists, alas, pay so much attention to cultural and institutional contexts that strategic action within them disappears. They have preferred to study the realm of "communicative" action, in which people are trying to understand one another, agree on a definition of the situation, and coordinate what they are doing. The "meaning" of an action, for most sociologists, lies in this shared social world, not in the minds of individuals. In traditions as diverse as ethnomethodology, symbolic interactionism, and Habermas's communication theory, reality has been seen as social, existing in interactions among people, in their communication, in their shared beliefs and feelings. This is true not only of what used to be called "consensus theory," but also of the tradition once known as "conflict theory," which emphasized that groups' mutual awareness of each other was crucial to each one's sense of identity. For all these schools, the social "situation" defines people's actions and intentions. In contrast, I examine actions involving people who do not necessarily share goals or even a common understanding of what they are doing and why. In many cases, one person is trying to do something different from what those around her think she is doing, and her success may require keeping them in the dark. Lies, secrets, and manipulation are regular parts of social action.

If sociologists and anthropologists assume communication in social life, game theorists—primarily economists and political scientists—take its presence or absence as one of their primary variables. This has allowed them to monopolize the study of strategic interaction. But they don't do justice to the game metaphor, for they ignore the thrills of the sport, its open-ended quality, the many skills involved, the many tactical choices open to a player. Theirs are games played by computers, *which are hardly games at all.* Game theorists can brilliantly sum up certain kinds of situations, and I have learned a lot about strategy from them. But students of strategy have largely ignored, and so can learn from, the messier human disciplines of sociology, history, and anthropology. They can learn especially about the cultural and institutional contexts of strategy, the rhetorical and emotional work involved, the crucial identities and alliances, the creativity and learning, and the complex goals and motives that drive action in the first place. It is time at last to examine the *social* aspects of strategic action.

My research on social movements showed me just how little social scientists have to say about strategy. Over the years many protestors have asked me what they might read to help them make better decisions. I had nothing to suggest, beyond Saul Alinsky. We knew about the political effects of strategic choices, especially effects on the state's reaction, which most scholars assumed to be the key issue. This was the most structural way of look-ing at strategy. We knew almost nothing, I discovered, about how activists (and others) make strategic decisions, much less how they might make good ones. This is not the how-to book those activists sought, but rather a soci-ology of strategy, looking at the underlying trade-offs that strategists face, trying to explain different choices and patterns, to understand how and why interactions unfold as they do. For it turns out that there are—and can be—no simple prescriptions. Strategic players face a number of dilemmas that cannot be easily resolved. That is why it is harder to predict strategic choices in advance than to explain them afterward. Strategic action is an art.

One idea lurking behind this book is *agency*, the term used by structural-ists when they reach the point where they throw up their hands and admit there is a lot their models cannot explain. They claim their job is to describe what is not agency, so it must be whatever is left over. They rarely try to look directly at it, as though they might turn to salt and blow away in the howling winds of intellectual history. It is time to describe the indescribable. As long as there are choices, there will be agency.

Sociologists especially are concerned with the hidden structures that shape our lives, and research into them has represented the forte of this dis-cipline since Marx, Weber, and Durkheim. For those with a taste for cogni-tive simplicity, this reduction is deeply satisfying. But once you have taken an introductory course or read some of the classics, it is obvious that po-litical, economic, and social structures do not explain everything. For those like me who have a taste for complexity, who revel in the world's details and surprises, sociology's structural emphasis is disappointing. It stops just when things get interesting. But how to talk about all the social life that's missing? All the choices, surprises, and creativity?

In earlier books (especially *Nuclear Politics* and *The Art of Moral Protest*) I tried to get at the open-ended aspects of social life through culture and biography. Culture offered meanings and feelings that humans could put together in new ways, changing themselves and their societies as a result. And biography—the ways in which individuals are idiosyncratic due to dif-ferent life experiences—also seemed to open a path for understanding so-cial change, as individuals bump up against each other and the structures around them, rejecting, changing, and reinterpreting them. In both dimen-sions, it was the clash of understandings, desires, and feelings that led to change and freedom, which necessarily took us beyond structures.

Culture and biography explain some of the open-ended freedom and in-determinacy of social life but not all of it, for they have a strong deterministic side as well: our culture and biography constrain us more often than they free us. They propel us, unconsciously most of the time, along predetermined paths. This is why understanding the life of a prime minister, say, helps us predict what she will do in a given circumstance. But we can never be certain of the choice she will make. By definition, agency cannot be predicted.

There are many moments in social life when we really cannot predict what someone will do, when people have genuine choices to make, often fateful ones. The many dilemmas with no single right answer, situations in which no social scientist could say, "This is the rational thing to do, and all other choices are errors," define the irreducible role of choice and agency. Much of this realm of freedom is covered by what I call strategy. For example, as long as you and your opponents have similar expectations about "normal" moves, or even the "best" moves, you have to break the rules to surprise them—at least sometimes. Doing the predictable thing is often a mistake. This means that "rational-actor" models like those of game theory can never be determinate, that strategic action must remain an art. I describe dozens of dilemmas that strategic players may encounter. For some players, the answer is obvious; for others, it is unconscious, but in many cases a conscious choice is made. (Even when the dilemma is not recognized as requiring a choice, it remains as a trade-off.)

Since this book developed out of my empirical work, I should probably thank everyone singled out in my earlier books. More specifically, though, conversations early on with Robert Zussman, Craig Calhoun, and especially Ian Roxborough generated useful ideas as well as encouragement for what I frequently feared was a mad project. Michèle Lamont, Frank Dobbin, Francesca Polletta, and Sarah Rosenfield refrained from scoffing at the idea. Nitsan Chorev, Chip Clarke, Carol Heimer, Ian Roxborough, and Chris Williams read and commented on early drafts. For comments on various chapters, I would also like to thank Samuel Bowles, George Brown, Edgar Kiser, and audiences at the American Sociological Association meetings, the University of Amsterdam, the University of Massachusetts at Amherst, Hitotsubashi University, the University of Jyväskylä, the University of Texas, New York University, the City University of New York Graduate Center, the University of California at Santa Barbara, the University of Georgia, and the Empty Cages Conference in Raleigh. I am running out of words to express my gratitude to several people who have become essential parts of my publication routine: the peerless Doug Mitchell, infallible copy editor Nick Murray, and indexer Martin White (one can rarely thank indexers, who work from page proofs, and who are at any rate woefully underappreciated). Because, as I march all too rapidly through middle age, I have come to appreciate the value of friends even more, I dedicate this volume to two men who have helped me formulate the ideas as well as to strategize in many different arenas, once colleagues and now good friends: Ed Amenta and Jeff Goodwin.

Royalties from this book go to the Global Fund for Women.

INTRODUCTION
THE POLITICS OF SOCIAL LIFE

We've all done it—every normal adult and any child who has had to deal with a playground bully. If you have courted a mate, sought a job, petitioned for divorce, planned a family reunion, complained to a boss, sat through a meeting, been to court, fought in a war, played one parent against the other, run for office, or engaged in any number of other normal activities, then you have thought and acted strategically. You have tried to get other people to do what you wanted them to. In doing this, you have puzzled over what was going on inside their heads, how they would respond, what they would feel about your actions. You have weighed different options and tried to anticipate their consequences. You have tried to pick the best means to attain your goals in the face of other people's goals. You have sought allies, worked to accumulate resources, managed the impressions you made on others, and tried to "win" against other people. Among other things, humans are strategic.

Scholars have examined strategic choice in diverse settings: formal organizations, markets, war and international relations, politics and protest, even interpersonal relations. Could there be common strategic challenges or principles across such different domains of human action? The answer, like that to all good social-scientific questions, is no and yes. There are no clear rules for what to do in any given situation, partly because the situations are impossible to specify completely. Even if there were rules, it is sometimes important to do the unexpected, to break the rules. Instead of precepts, we find dilemmas: two or more options, each with a long list of risks, costs, and potential benefits. Much of the time, there is simply no single right answer. On the positive side, the dilemmas we face may look similar across many institutional arenas. We engage strategically with others in certain fundamental ways, no matter what the setting.

Dilemmas mean that humans will always have choices to make and freedom to act. The modern middle class—which includes academics—is surprisingly uncomfortable with this fact. Our training and prestige are based on the idea that every challenge has a proper answer, that an algorithm exists for solving every puzzle. With enough scientific research, we can know the full truth. But what may work for quarks and amino acids does not work for human interaction. Social scientists have been misled into thinking they could eventually describe all the constraints on humans and develop a complete model of social life. In the end, they still encounter the choices we all make. To their dismay, social scientists must grapple with *human freedom*.

Game theorists have done the most to describe universal situations of strategic choice, producing a massive mathematical edifice meant to apply equally to individuals and organizations, footballers and nations. As any good approach to strategy must, game theory focuses on choices and actions, on preferences and outcomes. In most versions it emphasizes that my choice affects your outcomes, and vice versa, forcing us to take each other into account in making our decisions. It has generated numerous insights into common dilemmas, unintended outcomes, and unpleasant traps from which players have a hard time extricating themselves.

But game theorists' concern for mathematical elegance has led them to make unrealistic assumptions. Many of the resulting gaps could be filled by a descriptive language with more emphasis on culture and institutions: the contexts in which strategy unfolds. For instance, a strategic act may be a move in several different games at once, not in a single, easily defined game. Second, preferences are not easily ordered, even when the player is an individual (a *simple player*, I'll call her) but especially when it is a group, collectivity, or organization (a *compound player*, or team).[1] Compound players are almost never unified actors who agree on their goals. Third, we cannot always clearly distinguish means and ends, especially those related to the satisfactions of the play itself. In addition, few real-life games come to an end in a way that allows a final tally and set of payoffs. Most social life consists instead of ongoing streams of action, institutionalized, supported by cultural and psychological expectations. Most devastating for game theory, however, is the finding in experiments that people do not anticipate more than one or two moves ahead, meaning they cannot choose the "right" move by working back from the ultimate payoffs. It is important to anticipate the next moves of other players, but the complexity of strategic interaction makes it unrealistic to try to figure out what will happen any farther down the road.

These limitations suggest a different approach to strategy, one that emphasizes the complexity and importance of human choice more than the expected outcomes. With a little imagination, we can redescribe almost anything that happens in terms of payoffs, as game theory does. Sometimes this is extremely useful; at other times it misses most of what interests us. Even though game theory currently dominates social-scientific thinking about strategy, in the end it is not really a social science at all but a branch of mathematics, whose brightest future probably lies in evolutionary biology rather than human interaction.

Two images of humans have dominated the social sciences in recent decades. One is the autonomous individual of economics, a calculating decision maker whom rational-choice theorists claim to have discovered behind all human institutions. He is the character found in most game theory, who knows what he wants and searches for the means to get it. (Game theory's players need not be selfish or materialistic: sociologists' standard rejection of game theory on these grounds is misguided.) In stark contrast is the conformist favored by most sociological and anthropological traditions, hemmed in by culture, norms, discourse, and the constant negotiation she must undertake with those around her. She is the character of the *situation*, responding socially in order to construct a reality in collaboration with those around her. Far too many social scientists are either gamesters or situationalists, *explaining either our choices or why we have none.*

Ironically, both camps suffer from a distortion that makes human beings less complex and less interesting: they both tend to downplay emotions. The world of strategic interaction, with winners and losers, good and bad choices, friends and foes, appears to be an arena in which cognition alone might reign supreme, a world of pure calculation. Emotions could only interfere. But even here emotions are pervasive, and they do not always (or even usually) undermine rationality. They often contribute to it. They shape our goals, choices, alliances, and pleasures. Without emotions, we would have nothing to fight over. We wouldn't care enough to engage others. *Strategy is anything but the cold calculation of game theory.* It is full of hate and love, suspense and joy, disappointment and excitement, shame and pride.

I do not want to rehash old debates between gamester and situationalist. At various times, each vision has tried to colonize the study of politics, with a nearly total victory going to the economic model (in implicit as well as explicit forms) in recent decades. But life is rarely a game with outcomes or scores or an effort to conform to norms or fulfill values. I prefer a third image, a properly political image of humans that tries to borrow the strengths of each of the others. Here we find purposive humans who form groups, develop identities, engage in conflicts, construct goals, and pursue them. Such a character is neither the calculating robot of game theory nor the earnest conformist of the situationalists. Humans take others into account in an infinite number of ways, ranging from physical obstacles to overcome to romantic partners with whom we hope to erase all boundaries and physical limits. Groups are fundamental parts of the goals as well as the means by which they are chased. Instead of an economic or sociological theory of politics, I hope to suggest a *political theory of social and economic life*.[2]

In the political model, people strategize both as individuals and as groups—with group formation being a key strategy but also frequently a goal. And many of the strategic issues facing the two kinds of players are similar. The economic view either explains groups and organizations— although not very well—as the result of individual choices, or it misrepresents both individuals and groups by treating the two as formally equivalent. Situationalism can barely envision the individuals beneath the groups, making it difficult to see strategic choice at all. In the political image, dialogue and persuasion are front and center, allowing us to appreciate clashes between different points of view. Politics and culture allow us to connect the individual and the collective without eliminating either from view. We need to analyze simple and compound players together (not artificially separated as distinct "units of analysis") without collapsing one to the other.

※

Strategy comes from the Greek word for a commander, someone who thinks about the big picture as opposed to the lower officers involved in tactics and implementation. Funk and Wagnall's dictionary gives three definitions for the contemporary English term. The first involves the *military*: the science and art of conducting a military campaign on a broad scale. The second implies *trickery*: the use of stratagem or artifice, as in business or politics. Here we have the element of not fully showing your hand to others because their goals and yours may not coincide. The third definition gets at the *long-term* aspect of strategy: a plan or technique for achieving some end. In military terminology, which until recently dominated usage, strategy was what was done in preparation, when the enemy was not present, in contrast to the tactics deployed once contact was made. In this sense, a strategy (note the article) is a broad and long-term plan. This is one end of the spectrum of the definitions, in contrast to more immediate choices and tactics oriented toward goals (although the contrast between planned strategy and improvised tactics tacitly recognizes that engagements never go according to plan). Even in its military form, the word seems to have come into wide English use only in the nineteenth century, if the examples from the *Oxford English Dictionary* are any guide.

As I use the term here, strategy has five dimensions. As a strategic player you have *goals*, which are usually explicit. You also employ *means* intended to attain your goals. There is at least the possibility of *resistance* from other players with their own means and goals. Recognizing this, you work to win or avoid anticipated clashes. As a result, strategy is *social and interactive*, as you need to elicit some action or belief from specific others, who may be allies or third parties as well as adversaries. Finally, strategic thinking is oriented toward the *future*, as you have projects to accomplish. It thus entails imagination, creativity, will, and subjectivity—all of which social scientists usually try to ignore. Combining the definitions from Funk and Wagnall, I take strategy to encompass the immediate and the long run, narrow and broad actions, military as well as other spheres of action.

Strategy as the effort *to get others to do what you want* includes preventing them from doing what you do not want them to do. Constraints against action and enticements to action are equally important. Further, a strategy may be aimed at getting others to notice, believe, or feel something rather than directly at getting them to do something.

Strategic action need not be entirely explicit and conscious. One person can consciously adopt a strategy that someone else employs without thinking about it. Implicit strategies, I would guess, are more common with simple players (who need not justify their actions to a team), especially when they are expressing emotions that help them succeed. A simple player may not realize she is sulking, for instance, and those around her may give her more of what she wants without quite realizing why. Indeed, if she were explicit in her demands, others might find it easier to judge and refuse them. Pierre Bourdieu and other situationalists have elaborated this category of implicit strategy ("practices," they call it), in the end collapsing it to structure and losing its strategic aspects. But situationalists make an important point: *individual personalities* and *organizational cultures* come to embody certain strategic choices, which then disappear—for a while—from explicit contemplation. I hesitate to admit that strategies can be *entirely* unconscious, as that implies that anything we do can be taken as a strategy; I would insist on awareness of others and of our goals, even if our means sometimes slip beneath full consciousness.

The most important subset of strategic action is strategic *inter*action, in which you face other players who regard you strategically, just as you do them, and engage in a series of actions in response to others, anticipating their reactions in turn. In this case, they react to your efforts, whether with resistance, cooperation, prevarication, or delay. For example, when I teach, I usually grade students' first assignments harder than subsequent ones. This is strategic *action*: I want my students to get a little worried and study harder. Because they are not aware of my stratagem (until they read this book), it is a kind of *manipulation*. But if they in turn try to figure out if I have graded the first paper hard and anticipate what I will do as the semester unfolds—in other words what is in my mind—then we have strategic interaction. Each side is trying to figure out how the other will react, what that player is thinking and intending. The students and I do not disagree over long-run goals—at least I think my manipulation is for their ultimate benefit—but we do disagree over means (working harder to learn more versus getting good grades to look good on paper). Strategic interactions need not pit one side's goals or interests against the other's. Strategic interaction, because it is more interesting than strategic action, is the focus of this book.

Action becomes interaction when both sides are doing it with mutual awareness. This normally implies a small number of players. If there are hundreds or millions, you cannot get inside that many heads effectively. You can try to influence them, as advertisers do, but you cannot hope to anticipate what each of them will think about your actions, how you might respond to their responses. This is the difference, in economics, between competition in an anonymous market and the more direct conflict of an oligopolistic one. Competitive firms still compose strategic plans, but they do not directly engage their competitors—they interact only through price and market share. They begin to deal with their environment as one would the natural world rather than as comprising thinking, responding human actors. A high-school girl does certain things to make herself attractive to boys in general, but she does different things when she has her eye on a specific boy—for instance, one who already has a girlfriend. The latter actions are directly strategic.

Few strategic interactions involve only two players. Most involve allies, judges, supporters, advisors, and spectators, in addition to any number of contenders. Even when we focus on a single adversary, we support that battle through a number of other interactions that I refer to as *indirect* strategic interactions. They are indirect only in relation to the main, direct one, as they are strategic engagements in their own right. We gather resources, mobilize allies, shape third-party opinions, and so on.

So how do strategic action and interaction differ from other forms of action? Humans do not think strategically all—or even most—of the time. Other kinds of action have different goals and contexts. For the most part we follow *habits*, well-known routines that we can walk through without thinking about them, usually forced on us by the large institutions in our lives, from employers to television networks. We leave for work at 8 a.m., watch the news at 6:30 p.m. We do not have to think about our ends or means. Though we may follow routines most of the time, we are always prepared to rethink and revise them if necessary, and those breaks ordinarily entail strategic action: cogitation about means, ends, and other players. Long periods of routine are punctuated by changes that usually come through strategic action. Much strategic action aims at changing our routines, and successful strategic action often settles into routines.

Across another boundary of strategic action lies *instrumental action*, in which we do not take the minds of others into account. When we are dealing with the inanimate world—how to escape from a burning building, say— we may engage in elaborate decision making, taking the risks of various routes into account, but we are thinking instrumentally, not strategically. We do not try to get inside the head of the fire or the building to guess what it will do next; we use our knowledge of physics. We may be exposed to danger, but the fire is not *opposed* to us in any strategic sense. It does not care what happens to us. (We may, however, try to anticipate what our fellow trapped humans will do, especially if we are struggling to get out the same exit.) Dealing with nonhuman species is a mixed case: we try to anticipate what they are thinking and assure ourselves that we can do this. But all we can do is pretend that their minds are like human minds. For that is the secret of getting inside other people's heads: we begin with our own minds, assume some similarities in others, then try to add potential differences. We all know what it is like to think strategically—we have done it all our lives.[3]

When we are dealing with other humans, instrumental action turns out to be a rather small category. A surgeon replacing a knee sees his patient as a physical object in the operating room, but before and after the procedure, he talks to that patient, assesses her needs, wonders how diligently she will go to rehab. A robber with a gun to your head may try to dehumanize you to make you more docile, but in order to do this, he must have a sophisticated sense of what you are thinking—even as he is willing to shoot you, taking your mind away altogether. He is still thinking strategically. He has run out of other moves for making you do what he wants. (Even a night burglar, who hopes not to wake the people he is robbing, still plans what to do if they wake up, that is, if his action triggers interaction.) Whenever we try to reduce people to "things," their minds have a way of thwarting our plans.

Introducing other minds to the mix of factors we must consider changes things enormously, adding immense complexity. But this does not automatically require strategy. On the other side of strategic action from instrumental action is symbolic or *communicative action*, where our goal is to come to some sort of understanding with others rather than to elicit some eventual action from them.[4] Sociologists and other situationalists have favored this kind of action (analytically and morally), using it as the ideal type for all social action. Conversations depend on an enormous amount of shared, taken-for-granted understanding; speech itself requires considerable "filling in" with common expectations and, according to Jürgen Habermas, may even promise an effort to understand each other. Social constructionists show how humans work together to create scientific facts, define greatness in art, reject certain activities as immoral, and generally create the world they perceive around them.

Sociologists insist on the importance of this "social" dimension of the world, which resides in interactions among people, not in the objective physical world or in individual minds. They forget that these interactions are not always so cooperative. Recognizing that they are frequently conflicted reminds us that they often begin with individual intentions and plans, which may never be fully shared with others. (If only people stopped occasionally to deliver candid monologues, like actors in a play!) People are never socialized into complete conformity with the wishes of others; their interactions normally combine conflict and cooperation. They may not even agree on what kind of situation they are in together, what kind of action is occurring. In the very paradigm of rigid social structures, even *castes* are forever maneuvering to defend or improve their status.

To summarize, we operate according to routine rather than strategy when we have no awareness of our means and ends; it is instrumental rather than strategic action if the objects of our design are not humans with minds. Even when we are purposively interacting with humans who are aware of our actions, our interaction can be either strategic or symbolic.

The similarities between these last two categories allow situationalists to misinterpret strategy as communication—a bias I hope to correct in the chapters to follow.

✖

Most sociology and anthropology would lead us to believe that strategic action is rare, but nothing could be further from the truth. Anywhere you find power, you will find strategic action—on the part of both those with more power and those with less. *Power* has been defined in deceptively simple ways in social science, usually as the ability to force others to act against their will or against their interests. We only recognize it through its effects. But how do we impose our will on others? Only rarely do we reduce them to physical objects and move them like cattle. More often we trick, cajole, bribe, and cut off their alternatives. In other words, most of what we call power is successful strategic action. Sometimes, the powerful fail to get what they want, in which case social scientists usually say they were not so powerful after all. But this circular measurement will hardly do. In chapter 4 (true to the underlying energy metaphor), I define power as physical capacities, such as troops, technologies, and brute strength, but I also argue that these are not the only determinants of successful action. I suspect we can get along fine without using the term *power* at all, substituting more concrete entities for this misleading—but resonant—metaphor. (If success or failure equals resources plus strategies, where exactly does power fit in?)

We act strategically in situations of cooperation as well as conflict, for we may often clash over the details of our cooperation, our means rather than our ends. Coordination requires strategic thinking. Normally, this takes the form of persuasion, by which we convince someone else that our goals are compatible or the same, and that they are best pursued through certain actions. We help them see the world differently, perhaps relating action to goals more accurately. We may or may not need to trick or coerce them, assuming they are capable of rational debate and discussion. Even in the middle of conflict, such as war, we find areas of cooperation, and conflict crops up in the midst of the most cooperative relationships.

Most of the time, though, the balance between cooperation and conflict is determined by our goals. They may simply conflict (employees want to work less hard than employers want them to). Or they may be complementary: we may want the same thing, something that is better if shared (such as a party). Finally, we may each want something that is not easily shared (the family car) or that can only be shared in such a way that more for you means less for me (food, money). Producing changes in our own or other people's goals, in processes that look like conformity, is a regular and powerful strategy. In the end, the traditional distinction between cooperation and conflict works only when players have very simple goals (a.k.a. preferences or interests), a state we rarely find in the real world. In this view, we have conflict if our interests clash, no matter what our intentions, and cooperation if they are compatible, no matter what our mutual feelings. More realistically, we have complex goals and streams of actions that combine cooperation and conflict. It is arbitrary to label most of our strategic actions as either cooperation or conflict. As sociologist Georg Simmel commented, "[T]here probably exists no social unit in which convergent and divergent currents among its members are not inseparably interwoven."[5]

Even the most altruistic impulses sometimes require strategic thinking. Take a couple with different preferences for how to spend an evening. In a classic example from game theory, he wants to go to something like a hockey game, while she prefers the ballet. This example is often used to show that the person who chooses first prevails (since the other would rather go along than be alone), or to show that the man has an interest in having her believe he cares less about being with her than about seeing the hockey game (even though this may not be true). But suppose he genuinely wants to please his partner: he will insist on his interest in ballet even though he must lie. She may equally proclaim her fondness for fistfights on ice. Each may suspect that the other is doing this just to be accommodating, leading each of them to assert even more their stated preferences. So each (still wishing to please the other) tries to sound quite sincere about the feigned preference, trying to be consistent, enthusiastic, and so on. Over time, they try to demonstrate these as unfailing preferences—which they may indeed grow to be (unlikely as that seems in this example). Of course, each may eventually grow disgusted with the game (or be angry with the other for independent reasons) and blurt out the truth.

When we are trying to get others to do what we want them to (which may be something good for us or good for them), we have three broad families of strategies: *persuasion, payment* (reward), and *coercion.* The most effective (because self-sustaining) inducement is usually to persuade others to *want* to do what we want them to. This is obviously more effective when we share interests, principles, beliefs, or affective loyalties with them. I would classify appeals to moral principles and intuitions under persuasion. Appeals may be both explicit and implicit, and we might call the latter "inspiration" rather than direct persuasion, since in that case we persuade others by setting an example or arousing excitement. Finally, persuasion is not limited to words. We convey messages through dress and body language, through architecture and design, through *how* we say something as well as what we say. A judge's robe, demeanor, and (in Britain) wig say something as surely as his pronouncements. Since most people are interested in money, they will do things they otherwise would not in exchange for it—this is the basis of our modern economic system. If we lack persuasive powers or sufficient funds, we must coerce them when they resist our will. With a fistfight or war, we resort to brute force, but coercion also includes other physical deprivations short of destruction. Persuasion helps them see their options differently, money increases the value of certain options, and coercion lowers it. In real life we usually find combinations of two or three of these—as with lobbyists who do not simply buy legislative votes through campaign contributions but also buy access through which they try to persuade legislators.[6]

Of the three mechanisms, payments and coercion have been the favorites of economists and political scientists; these are the supposedly "hard" resources that stand behind politics and culture. They promise tight explanatory models of history moved by economic or military might. In recent decades money has edged out fists as the favorite, and all of social life has been analyzed through the metaphor of exchange. The *political* metaphor of a *forum*, in which rhetoric is deployed for the strategic purpose of persuading others, has been underutilized—that is one reason I highlight it somewhat in the pages that follow. Persuasion is only one of three kinds of strategic moves, but it is perhaps the central one. If money and fists are resources, words are a form of intelligence that can compensate for a lack of resources. (Sociologists have favored one form of persuasion, moral suasion based on shared norms, ignoring others.) Rhetoric is now mostly a lost art.[7]

Because strategic action, like other forms of social action, is performed with an eye toward one or more audiences, it has been compared with the theater. This is why persuasion is so important. There is a lot of posturing and gesturing and positioning that goes on in strategizing, in front of several audiences simultaneously or separately. Much of the point of strategy is to boost one's own credibility, making others more likely to trust you, and to damage the credibility of opponents. Much depends on extremely fragile and fleeting qualities like trust, which in most cases are as important as the physical resources that players command. The theatrical metaphor demonstrates that much strategic action involves shaping understandings of the world—our own and those of others. This can involve specific information, but it also includes deep assumptions about how the world works and the characters of the actors in it.

Cultural meanings permeate strategic action at every moment—an influence that game theory has traditionally hidden, thereby limiting its own utility. Participants' know-how, usually gained from their cultural traditions, shapes the moves at which they are competent. Their understanding of the world affects their goals. Their moral perceptions determine the satisfactions they expect from various moves. Their emotional ties to the world around them affect their allies, their enemies, their enjoyment of the game, and their payoffs. It is hard to find any aspect of strategic action that is not filtered through meanings and feelings. (Physical resources come closest— the availability of tear gas for riot control, say—but people must still understand *how* to use the resources and be *willing* to use them.) What is more, culture offers a vocabulary of tropes and images with which we put together arguments to persuade others; to this extent, culture is a tool kit we use in our strategic efforts.[8]

In addition to their cultural contexts, strategic interactions unfold in complex institutional settings, which I examine under the rubric of arenas. One aspect of institutional context distinguishes two kinds of players, whom I shall call private and public. *Public players*, either simple or compound, can expect their strategic actions to get media attention. Whether individual celebrities or well-known organizations, they act in the public realm; they are public figures. *Private players*, who interact with a more limited number of others, sometimes become public players, for instance if their actions are outlandish enough to make the evening news (ask Joey Buttafuoco). Public players face an additional set of bystanders.

There is a paradox at the heart of all theories of strategy, which I think of as their *vacant core*. Because strategy is an eminently pragmatic domain, theorists inevitably mix prescriptive advice into their descriptions and explanations. But that how-to advice, in books on management or the military for example, consists of little more than vague platitudes, or at best checklists of mistakes to avoid (see the appendix for examples). They have little to say about what a player should actually do in any given situation, in part because the situations themselves can never be fully specified. A pair of political scientists, for instance, wondered, "What is it about the American presidency that defies theoretical precision? Why can't we devise propositions that predict the behavior of presidents and explain presidential leadership?"[9] But it is not just presidents who are hard to model: all strategic actors defy our attempts to say exactly what moves they should make. That vacant core is where choice occurs. Social science can only bring us to the moment of choice, not make it for us.

In the following chapters I label a number of common dilemmas that strategic players face. The list, far from exhaustive, is meant to show moments when players can make choices. At best, we can warn players what risks their decisions entail, the hazards of taking one path rather than others. Several of these dilemmas have their counterparts in the ecology of nonhuman entities—primates, reptiles, even plants—but I have not cited this literature because these are not strategic players in the full sense that humans are.

Whether you are interested in organizations, politics, markets, war, the professions, international diplomacy, marriage and the family, or almost any other domain of social life, you will understand them more fully if you appreciate the dynamics of strategic action. Structural models of union decline, for example, will never explain much as long as they exclude union and employer strategies. Even if you are more interested in structural constraints than in how agents maneuver within them, you cannot see one without appreciating the other. Strategic dilemmas and choices are an important part of freedom and agency, and without them human life (for practitioners *and* those who study them) would not be very interesting. Strategic action is not the whole of social life, but it is a big part of it.[10]

⚒

The following chapters lay out basic aspects of strategic action. I start with how strategic interaction begins, showing among other things that there are many barriers to engagement. Chapter 2 shows that a sense of threat is a central component to most engagements, overlooked in traditions that picture humans as passionless calculators. Chapter 3, on goals, primarily tries to show the diversity of human desires, overly simplified models of which will always distort what we see and expect. I then examine the kinds of human competencies and physical resources that are helpful in strategic interaction. When I turn to players in chapter 5, I emphasize that they are audiences interpreting actions and words, insisting on the cultural filters of all strategic action. The final chapter addresses the arenas within which interaction occurs, looking at different kinds of arenas, different relationships among them, and the switching that frequently occurs between them as players search for the most favorable settings. In the conclusion, I discuss dilemmas and how to think about (and with) them, and I suggest how a number of fields of inquiry might benefit from attention to strategic issues.

----→ STARTING POINTS

If a country abounds with woods or mountains, you may lie in ambush and, when he least expects it, fall suddenly upon an enemy and be assured of success. [But] if it be an open plain, you cannot conceal a part of your forces as would be necessary.
→ MACHIAVELLI

I had only lived in New York a week when I was mugged—in Times Square no less, in the middle of the day, with crowds of people all around. I was looking in a shop window when I felt a hand in my left pocket. As I turned around, it pulled out, taking a lot of cash with it. I was a bit confused about what was happening, but I took a step toward the short man backing away from me. I probably said something cogent like "Hey!" The same instant, a much larger man knocked me down—hard. My girlfriend was backing into the store, clutching her expensive camera. The two men scrambled for some bills that had fallen to the pavement, and one grabbed at my hat, which had fallen off. Not my hat! I grabbed it back, and the two of them ran off. It had taken no more than a few seconds. Neither of us had really had time to react, much less to cry out. This is simply not what we had been expecting. In contrast the two men, who had followed us for blocks, knew exactly what they were doing. This was their business. For them, it was an easy job.[1]

Often, by the time you realize someone has begun to interact with you in a strategic fashion, it is too late to do much about it. Sometimes, you have already lost. You have already been fired from your job. Worse, you're already dead. Taking the initiative can have clear advantages, especially when much of the initial activity can be kept secret. But this merely increases the biggest advantage, surprise. What is perhaps less obvious are the barriers and disadvantages to initiating strategic interaction.

INITIATION IS RARE

In this chapter I look at who begins strategic action, why, and how. I do not think people initiate strategic interactions very often. We rarely sit down and ask, what do I want? How can I get it? Mostly, we are already embroiled in routines and habits, following laws and bureaucratic rules. We rarely stop to think about ends or the means to attain them. But sometimes we do. And sometimes we act on those thoughts.

We can get involved in a strategic engagement in several different ways. We may formulate a project and take the first step toward accomplishing it. Or we may join an interaction someone else has begun; we may be the direct target or simply be drawn in indirectly, as ally or witness. Finally, we may choose a strategic response to someone else's actions that were not intended strategically. I have listed these in what I suspect is their increasing order of frequency. Let's begin with the first case.

Who initiates strategic action? First, some personalities seem prone to launching strategic action: the gang member who cooks up the next convenience-store heist, the sibling who plays a trick on another, the friend who is always thinking up ways to make a buck. They have a kind of strategic creativity, perhaps due to a willingness to break rules or a penchant for viewing people as strategic players rather than as loved ones. Paranoids see more intentionality in the world than the rest of us, interpreting others' actions as attacks and responding in kind.

If individual personality is important in the origins of strategic interaction, then social roles and positions are probably more so. Some people and organizations initiate strategic action as part of their jobs or missions. Corporate executives are forever launching "strategic initiatives," their name for almost anything they decide to do that they can pretend is new and different. Presumably certain employees or consultants devote their time to cooking up these strategies (although they are not always strategies in my sense, merely plans). Inventors develop products that may cause strategic battles when they are launched. Policymakers and interest groups make proposals that set off chains of strategic interactions. Every day hundreds of U.S. Army colonels sit at their desks trying to imagine the implications of engagements around the world.

As these examples suggest, some parts of any society are designed for strategic engagement, and some players are permanent and ongoing. We will look at particular arenas, such as law courts or electoral politics, later. If you are going to be a lawyer or politician, you will interact with others strategically. Legal and political settings require this.

In personal life, initiating positions are less obvious. People spend most of their time following personal routines and workplace procedures. But when they call someone for a date, decide to look for a new job, or try to buy a house, they launch strategic interactions with others. In the heterosexual world it is still usually the man's role to ask the woman on a date; some take the step of registering with an Internet dating service. And there are certain characteristic moments in life when people move or look for new jobs—one reason that even these interactions are partly routinized.

Cooperative interactions like these are easy to initiate, since the other party has something to gain as well. Real estate agents are paid to hook you up with that new home. They may even seek you out, taking the initiative in this interaction. Most market transactions involve players who are interested in cooperation. But not all cases are so clear. You may have to persuade others that the interaction will indeed be cooperative rather than conflictual. The man must persuade that potential date that she will have fun; the possibility that she will turn down his invitation shows the fuzzy interpenetration of conflict and cooperation.

The real estate transaction reveals several aspects of strategic games. Most have three or more players—in this case the buyer, the seller, and the agent. Typically you are simultaneously cooperating and in conflict. The agent wants the deal to go through, and this may require the seller to accept less than she wants or the buyer to pay more. In this example, the agent is supposedly cooperating with both sides but also acting on behalf of one of them—against the other. (This arena is so confused that in New York, you must sign a form saying that you understand your real estate agent is not in fact acting as your agent on your behalf!) Second, the conflict between the buyer and seller over price and other details takes place within a broader context of cooperation: both desire the transaction, but on the best possible terms.

Some academics are adept at creating one kind of strategic game: competition over faculty. If you can get two universities enthusiastic about hiring (or retaining) you, you have your best shot at increasing your salary and status. You become a "hot property," while two institutions battle for your loyalty; others may hear of this, conclude that you must be worth the fuss, and join the competition. Some individuals manage to do this year after year, in many cases never actually moving to a new job. (I have noticed that rational-choice scholars seem especially adept at this kind of self-interested game.) Here again, you get what you want from potential employers by shifting the interaction from a direct conflict between you and each university to one between the universities, which allows you to have a more cooperative relationship to each. On the down side, too much of this activity is considered bad behavior by colleagues—revealing a general anxiety and fear about those who initiate strategic action. They cause trouble for the rest of us.

In addition to starting an entirely new engagement, you can initiate action within an ongoing interaction. Within an existing conflict, you may suddenly open up a new arena; or within a routine interaction, you may try something new. Baseball provides an example. Within the "normal" flow of a game, a coach may signal for a player to make a surprise move, such as a bunt. If the opposition knows a surprise is coming, they may figure out what it is (options are limited), so you need to hide the very fact that you are sending a signal or preparing a surprise. Even so, a player may give it away. Yogi Berra, as a young player, chattered constantly while on base—except when he had been given special instructions. When he fell silent, he was ripe for being picked off. (He was quickly retrained to chatter all the time.)

All of us have initiated strategic interaction at one time or another. But the existence of certain personalities, positions, and organizations that "specialize" in it shows that it is relatively unusual. Starting something has both advantages and disadvantages, as we will see; more importantly, however, engagement brings a great deal of risk. You can never fully control how others will respond, how interactions will unfold. You may not be as good a strategist as others are. In Venezuela, for example, opponents of President Hugo Chávez tried to oust him, first through a coup in the military and then through a strike at the national oil company; he ended up with tighter control over both. For another example, you may suggest to your partner that the two of you need more time apart, with other friends, intending some rethinking of the relationship. Your partner embraces the idea all too enthusiastically and is soon out the door forever—not exactly what you intended. Such risks form a basic dilemma, what I call the Risk Dilemma, that appears in different forms in later chapters.

THE RISK DILEMMA → Most engagements and moves within engagements entail unknown and known probabilities of a number of outcomes, both good and bad—and these are often not easily compared. Increased odds of a big gain often accompany those of a big loss. There is typically a *prudent* choice to risk less and an *enterprising* one to risk more.[2] The levels of risk that players will tolerate is a fundamental choice facing all of them. Entering a strategic interaction always risks an unknown outcome, and hence is more enterprising than avoiding or refusing interaction. (See the Engagement Dilemma below.) Prospect theory in psychology and economics has shown how the framing of this dilemma affects the choices made—all the while establishing the centrality of the trade-off.[3]

With characteristic good sense, Anthony Giddens shows the link between strategic engagement and riskiness by defining *fateful moments*, "when individuals are called on to take decisions that are particularly consequential for their ambitions, or more generally for their future lives." Such moments may be planned or forced on us by events. In my view, most are choices whether to embark on strategic projects and what kind to undertake. They are times, Giddens points out, "at which, in more traditional settings, oracles might have been consulted or divine forces propitiated." Our destiny is partly in the hands of fate, with all the uncertainty it brings. At fateful moments, "the individual must launch out into something new, knowing that a decision made, or a specific course of action followed, has an irreversible quality, or at least that it will be difficult thereafter to revert to the old paths."[4] Much is at risk.

Sometimes we work hard to avoid engagements. Erving Goffman described the obvious example of our actions on a modern city street, where we use "civil inattention" to avoid interactions with strangers. We glance at passersby, then immediately look away. When arguments break out, even among friends or family, we often remain silent to avoid "getting involved."[5] Many engagements are simply unpleasant. Of course, civil inattention can get us mugged when others are determined to engage us.

Cynical resignation, or at least grudging acceptance of the status quo, underlies much of our reluctance to engage. Especially in dealing with the many bureaucracies of modern life, we tend to feel that the outcome will be the same whether we get involved or not. Things may even work out for the better. (Giddens points out that this resignation can have either a pessimistic or an optimistic tinge.)[6] Whether we call it fatalism or mere adaptation, this form of acceptance is ubiquitous. Such moods can be a cultural tradition or a recurrent personality trait.[7]

Besides our inclinations and intentions, many sources of inertia work against strategic action. In some cases inertia prevents interaction altogether; in others it brings it to an end. Calculations of likely outcomes often suggest that a player should avoid an engagement. Emotions such as anger and outrage frequently overpower these calculations and draw players into battle. Passions like these are not necessarily irrational, but they do not conform to the narrow, calculating definition of rationality used by most game theorists.[8] (Inertia also attends some paths of action once initiated, keeping them going once they have been launched, such as organizational routines that are hard to dislodge.) Even when calculations suggest engagement, people may still need an emotional spur to get them to do what furthers their goals.

Another reason initiation is rare has to do with the *fragility of sustained action*. Projects are easier to prevent or halt than to start or continue.[9] First, most strategic action is costly. Skills, resources, attention, and coordination must all be combined, then expended. Many arenas impose high costs of entry, like licenses to practice law or seats on exchanges. "Friendly fire" too is an unavoidable cost of war—even when you win. All strategic interactions produce *some* form of collateral damage. For most people strategic actions—and especially the responses from others—are extremely stressful (although some people thrive on the excitement).[10] A strategic engagement usually requires lots of attention, crowding out other aspects of players' lives. A great political leader may ignore her family or finances, for instance.[11] Professional military leaders are often reluctant to enter "dirty" wars like ethnic rivalries not only because of the risk to resources but even more to morale (loss of lives counts in both columns, at least in today's culture).[12]

Action is also fragile because it is easy for one reluctant or inept player or defector to bring the enterprise to a halt; many have some degree of veto power. If your spouse does not want to leave the house on time, the two of you won't; if one partner doesn't want to have sex, it won't happen. It is easy to refuse to cooperate simply by delaying or absenting yourself at the right moment. (This need not be intentional; attacking troops for instance often develop "weak knees" and other bodily failures that take them out of the action.)[13] In the case of a filibuster, opponents can "fill up" an arena with other issues, preventing you from pursuing yours. Coercive powers are rarely absolute, as you usually need some cooperation from others. It is easier to prevent them from acting in certain ways than to require performance of some kind: it is easier to pull on a rope than push with it. The

Shah of Iran learned this when he tried to keep newspapers, oil operations, and electric production going despite mass strikes. It took more troops than workers to keep the latter at their stations, and they left as soon as the troops did. (Numerous coordination and control mechanisms have been designed to overcome the fragility problem, but none are foolproof.) Inept players are just as dangerous: if you lack confidence in your lawyer, you may accept the certainties of a plea bargain to avoid the strategic uncertainties of a trial.

In addition, chance events happen that thwart strategic action even when all the players are agreed. The world is chaotic and "foggy," as Carl von Clausewitz said.[14] Some factors, like the weather, are accepted as being out of our control. Our tools, on the other hand, promise control but sometimes break that promise. (Talcott Parsons termed the former "conditions," the latter, "means.") Hannah Arendt thought these sources of friction trivial compared to humans themselves, who use strategic actions to reveal complex identities that inevitably transcend their stated purposes of action. She spoke of "the notorious uncertainty not only of all political matters, but of all affairs that go on between men directly, without the intermediary, stabilizing, and solidifying influence of things."[15] An important contribution that leaders and ideologies make to their teams is to create an illusion of a world that is orderly and responsive to our action, an arena in which strategic projects make sense.

Another source of uncertainty is that you can never be sure who the other players will be. If you enter an arena, so can others. Opponents bring allies; bystanders suddenly appear. If your company enters a new market, others might too. Controlling with whom you interact is an important but difficult strategy.[16] And as Arendt said, it is hard enough to control your own team, to keep them all in the current game. Timely exits are as influential as timely entrances. As Charlie Chaplin quipped, the secret to good performance is entrances and exits. This is as true of strategic engagements as of film and theater.

Games mutate. Beginnings do not always seem like beginnings. One party opens a different kind of game, like the spouse who begins to want out of a marriage long before she signals this to her partner. Or you may try to hide the strategic nature of your actions, like the time-study agent who surreptitiously times a machine operator, who responds strategically only if she notices him doing so.[17]

Denying the strategic nature of your act is often a good strategic move, especially in cultures that disapprove of strategy and conflict. Corporate executives inevitably accuse union organizers of stirring up conflict. Movements for social change deny that they are "political" by insisting, for instance, that their actions are "spontaneous" rather than organized and premeditated.[18] Suburbanites go to great lengths to avoid contention with neighbors.[19] So we may deny strategic action even in the middle of it—making it hard for others to know when it has commenced.

Who goes first is important because the order in which things happen matters. Partly this has to do with the availability of information necessary for action. Who knows what and when they know it affects how they can act. Partly it is also due to the cultural impressions that information and events leave behind, the emotional impact of learning or seeing something at a particular time. First impressions are, as the maxim (confirmed by cognitive psychologists) goes, especially influential. They make the difference between shocked outrage and weary resignation. And finally, the action itself matters. A number of things must be in place, planned and carefully prepared, before an action can succeed. When several players are involved, coordination is vital because the precise order of actions is important. Starting an interaction has both advantages and disadvantages.

ADVANTAGES

When you know you are launching an interaction that will be primarily conflictual, and when you can afford to alienate others because you are not looking ahead to eventual cooperation, then you have a special interest in making a devastating first move (mugging is a good example). In fact you may try to make a lot of moves before others are aware of what you are doing and begin to respond. You may be able to leave them only responses with few advantages or even gain a decision that permits them to do little but capitulate. By speaking with third parties surreptitiously, you may be able to undermine the reputation of your opponents, or frame authorities' beliefs about what is happening and what is at stake. You may be able to strip your opponents of potential allies as well as goodwill. And as long as you campaign in secret, you are less likely to have your claims and perspective challenged.

The central advantage of making the first move is *surprise*. Others do not know what is coming or even that anything at all is coming. They are not prepared to respond; they have not marshaled the necessary resources or attention. It may take your opponents considerable time to mobilize. Whether you are invading Normandy or trying to take over a corporation, surprise will help you get what you want in the face of (eventual) resistance from others. The advantage of surprise depends on your arena, of course. Like the woods or mountains that Machiavelli recommended, some provide more places to lay your ambushes than others do.

In addition to mobilizing allies and resources, those who initiate interaction can also do useful emotional work in advance. They can praise potential allies and demonize expected opponents. In a couple, the one who initiates separation or divorce has already grieved for the end of the relationship before she ever informs her partner they are finished. Diane Vaughan makes this point in a book about "uncoupling" that systematically compares the role of "initiator" with that of the other partner.[20] The initiator begins to build a life outside the relationship, develops a sense of self as an individual rather than part of the couple, finds sympathetic allies and confidants, recasts the history of the relationship in a negative light, perhaps even transfers funds into a secret account. One partner begins to see their interaction as conflictual while the other still views it as cooperative. They interpret everything differently: one partner raises serious complaints that the other dismisses as trivial. One sees joint therapy as a way to get out, the other as a way to mend the relationship.

A good initial move can change the emotional balance, especially when it comes to morale. The initiator strengthens his own sense of agency, building his confidence—and to the same degree undermining that of his adversaries. Their response may be delayed or lethargic, since those attacked may be demoralized or resigned in the face of a devastating assault. In traditional warrior cultures there is typically honor in attacking and shame in defending. One is seen as active, the other passive. In extreme cases, there is more shame in passivity than in defeat.[21]

Your opponents may be surprised not by your making a move but at your strength. They may not view you as enough of a threat to require mobilization until it is too late. They may think you have few resources, not counting on you to compensate for any shortfall through clever strategy. How many of us expected a few Islamic fundamentalists to transform jet aircraft into devastating fire bombs? If we have "characterized" opponents as ineffectual, we are especially surprised when they act out of character. We are further demoralized if we suddenly have to recharacterize them as powerful.

Those you have attacked may even be willing to let you keep whatever you have gained, figuring it is not worth their while to engage you further. Some protest movements, for instance, have advantages in their early stages that they later lose as opponents mobilize. American antinuclear protestors in the 1960s, before they had really formed a visible national movement, were able to block several nuclear plants proposed by electric utilities, which figured they could easily find other sites for their reactors. But as the antinuclear movement grew, local utilities began to resist and even fight back, spurred on by nuclear manufacturers who were seeing the same kind of resistance across the country. Local protests were not flukes but part of a trend that had to be confronted head on. In the 1970s and 1980s, no reactors were canceled because of the antinuclear movement (although some were for reasons of cost). Their opponents had fought back effectively.[22]

A final advantage to taking the initiative is that other players may never realize what you are up to and never get into the game at all. The most successful strategic action is one that never becomes strategic interaction, that is, one that your opponents do not resist because they never realize your intention. We could label these actions manipulation, but the issue is also one of extreme stealth.

DISADVANTAGES

Most of these advantages disappear if opponents see you coming. In a kind of judo tactic, they can use your own movement against you. If they know your move, but you do not know they know it, they can lay a trap, an ambush. Their tanks suddenly appear at the top of the hill, or archers at your weak flank. Opposing lawyers are prepared to devastate the "surprise" testimony of your witness. The spouse you are preparing to divorce has been saving the e-mails you have exchanged with your lover. If you believe you have kept your initial move a surprise, you will be staggered instead to find your opponent fully prepared for it.

Whether or not they have been taken by surprise, those assaulted may be indignant. They may feel like—and present themselves to others as—innocent victims who had been minding their own business until this aggression. Strong emotions, I said, are often necessary for a player to overcome the inertia working against strategic engagement. This is true of those who react as well as those who initiate. Victims arouse compassion and indignation, which can be transformed into anger, outrage, and hatred of the villains who assaulted them. Thus, in traditional cultures, it is typically forbidden to initiate magic against someone but not to use it in response to those who "started something."[23]

Indignation has a moral tinge to it that is powerful for mobilizing people, and players often use it to transform bystanders into supporters or at least sympathizers. Most modern cultures take a dim view of "aggressors," if you can portray your attackers in this light. This may involve tracing the initial steps they took behind the scenes—secrecy being another dubious quality in modern democratic societies with strong journalistic traditions. Much depends on the meanings and feelings available in local cultures. But note that Americans, who had little sympathy for the "camel jockeys" of Kuwait, the central pillar of demonized OPEC, could be persuaded that Saddam Hussein was an even greater evil, whose villainous aggression deserved an armed response—twice. Among common character types, those who initiate action can often be portrayed as villains. (This is one reason Bush II met worldwide outrage in attacking Iraq in 2003—try as he did to portray the United States as a victim reacting to the 9/11 attacks.)

To shape sympathies, strategic actors go to great lengths to define actions as offensive or defensive. Many parties deny that they are initiating an interaction, insisting instead that they are merely continuing (and hopefully ending) a long-standing engagement. They are defending their honor, demanding their due—anything but aggressing! Thus the creators of modern Spain (and their successors) portray the expulsion of the Moors as simply the "reconquest" of the Iberian peninsula: not a new conflict but the completion of an old one.

Even buildings can be part of this attempt to shape sympathies by pinpointing aggression. The Branch Davidians built their compound in Waco and bought arms to protect themselves from the invasion that, in their paranoia, they expected. Yet government officials insisted that the farm was an offensive, somehow threatening, structure. Even after they attacked the Branch Davidians, on rather flimsy pretenses, the Treasury Department opened its report on the event by saying (referring to an earlier incident that had triggered the siege) that "David Koresh and members of his religious cult, the Branch Davidians, ambushed a force of 76 ATF agents."[24] Ambush? The Branch Davidians had felt themselves on the defensive so much that they even dialed 911 as the ATF attack commenced.

Those who initiate strategic action may try to dull others' outrage by issuing a threat before commencing. This may work if you can persuade others that your threat is a fair warning, but not if they dismiss it as a pretense. The cost of threatening before acting is that opponents can prepare. You lose the advantage of surprise. Conspicuous preparation for action increases the credibility of your threat but also alerts others.[25] You may hope that your threat is so effective that you need not follow up. If you do, you aim to give your opponent too little time to prepare effectively—which is not always easy to do. There is a Threat Dilemma that is a subcategory of the Engagement Dilemma, which we are about to articulate: if you threaten, you may later have to decide whether to carry through with your threat.

Of course, some organizations expect aggression as part of doing business. A corporation cannot usually present itself as an innocent victim of a competitor's ad campaign. But even here, it is possible to go beyond the pale. Unfriendly takeover bids and predatory pricing meant to drive a competitor out of business are generally frowned on as unfair practices. But a company can do little unless laws are broken. Public sympathy counts for little in many arenas.

If your initial aggression is successful, the next risk is overconfidence. Flush with self-assurance, you overextend your campaign. You try to do more than your resources will support: you borrow too much money to extend the game, try to engage on too many fronts at once. Feelings of grandiosity overwhelm you. For this reason, confidence and initiative often see-saw from one side to the other in a conflict. (I examine confidence further in chapter 4.)

The risk of initiating an engagement is ultimately that your opponents may mobilize more effectively than you have, leaving you in an even worse position (as we saw with the nuclear industry's countermobilization). This is a variation on the Risk Dilemma.

THE ENGAGEMENT DILEMMA → The decision to enter into strategic interaction is not taken lightly. Most of us, most of the time, avoid it, and it usually results from strong emotions. People who see themselves as "nice" often feel uncomfortable thinking and acting strategically—unless they feel they must do so to right a wrong. Even those who initiate interactions enter a world in which they cannot know outcomes with certainty; those who begin with the strongest positions sometimes end up losers. Considerable confidence, often unwarranted, is usually necessary. So is information about the possible results. Initiators are not the only ones who must decide whether or not to engage in interaction. Those they engage must also decide whether to react in kind. Often they have no choice but to defend themselves. But just as often they tolerate small losses in order to avoid broader conflicts.[26] Engagement puts good reputations—for power, courage, success—on the line, where they can be ruined. Nothing ventured, nothing lost. On the other hand, you gain those reputations primarily through engagement (and good PR). Many debates among political realists revolve around the Engagement Dilemma, with some touting bipolar and others multipolar systems as generating less conflict.[27]

For hundreds of years, military theorists have flip-flopped between favoring offense or defense. Perhaps the lesson is that too much confidence in and reliance on either one is risky. Compare the preparations for World Wars I and II. Before 1914 the cult of the offensive dominated, but it was quickly discredited by the trenches. Allied planners took this new lesson—the power of defense—into World War II, when they were quickly overrun by Panzer tanks. (There was an unintended effect on alliances: the offensive cult led all allies to mobilize immediately in 1914, believing that the first offensive drives would be crucial; in World War II their faith in defense prevented them—alas—from coming quickly to their allies' aid.)[28] Although technologies can shift the balance between offense and defense—especially in war—usually a trade-off remains between them. Initiating an engagement always entails a risk.

All the advantages and disadvantages I have discussed for the initiation of action seem amplified for public players (those in the public eye, whether simple or compound). The media are especially likely to cover actions aimed at changing things, ignoring the many actions intended to protect the status quo. News is about the new.

KNOWING THE TERRAIN

Familiarity with your arena reveals the subtle interplay of aggression's advantages and disadvantages. Clausewitz believed that defenders have a natural advantage over aggressors, a claim that seemed to be confirmed a century later by the trenches of World War I. They know the terrain they are defending, have regular lines of communication and supply, and are familiar with paths of retreat if they need them. They usually have the support of the local populace. And they often have a strong emotional inspiration, since they are fighting to protect their homes. Of course, some structures and tools are designed for defense: it used to be easier to defend a walled town or castle than to take one; the pike is an excellent weapon for knocking charging knights off their mounts; legal defendants are innocent until proven guilty; "poison pills" make corporate takeovers expensive.

Several of the points about war are valid more generally. The emotional energy of defending what you believe is rightfully yours (or at least what you are accustomed to controlling) is powerful and usually gives you an emotional edge over aggressors. Bystanders or judges may also be sympathetic, especially if they agree with your claims of justice. Or they may root for the home team, secretly or openly. In addition, aggressors who are entering a new arena will be less familiar with its customs, resources, and players than the "home team."

The balance of power between offense and defense shifts with the invention of new tactics and technologies. Air dominance allows offensive strikes deep in another's territory—although they are meant to demoralize or paralyze the other side rather than to seize land. But airplanes can also carry paratroopers, whose use allowed Hitler to seize the "impenetrable" Belgian fortress of Eben Emael with only seventy-eight men (only six of whom were killed). The bridges of Holland were captured in the same way, before the country's defenders could destroy them. No defense is proof against all types of assault. Castles eventually became obsolete.

Moreover, initiators often choose and influence the arenas. You can "set the stage" for an interaction in more figurative ways. You invite someone into your office and offer her an awkward or a comfortable chair depending on the effect you seek. You give a lover bad news in a restaurant in the hope this will dampen emotional display. You control others' responses by selecting the time and place for your moves. Within the setting, you can set the agenda by posing certain questions or issues, providing new information. You can also shape events by controlling who is present, inviting some people but not others. By posing a problem in one way rather than another, you even help define who the players will be and what the conceivable responses are.

Too much reliance on strong defense can undermine your sense of agency, leading others to greater aggression. Alexander the Great learned this in an early battle with the Thracians, who chose to defend a narrow mountain pass with heavy wagons they could roll down on the advancing Macedonians. Alexander took this as a sign that the Thracians had little stomach for combat, and they had little backup after they had used the wagons. Alexander drew from the experience a lesson he used often in his campaigns: "When he detected that the enemy had artificially enhanced the strength of a strong position—by fortification or the emplacement of obstacles—those signs seem to have clinched his conviction that it was there he should attack, since they signified that there the enemy was most vulnerable to attack, in psychic if not material terms."[29]

The confidence that strong defenses offer can actually make you more vulnerable.

Such confidence also makes you less flexible. You are less likely to formulate backup plans, in case your strong defenses fail. This is the Basket Dilemma (see chapter 6), in which you must decide whether to put all your faith in one powerful move or strategy or to spread your risk across many. When Hannibal invaded Italy, the Romans retreated to a strong defense of Rome, destroying the bridges over the Anio and the Tiber, but leaving Hannibal free to ravage the countryside. The Romans were unaccustomed to retreat, although in this case it allowed them—barely—to triumph in the end.

Machiavelli's advice about the best terrain for an ambush needs qualification. Best of all is an arena where your opponent *thinks* he can see everything but cannot, rather than one where he can see that there are hiding places. Seeing the woods makes him think about ambushes. This was one of Wellington's advantages at Waterloo: behind a long hill that looked fairly flat, he managed to hide large numbers of troops. The point is more general: try to find an arena that appears transparent but holds literal or figurative "hiding places." I felt safe in Times Square, unaware I was being stalked.

This gets to a larger point: what is crucial is *knowing a lot about your arena*. Such knowledge usually belongs to the home team, but outsiders can learn the terrain. Wellington was not Belgian, but he had spent time there. Familiarity with an arena includes knowledge of the local rules, the hazards to expect (morning fog, unfriendly questions from a judge), and what resources you can seize, so that you can "blend in" better if you need to. In the end, home turf provides most of these advantages, but they are often accompanied by a constraining fondness for the arena (whether a place or institution).

THE HOME-TURF DILEMMA → Fighting on your home turf constrains you as well as enabling you, for along with familiarity goes fondness. Paradoxically, defending your home can sometimes conflict with defeating the enemy that threatens it. Individual soldiers defect to protect their farms and families. You avoid scorched-earth and other tactics that destroy the land, even when these would hurt your opponents. A student of the conquest of the Yucatan reports the main advantage the Spanish had over the Mayans: "While the Indians were fighting on their home ground, with all that implies of inhibition, vulnerability, and anxiety for the morrow, the Spaniards could move through the land with no scruple as to destructiveness and the human cost of their actions: those considerations could wait on victory."[30] An advocate may be less aggressive in a courtroom she returns to regularly, limiting her options in the current case for the sake of future ones. Loyalties curtail your options at the same time that familiarity increases them.

At the extreme, trying to control an unfamiliar territory, organization, or arena is almost always harder than gaining a victory within it. Hostile takeovers transform the "natives" (whether peasants or functionaries) into additional opponents, whether they were previously or not. Passive, if not active, resistance is always possible. "The conduct of a general in a conquered country," said Napoleon, "is full of difficulties. If severe, he irritates and increases the number of his enemies. If lenient, he gives birth to expectations which only render the abuses and vexations inseparable from war the more intolerable."[31] Bush II learned this—or should have learned it—in his Iraq venture.

Personal traits may make individuals better suited to offense or defense. In his book on courage, William Miller contrasts "aggressive honor versus stoic and Christian fortitude, challenge and aggression versus sufferance and patience, physical courage versus moral courage, fear versus disgust, masculine versus feminine."[32] Think of Achilles' thirst for honor versus Hector's love for his home. We associate offense not only with masculinity but with a host of associated pathologies: rashness, fury, hardness, cruelty, stupidity, even criminality—which add to our distrust of those who initiate strategic action.

The inherent strengths of defense or offense, if they exist, are more advantageous in literal wars than figurative ones, as most conflicts are not about seizing someone else's territory. Knowing an arena, controlling it, and caring about it are not the same thing, although they are frequently linked. But familiarity with your arena is always an advantage. Nonetheless, the distinction between offense and defense is somewhat artificial. It is almost impossible to use only one or the other rather than a combination of the two. A good soccer player is always thinking about both: how to keep the other side from scoring, but also how to set her own team up when they get the ball back. And a great show of defense often feels offensive, in that it mobilizes resources and people who, once gathered, could be used for offense.[33] Nuclear missiles may feel defensive to those who install them but offensive to neighbors. Barry Buzan comments that defense "can involve preparation for forward or pre-emptive action designed either to meet threats which are still remote in time, space or magnitude, or to eliminate all significant sources of opposition or threat."[34]

ACCIDENTAL ENGAGEMENTS

We often act strategically only in response to others who, while not intending to act strategically, do something that arouses a strategic response in us. The drunk driver is not acting strategically when he runs off the road and kills a child, but the grieving parent is when she then devotes her life to lobbying for tougher drunk-driving laws. A nation increases its security through extra military spending, and its neighbors feel threatened (the Security Dilemma; see chapter 5). Often the action of an ally or subunit of our own team draws us into engagement (especially when tensions are already high). They may initiate action that involves the larger player—as happened frequently when local soldiers got into trouble with natives as the American frontier moved West. General Andrew Jackson invaded Florida without permission, but the U.S. government then had to back him.

As the next chapter shows, it may take a shock to shake us out of our routines, giving us the jolt of energy we need to "do something." A woman comes home to find her husband in bed with someone else. Your boss asks you to fudge some numbers in a report. Plans are announced for a toxic waste dump down the road from your summer home. Such events disrupt our sense of the world as a comfortable and benevolent place, and our response is sometimes to initiate a new line of strategic action. Instead of following along someone else's line of action, we inaugurate a new game— of divorce, whistleblowing protest, or job-hunting.

That simple players respond to strategic actions initiated by others is partly a logical point of arithmetic. We know a lot of people—friends, family, coworkers, neighbors—who are also capable of initiating sequences of strategic actions that involve us. Most often, we are responding to their overtures and moves rather than beginning something new. There is only one of us but dozens or hundreds of them, so we normally spend more time reacting than initiating—most of us, that is. Only in the world of game theory do people continuously scan the horizon for strategic openings. The same arithmetic holds for compound players: any organization or nation is involved with dozens of others who can draw it into engagements.

Because starting points are so frequently accidental, it is hard to say that certain kinds of players are more likely to be drawn into conflict than others. The characteristics of the players, the nature of their relationship, and their alliances with others all play some role, to be sure. Two nations are more likely to go to war if they share a border, if one or both has an authoritarian government, if they lack industrial economies, if their relative power is shifting or relatively equal, or if only one has an alliance with stronger powers. Since wars are often over borders, the first factor is merely a horizon of opportunity: you clash with those you interact with. The second may indicate either the bellicose nature of dictators or the awkwardness of declaring war when multiple audiences must be satisfied. Economic development may discourage war because citizens and elites have more satisfying things to do with their time (although both must be developed to make war less likely), or it may be that the ties of trade between countries discourage war.[35] But *none* of these factors is a strong predictor.

It is almost impossible to predict, on the basis of the characteristics of players, which ones are more likely to end up in strategic interactions, beyond the fact that some are put together precisely for this purpose. As one research team suggests, "Population pressure, geographic size, economic development, business cycles, national culture, and political system-type appear to be unrelated to state-level involvement in militarized conflict or war."[36] Not surprisingly, the factors correlated with conflict are those that have to do directly with conflict: level of militarization, position in international alliances, shifts in military power relative to others. Strategic interaction is open-ended enough to lead in different directions that cannot be predicted easily in advance, despite the efforts of hundreds of political scientists. Even its initiation is frequently accidental.[37]

Any simple or compound player can be drawn into strategic interaction, and any interaction can involve conflict. Yet relatively few players initially intend either.

❌

Starting points are just that. They are rarely conclusive, so that our discussion merely points toward other issues for later chapters. For example, we saw that making the first move strengthens your sense of agency, the feeling that you are in control of events rather than simply reacting to the actions of others (which is actually more common). This is an important message to send yourself, your team, your allies, and other players. According to Machiavelli, if the enemy is about to force you and your army to do something, go ahead and do it first. If a sect is about to expel you for doctrinal disagreements, you should quit and denounce it first. If you are going to be sued, sue the other person first. Then their action looks like sour-grapes retaliation. However things turn out, you have a feeling of being in charge. Chapter 4 shows how this sense of mastery and confidence is an important asset for strategic actors.

The success or failure of your initial move depends primarily on surprise and information about the arena. How long can you keep your moves secret? This is the difference between a pickpocket and a mugger; if the former is discovered in the act, he typically flees, but the latter expects the victim to feel that hand going into his pocket and is ready to respond. He must be ready with forms of intimidation, to further confuse his victim, to insure the success of his strategy.

Whether certain players are more likely than others to initiate an engagement depends on their complex sets of goals. They may inordinately value the prizes to be won in strategic arenas compared to other satisfactions (as discussed further in chapter 3). Their willingness to engage also normally depends on their available resources and skills (see chapter 4).

Initiating an interaction, whatever the advantages and disadvantages, can always backfire. Declaring a war involves the risk of losing. The final decision in a legal proceeding that you initiate may go against you. Once you raise a new issue in a debate, you cannot take it back. In any number of cases, those who initiate strategic interaction fail—a problem addressed in future chapters that reminds us of the unpredictable nature of strategy. Because strategic interaction is so risky, most of us join the fray primarily when we feel threatened, since threats arouse the emotions that help us engage.

CHAPTER 2

THREATS

What made war inevitable was the growth of Athenian power and the fear this caused in Sparta. → THUCYDIDES

In the mid-1970s, Lois Gibbs's attention was focused on raising a family. She and her husband, a chemical worker, lived a normal suburban existence in a three-bedroom house surrounded by tree-lined streets and weekend do-it-yourselfers. Lois had stopped working when their two children were born, and neither she nor her husband was interested in politics or active in any community organizations. Lois thought of herself as painfully shy, incapable of public speaking, and apolitical. When she began to see articles about Love Canal's health hazards in the *Niagara Falls Gazette*, she did not realize at first that they were talking about her neighborhood. From 1946 to 1953 the Hooker Chemical Company had buried twenty-two thousand tons of chemical wastes there. Soon after, the city had bought the site for an elementary school and sold the remainder to real estate developers.

When Gibbs recognized her own neighborhood in the articles, she grew alarmed, as her son Michael had just completed kindergarten in the school built right on top of the old canal. Could this, she wondered, explain the seizures he had begun having right after starting school, or the sudden drop in his white blood count? Her brother-in-law, a biologist at the Buffalo campus of the State University of New York, confirmed what the articles said: Many of the chemicals buried in Love Canal were known to damage the central nervous system. They decided Michael should no longer go to the 99th Street School.

The county superintendent refused to transfer Michael to a different school, despite two doctors' letters pointing to his special sensitivities. The president of the PTA seemed uninterested as well. Indignant, Gibbs carried a petition door to door, beginning with her own friends and acquaintances. She was surprised to hear about so many mysterious illnesses, crib deaths, and other cases of suffering children. Shy Lois Gibbs was soon testifying before government hearings, addressing rallies of local residents, and leading a movement incensed with the government for not doing enough to help. The Love Canal Homeowners Association, which she helped found, was a major reason the government eventually responded, paying to relocate those residents who wanted to move. The sudden, overwhelming sense of threat—especially to her son—was what pushed Gibbs and others to political action.

Hooker Chemical and the local government that bought its landfill never thought they would be embroiled in strategic interaction after their deal, but normal manufacturing routines set in motion events that would eventually feel mortally threatening to many Niagara Falls residents. Going about their daily lives, these citizens found themselves compelled to act. Both sides were forced to interact strategically with dozens of players, right up through President Jimmy Carter.

THE POWER OF THE NEGATIVE

Fear of some perceived threat is probably the most common reason for initiating strategic interaction. In many cases, as with Hooker Chemical, an individual or organization does not intend to threaten others, who sense a menace nonetheless. Those who feel threatened often respond with the first explicitly strategic action. A manufacturer decides to build a new plant without anticipating local opposition; one country designs a new weapon without reckoning how its neighbors will feel. Normal processes of innovation and development can ignite conflictual interactions when someone else decides that "something must be done." It is the unexpected strategic response that suggests the accidental quality of so many interactions.

In some cases there is a mutual sense of threat, again often unintended: this has caused many wars, like that between Athens and Sparta. One country takes steps that it sees as defensive measures, but its potential opponents see them as threatening. When they respond in kind, the result is often a spiral of hostile actions that may lead to a crisis or war. Every response to a perceived threat merely confirms the other side's perceptions of a trucu- lent menace.[1] Similar dynamics lie behind family feuds and office battles. Hostile spirals can occur in most strategic engagements, leading to anger, hatred, and polarization.

A player usually assumes the costs of strategic action in order to fend off even greater harm: many or most engagements seem to involve searching for the least harmful outcome rather than the most beneficial. Even in the abstract world of game theory, most examples appear to involve choices among negative threats rather than positive opportunities for gain. A per- son may accept a minor jail term to avoid a longer one. Another may coop- erate to avoid a deterioration in the environment, or "the commons." People feel forced to play the game in order to try to gain a "less bad" outcome rather than a worse one. Herein may lie a truth about strategic interaction: Most people are drawn into it *reluctantly rather than enthusiastically*, nor- mally preferring the bland security of the status quo to the risk of conflict. This is just as true of fatalistic peasants as it is of the modern middle class. (Perhaps warrior classes, whose status depends on demonstrating valor in battle, seek out engagements more readily; at least they pretend to. Even today, certain occupations and positions carry special rewards for strategic action, as we saw in chapter 1.)

Threats capture our attention immediately because humans tend to take the world around them for granted in a number of ways. We are confident that the floor beneath our feet will not suddenly start moving, that the boss will not peel off her skin to reveal a lizard's face, that our stockbroker will not flee to Tahiti with our life savings. Anthony Giddens terms this con- fidence "ontological security," or "confidence or trust that the natural and social worlds are as they appear to be."[2] This predictability and control over our bodies and immediate environments, he says, are necessary for normal daily life. We do not expect the world to be entirely safe, but we think we know the sources of danger. In fact we work hard to transform unknown fears into known ones—a primary function of myth, according to its many analysts.[3] We accept many threats if we understand them, have some con- trol over them, and feel they are fairly distributed.[4] When our confidence in the world is threatened, on the other hand, we usually try to remove that threat.

Economists and psychologists have discovered that people tend to be "risk averse," placing a higher value on what they already have than on what they might additionally acquire. They are more upset about the loss of a given amount of money than they are pleased by receiving the same amount. In a standard example, most of us would demand more money to get off a plane that was about to leave than we would bid to get onto the plane if we were in the terminal. We value the identical "good" more highly if we already possess it than if we are about to acquire it—this is called the "endowment effect." We feel entitled to what we already have. "Men generally fix their affections more," observed David Hume, "on what they are possessed of, than on what they never enjoyed. For this reason, it would be greater cruelty to dispossess a man of any thing than not to give it him."[5] We launch into strategic action to protect the status quo; or, if the status quo has recently been disrupted, we may act to restore it.[6]

Entire schools of psychology have envisioned the management of fear as the driving force behind human thoughts and actions. According to Harry Stack Sullivan, we learn in infancy to fear anxiety more than anything else, because it is so nightmarish then. As a result, most of us seek the familiar throughout our lives, expressing a need for security that is as important, Sullivan thought, as the aggressive and sexual drives that Freud highlighted. The more anxiety we experience in infancy, the more rigidly we try to control ourselves and our environments through "security operations" in order to prevent future recurrences. Some individuals feel a greater need to control threats than others, to actively protect their ontological security.[7]

What people feel threatened by depends on what they value, as well as on psychological dynamics and cultural meanings. Before we recognize a change in our environment as a threat, we must process information cognitively and emotionally—at least for anything more complicated than a startled response to a figure lunging from the shadows, which may be hardwired into us. These processes are complex, as we shall see when we examine different kinds of threats separately.

Action seems to be triggered in most people by some *sense of urgency* and the adrenaline called up by the emotions that accompany it. If we do not act now, things will be worse in the future, including our capacity to respond. We will have fewer strategic options. Again, emotions intervene, determining whether urgency is translated into agency or paralysis.

Institutions also filter our threats. In bureaucracies, some positions are more exposed to external menaces than others. In families, parents normally try to shield children from many potential threats—although this protection often simply reshapes them into vague anxieties (as it perhaps does for bureaucrats too). Like other kinds of information, that about threats is usually not distributed evenly. Even serious threats, maybe to the team's survival, are sometimes kept secret. Leaders use revelations of threats, like other meanings and information, for a variety of purposes: to retain power, to get their own way, to stimulate morale. This *social distribution of threat perceptions* distinguishes simple and private players from compound and public ones. If an individual is part of a compound player, others can manipulate her perceptions of threats. Public players have even more power to do this: there are political operatives and news media whose intent is to deploy a sense of threat for some purpose (to win an election, to sell newspapers). We have experts in threat and negativity.

In threats we see *the power of the negative* to focus attention. Sociologist Georg Simmel was so struck by this that he posited a "wholly primary need for hostility."[8] We rally against people and things more readily than for them. A California school superintendent discovered this when he proposed random drug testing of students. Twenty people attended the meeting where it was first proposed, "and they were mostly for it." Word got out by the next meeting, which a hundred and fifty people attended, almost all of them opposed.[9] Revolutions, too, are made by coalitions who agree on nothing except the unsuitability of the incumbent. According to Simmel, "In general, common enmity is one of the most powerful means for motivating a number of individuals or groups to cling together."[10] In Nigeria's Biafran war, for example, the Igbo developed from a collection of unconnected lineage groups into a unified player only when threatened by other players.[11] Negative feelings trigger action.

The power of the negative is apparent in the English language, where words for negative feelings far outnumber those for positive ones. Philosopher Robert Solomon points to "the wealth of meticulous and fine distinctions we make in describing our feelings of hostility: hatred, loathing, scorn, anger, revulsion, resentment, envy, abhorrence, malice, aversion, vexation, irritation, annoyance, disgust, spite and contempt, or worse, 'beneath' contempt. And yet we sort our positive affections for the most part between the two limp categories, 'liking' and 'loving.'"[12] There is poetry in the negative.

Political scientists have repeatedly documented the power of the negative, finding, for instance, that negative information carries more weight in political judgments than does positive information. This is especially true in impressions of others, such as candidates.[13] Negative emotions are central to mobilizing action in the short run, even to the extent of disrupting normal group loyalties such as party affiliation.[14] A single piece of negative information can dominate our impressions of another player, polluting otherwise positive knowledge. And the rhetorical power of denouncing "enemies" has long been known.

The dynamics of fear and urgency that initially draw people into strategic action can also keep them in the alliances formed for the purpose. External threats heighten the sense of boundaries between insiders and outsiders. Every brushstroke added to the portrait of outsiders as threatening and evil also makes the insiders appear more benign, innocent, and in need of mutual support. Allies of convenience become treasured teammates. The Cold War is a chilling example of this kind of polarization. In the West dissent was suppressed in country after country in the interests of national defense, and a uniformity of opinion was continually demanded of NATO countries. In the East, too, the Soviet occupation of central Europe gained whatever legitimacy it had from the argument that there was a constant threat of invasion from NATO. Each side saw the other as malevolent and expansionist, a direct and dangerous threat. Solidarity arises naturally in the face of threat, but it is also frequently enforced for strategic purposes.

Threats easily escalate symbolically well beyond any player's intentions. Vague threats can frighten us more than well-defined ones. Poorly defined threats have no limits, and our imaginations can exaggerate them. In analyzing public opinion data, David Sears and Carolyn Funk concluded that "self-interest emerged in these cases because of the combination of uncertainty and severe negative possibilities. The uncertainty, we suspect, allowed for the most threatening sorts of fantasies about one's possible fate; the imagined threats could reach extraordinary peaks, helped along by the far-reaching rumors that gain circulation in a time of uncertainty and ignorance."[15] Uncertainty characterizes much intense strategic interaction, and ignorance is especially strong in certain kinds of interactions, such as that with other nations (allowing some team members to manipulate the fears of others).

With mutual threats, such as an arms race or name-calling in a nasty divorce, escalation carries the possibility of devastating consequences on both sides. Unlike most strategic situations, a situation of mutual threat may lead reasonable players to give their opponents time to think and to make rational (less destructive) decisions. Recalling the Cuban missile crisis, Robert Kennedy said, "Against the advice of many of his advisors and of the military, [President Kennedy] decided to give Khrushchev more time. 'We don't want to push him to a precipitous action—give him time to consider. . . .'"[16] It was important to leave a variety of options open to Khrushchev rather than backing him into a corner. Pushing adversaries into tight corners is the usual goal of strategic action, but in this case the nuclear corner was simply not a desirable one for anybody.

As this example shows, players on both sides would sometimes like conflict to include elements of cooperation or reconciliation. One student of diplomacy sums up lessons in crisis management that are designed to prevent devastating outcomes in which everyone loses (World War I looms as an example of this). He suggests instituting multiple advocacy to be sure that all alternatives are considered; restricting one's own objectives as much as possible; maintaining flexible options on both sides; reducing time pressure for decision making; understanding one's opponents as fully as possible; keeping communication open at all times; and controlling the military so that it does not pursue its own game (more abstractly, this means keeping your team and allies together as a united front).[17] These steps are intended to allow both you *and your opponent* to feel less immediately threatened.

I draw on the language of crisis management because a crisis occurs when the stakes are too high to maintain one's normal routines. The sense of such high stakes may be due to the perceived threat that inspires strategic action in response. Or it may arise in the course of strategic interaction, when the risks grow so large that "normal" strategic action no longer seems appropriate. Threats can force players into cooperation as well as conflict.

In sum, most strategic players are drawn into interactions begun (intentionally or not) by others—whether those others are other players or members of your own team. In some cases you see opportunities for your own gain, but more often you see potential losses. You feel threatened in some way. If you do not respond, and respond well, you may lose something you value—a good reputation, a particular legal standing, material benefits, political office or access, treasured allies, and so forth. In chapter 3, I group these crudely into reputation, sensual satisfactions, impact on the world, and curiosity; here we can analyze threats to the first three of these (curiosity is not threatened as readily and is less strategic than the others).

INSULT

Honor is a fundamental human value. Individuals, groups, and nations can all have reputations they care about. Attacks on someone's reputation can unleash powerful passions, which lead victims to place a high value on regaining the lost honor and a low value on the costs of doing so. Certain images of honor place a premium on rebuffing all insults. In the frontier culture of America's so-called wild west, young men were quick to take umbrage at perceived slights and to regain their honor in physical combat. Medieval knights similarly resorted to a kind of righteous rage at any small slight. (Emotions like anger are more than simply irrational irruptions: they often have strategic intents and effects.)[18] Such cultures of honor fade with industrialization, but other sources of personal reputation come to the fore.[19]

The collective reputations of imagined communities can be just as highly valued as individual reputations. National pride has been one source of sensitivity, especially during the apogee of nationalism from roughly the middle of the nineteenth to the middle of the twentieth centuries. Time and time again, most bloodily in 1914, perceived slights to national honor propelled the nations of Europe close to or into war. Take the Agadir crisis of 1911, a near miss for starting World War I. Morocco was supposed to be left open to commercial exploitation by all European nations, but tensions were especially strong between France and Germany. France occupied Fez, the country's capital, which led Germany to send a gunboat to the port of Agadir. But the main action lay in the aggressive words of both those countries and Britain. There, David Lloyd George (at the time chancellor of the exchequer) gave a speech typical in its concern with not being humiliated. After praising British contributions to Europe's peace and liberty, he continued, "But if a situation were to be forced upon us, in which peace could only be preserved . . . by allowing Britain to be treated, when her interests were vitally affected, as if she were of no account in the Cabinet of nations, then I say emphatically that peace at that price would be intolerable for a great country like ours to endure."[20] Obscure though his meanings are, everyone at the time thought they knew what the "greatness" of Britain meant and what being "of no account" was. This speech aroused similar proclamations in France and Germany, further expressions of national pride and fear of insult—"fighting words," in brief. Such words can feel threatening in and of themselves, and Germany's willingness to back down in its rhetoric (the Kaiser's own decision, apparently, against the wishes of his secretary of state) avoided war in 1911. Three years later, similar words and sentiments would lead to much worse.

Reputation has many facets, and players may see insufficient recognition of any of them as a threat worthy of strategic response. The threat can be to your personal reputation or that of some collective with which you identify. The insult can portray you or your group as villainous and malevolent or as weak and ineffective. Any source of pride—bloodlines or accomplishments, beauty or intelligence, pets or mothers—can be insulted, triggering action.

Some attacks on reputation are based on concrete information, taking the form of *revelations* rather than insults. And they can be part of an interaction rather than the act that inaugurates it. In her discussion of couples, Diane Vaughan points out, "[Our partners know] us in a total way that the rest of the world does not. This knowledge of the other that accompanies intimacy can at any moment convert that safe haven into a dangerous place, for we each possess information that can be used to do the other in."[21] We are especially vulnerable to breakdowns in our alliances, as former partners have the most devastating information about us—and an incentive to use it.

Some attacks on our reputation can paralyze rather than inspire us. Shame, the utter degradation of our reputation, is devastating. It strips us of our ability to accomplish anything, even our willingness to be seen by others. At the extreme, if we feel utterly cut off from our society, we commit suicide. Japanese executives kill themselves when their companies have violated moral expectations. In the West suicide due to shame is less frequent, but the exposure (even threatened exposure) of embezzlement, pedophilia, and other actions considered immoral often triggers suicide. Unlike guilt over a specific action, shame makes us feel as though we are thoroughly bad. But when we see another's action as a strategic effort to shame us, we are often propelled through indignation into action.[22]

Rather than taking us out of play, milder forms of shame can deeply affect strategic actions. When shame is not acknowledged, a frequent result is aggression. Social psychologist Tom Scheff has written extensively about these dynamics, which he locates both in quarreling couples and vicious international conflicts. When we are insulted, we don't always acknowledge the shame we feel as a result. Instead of reacting to the insult with angry outrage, we instead become angry about feeling ashamed—as well as ashamed of feeling angry. (This is especially true of relationships that are mistrustful or deceitful to start with.) According to Scheff, these feelings "can become a self-perpetuating loop of intensely painful feelings, usually much more painful than the original shame being defended against."[23] We may in turn insult and attack the other, as revenge (hurting the other) becomes a primary motive that crowds out other goals. Like "normal" shame, unacknowledged shame often contorts our strategic projects.

If shame results from our own actions, humiliation is an equally devastating insult that typically does not. While some insults seem culturally variable—it is difficult for us today to grasp the logic of dueling, for instance—others are probably universally destructive to those on the receiving end: those who are stripped of whatever props make them human, make them members of a social order and community. The deepest insult is to take away our basic human dignity, whether through concentration camps or caste structures that make certain groups untouchable or unseeable. Yes, resistances and accommodations may make the humiliation bearable (many institutions seem designed to "normalize" inequalities and deprivations), but it remains a devastating threat. Humiliation fosters hate and rage that can lead to strategic action years later if the right team or leader can tap into them. As long as Israel continues its daily humiliations of Palestinians, for instance, it will have a stream of enthusiastic martyrs on its hands. (Rationalist formulations that view martyrs as motivated by a calculation of rewards in the hereafter or altruistic identification with the group ignore this emotional dynamic: Revenge for humiliation is directly satisfying.)[24]

DEPRIVATION

Other basic threats involve our physical safety, even our lives. These range from our gut-level reaction to a blurred figure coming toward us from the shadows to a more cognitively filtered fear that the hazardous waste dump down the road is making us ill. But direct harm is only an extreme form of a wide class of threats to our sensual being, our bodily pleasures and needs. We can be deprived not only of the use of our bodies, but of our ability to move around at will, our pursuit of accustomed pastimes and pleasures, or connections with loved ones (which are not necessarily physical but have the same gut-level quality even when they are Platonic). And when loved ones are threatened, like Lois Gibbs's son, it feels as though we ourselves are—or worse.

The threat of harm is especially likely to arouse the emotions and adrenaline sufficient for frenzied activity. After a military rout, those pursuing rarely have the energy to catch those running for their lives. But in the brutal world of a warrior class, in what we think of today as primitive societies, physical pain may have been less frightening than the possible loss of honor. In flight we become physical objects to be hunted down; in fight we retain our agency. But even in flight, we can recover agency through choices about hiding, regrouping, or surrendering.

Just as shame can paralyze, so can physical fear. We are frozen, in a kind of shock that prevents the brain from processing information and making quick decisions. To succeed, players must find ways to overcome paralyzing fears; this is one reason that troops are so well trained. But short of this extreme, physical threat usually puts us into action. Our responses may be organized and calculated, and frequently delayed, but this should not hide the fears helping to motivate them.

Different kinds of physical threats lead to different responses. Institutionalized violence, like that of a dictatorial regime that "disappears" people, requires a different reaction than the one we have to the personal violence of a mugger. Violence, in turn, feels different from an illness. Sudden threats—a gunshot or car accident—may be more shocking than chronic ones such as lead-paint poisoning. Threats that can be traced to human choices trigger a different emotional response than those that seem to be true accidents. Combinations are possible: hazardous waste dumps are a physical threat, but the decision to place them in our neighborhood can be framed as an insult (would they have put it in a rich suburban neighborhood?). Physical threats are rarely pure: they are frequently assaults on our reputations as well. Many of these differences are captured in the idea of blame, as we will see below.

INCAPACITY

In addition to the satisfaction we gain from our reputations and our physical existence, we get satisfaction from our ability to have an effect on the world around us, and so this too can be threatened. Try taking away people's right to vote or other ways of having a say in what happens around them. Their reaction is unmistakable. Early labor mobilization was spurred by economic threats, but what workers most demanded was some say in politics and the ability to form unions so that they could manage their own affairs. The Berkeley Free Speech Movement is a dramatic example of a strategic response to the withdrawal of a relatively minor right, namely the right to hand out pamphlets at the main entrance to the Berkeley campus (on a strip of land outside the gate but owned by the university). Students had come to take the pamphleteering for granted, and were indignant when an old prohibition was suddenly enforced.[25]

People can also be incapacitated in their productive activities. According to the young Marx and others, this is the essence of alienation: the industrial proletariat no longer recognize their products as their own, no longer feel a sense of pride in having produced something from raw materials the way that peasants supposedly do (or did). This ability to create something in the world (artists are an extreme example) is another aspect of dignity, alongside reputation in others' eyes.

We may want to affect the world for all sorts of reasons, in pursuit of almost any goal. We may wish to create, protect, or aid our children, prevent evil and punish evildoers, contribute to history or progress, or save other species. Most goals require action in the world around us. Seeing our product, our effect, is deeply satisfying to most of us. And one of the worst effects of deprivation is that it strips away our sense of agency, our confidence in our strategic and other capacities.

MORAL SHOCKS

In any of these categories—insult, deprivation, incapacity—a perceived threat strong enough to trigger a strategic response administers what I have elsewhere called a "moral shock."[26] As the term implies, powerful threats do not merely provide new information, they arouse emotions and usually a sense of moral indignation. You find that your best friend is sleeping with your husband, your boss is embezzling funds, one of our closest allies has moles in our defense ministry. How could they do this to us? When we suddenly realize that the world is not what it seems, that our basic assumptions have been wrong, the resulting shift is not merely cognitive. We may get enough of an emotional jolt to propel us into action. By definition, we don't expect shocks, and the surprise we feel gives us emotional energy that propels us forward. Shocks rattle the complacency of our daily routines. One goal or moral intuition may rise to the surface to crowd out others. Narrative theorists have referred to moral shocks as "inciting incidents."[27]

The passion of most shocks comes from our sense of betrayal. In some cases people we love and trust have betrayed us, but at a deeper level in all cases the *world* has duped us. We were wrong about what the world is like. This shock fuses cognitive shifts with emotional responses, since there is always a twinge of indignation, and perhaps shame over our own naïveté. How could we have been so wrong, so gullible? "The deepest hatred," remarked Georg Simmel, "grows out of broken love."[28]

In addition to new information, we may also get a shock from the juxtaposition of two people, settings, ideas, or actions in a way that forces us to compare them. We may realize how bad our job is when we return from an extended vacation, how vacuous our buying habits are when we go to the mall right after church. Diane Vaughan refers to this as "re-entry shock." In her example, people thinking of leaving a relationship are pushed toward this when they return to their partners after being away: "Often the initiator's moment of certainty occurs after the initiator has had an intense experience elsewhere, then rejoins the world shared with the partner. Perhaps the initiator returns from a reunion with family or old friends, a business meeting in another city, a stolen weekend with a lover, or from a satisfying time alone."[29] Shocks remind us of our basic goals and values: What do we "really" want from life? Sometimes questions like these inspire new strategic projects.

Some shocks cripple us, forcing us to abandon some stream of action or identity. Far from arousing indignation, they often impose on us a kind of moral collapse or shame, as we are the ones who have done something wrong. (The mistake could be a grave moral error or a strategic misstep.) As with other shocks, some supporting component of our world has been kicked out from under us, along with the stream of action it sustained, but we may not have moral and cognitive reserves to fall back on in order to fabricate a new strategic path. Jack Katz provides an example, describing the moment when a murderer's story collapses under interrogation. "Martin is first shocked by the revelation that the police have eyewitnesses. He receives the news with a blank face and then with evasions." Martin soon cries, recognizing that the story and "self" he had crafted so far had failed to persuade. "His crying is not a giving up or a giving in, but the third step in a quickly improvised strategy of self-preservation. . . . [It] is a dramatization of a dissolving self enacted in the process of searching for a new overall understanding of the interrogation situation he is in."[30] Martin does not entirely give up, but tries another tack, presenting himself as a victim to be pitied. He has suffered a serious strategic check, from which he will not in fact recover.

Clifford Geertz gives a characteristically existential twist to the bafflement we sometimes feel—not only from moral shocks but from other events as well. He emphasizes the cognitive work we do in response rather than the strategic:

> There are at least three points where chaos—a tumult of events which lack not just interpretation but *interpretability*—threatens to break in upon man: at the limits of his analytic capacities, at the limits of his powers of endurance, and at the limits of his moral insight. Bafflement, suffering, and a sense of intractable ethical paradox are all, if they become intense enough or are sustained long enough, radical challenges to the proposition that life is comprehensible and that we can, by taking thought, orient ourselves effectively within it.[31]

Geertz is not clear about who does the cultural repair work that is necessary; he leaves it vaguely to the community as a whole.

We respond to shocks, evidence of a changed world, in various ways. We may be overwhelmed, depressed, or cynical to such an extent that we resign ourselves to fate. We may lack the self-esteem or confidence to confront evildoers, if there are any. Or we may not consider the shock serious enough to be worth the effort of a strategic response. We stick to our routines and wait for the threat to blow over. But if we can figure out what to do, and have the confidence and resources to do it, and, perhaps most important of all, can figure out whom to blame, the shock frequently triggers strategic action (although that's a lot of "ifs"). By helping us to clarify our goals and forcing us to evaluate our lives, moral shocks can help us decide to engage in action.

This is the reason our opponents often try to talk down our shock, hoping to minimize our strategic response. Erving Goffman famously referred to this as "cooling the mark out." In a team of con artists, one may stay behind to engage the mark as he realizes he has been taken. The cooler helps the mark interpret what has happened to him so he does not complain to police or chase after the other perpetrators. Instead, he may blow off steam to the cooler, delay out of uncertainty, or simply write the event off as a learning experience. Organizations use similar techniques to deal with disgruntled employees, clients, and customers, discouraging them from opening a new strategic arena by complaining to authorities.[32]

Death deals the most extreme moral shocks. It "focuses the attention," as Samuel Johnson put it. The loss of a loved one, threats to our own lives, even gruesome news of a stranger's death can propel us into action. Feuds, lawsuits, wars, and social movements are all potential results. Like other shocks, death forces us to think about what we value most in life and to ask ourselves what we should do to get it. It is a compelling context for launching strategic initiatives. A person may decide to quit her job, start a new career, divorce a spouse, or reform her business practices. Like birth and sexual relations, death is a basic life passage that helps us define our humanity, so any threat to our expectations here will arouse strong emotional responses.[33]

Failure can shock us out of our complacency, focusing the attention and encouraging innovation. Defeat is probably the greatest inspiration for learning and change in strategic teams. Personnel and practices are both shaken up. As long as the failure is not fatal to the player, it is a source of rationality, defined simply as the ability to learn from mistakes. The more severe, dramatic, and memorable the failure, the more change it normally imposes. Defeats have always been the main source of innovations in military practices, for instance.

Moral shocks highlight emotions, but they are involved in most decisions to enter strategic engagements. Unless we are paid to engage others strategically (and often even then), we are driven (at least it feels as if we are driven) by outrage, shock, anger, fear, and other emotions. Gamesters are wrong in presenting strategic choices as resulting from cold calculations of interests; they more often spring from the hot impulses of emotions. It takes moral passion to get people into the street, to file a grievance, or to betray a friend. Emotions motivate action. They force us into fateful moments.

We can be equally shocked by actions that are intended strategically and those that are not. Either can strike us as immoral or repulsive, triggering action on our part. We may not take the time to ask whether an affront was strategic, frequently assuming that it was, without any evidence: How could anyone do this without knowing the effect on us? Our response nonetheless has more energy if propelled by the greater indignation we feel at intentional actions. Our ability to point a finger at someone is key.[34]

BLAME

Can we find someone to blame for a threat, someone whose conscious act caused our troubles? If we can denounce a corporation, nation, individual, or other player, we may seek redress through a strategic response. But if we are threatened by something we feel is an act of god or nature—a flood or hurricane—strategizing usually seems less appropriate (beyond a promise to attend religious services more regularly if our god will help out this one time). According to Goffman, this choice between social and natural is a basic component of how we frame events.[35] Nature does not respond to our strategic moves. Job was indignant at the way his god treated him, but his strategic response was limited to complaints. More would have been fruitless. (Their intransigence is what makes gods and nature trumps in rhetorical arguments: You cannot "reason" with them.)[36]

When we are dealing with humans, rather than a god or nature, we attribute the "intentional stance" to them. This is philosopher Daniel Dennett's term for how we interpret what other people believe and how we anticipate what they will do. It differs from the physical stance, in which we use folk physics to make predictions, especially about the natural world, but also from the design stance, in which we assume that an object will work as it was developed and designed to work, without knowing anything about its physical details. It is tempting to treat organizations and other teams as designed systems, but ultimately the design stance will mislead us, especially when it comes to strategic interaction. We switch to an intentional stance, which assumes goals based on people's experience: "One starts with the ideal of perfect rationality and revises downward as circumstances dictate." As Dennett goes on to say, the intentional stance "works with people almost all the time."[37] We can predict what they will do, but we also blame them for the effects of their actions.

Many threats lie between the extremes of the natural and the human, like the global air pollution that hurts our lungs but is tough to blame on any particular source. Ecologists must work harder to blame power plants in far-off regions for acid rain than to rouse fears about the nuclear power plant being built down the road. A definable, observable threat, embodied in tons of ugly concrete, owned by specific companies and regulated by known agencies, allows more blame and indignation.

The intentional stance interacts with the power of the negative in the "ultimatum game" and related experiments. One player decides how to share a sum of money with a second player, with the proviso that the second player can reject the offer altogether, in which case neither gets anything.[38] A monetarily maximizing player should never reject a positive offer, since she is giving up money, but players typically reject what they consider unfair offers by the first player, who is keeping too much for himself. They are "paying" to avoid unfairness. But if "offers" are generated randomly by a computer, which they cannot blame, they generally accept unequal ones. In variations on ultimatum games, players respond more strongly to unfair offers than to fair ones. "Positive reciprocity," comments Colin Camerer, "is weak relative to negative reciprocity. (As in life, laboratory subjects are quicker to avenge perceived attacks than they are to write thank-you notes.)"[39]

Economic threats, easy to blame on human instigators, often result in strategic action. Layoffs, wage cuts, plant closings, and job deskilling threaten human dignity as well as physical well-being. They have been the main causes of labor insurgency, especially in times and places where unions are illegal. The corporate executives who make or implement adverse decisions try to present their actions as responses to forces of nature, imposed on the corporation by international competition. Talk of "globalization" serves this purpose well.[40] It shifts the blame and defuses strategic reactions (or channels them into demonstrations against, say, the Japanese). American culture has proven especially receptive to this argument. Our capacity to earn a living is a complex accomplishment, so threats to it combine insult, incapacity, and potential deprivation. And yet few mobilize, because they do not know whom to blame.

Blame for complex technological failures is always controversial, as they can never be truly attributed to "nature." Formal organizations, especially corporations, try instead to blame operator error, deflecting attention from their own structures and the risky technologies they have developed. One exception is the space shuttle, partly because astronauts have so little control over it to start with and partly because so much effort has gone into making them heroes in the interest of keeping funding robust. NASA simply could not pin the blame for failures on them. Best of all is to blame your opponents for accidents, as Union Carbide did when it insisted—with no hard evidence—that sabotage had caused the catastrophic Bhopal accident in 1983.

The boundaries of blame are cultural creations that shift, often as the result of strategic action. Over time, we have come to expect more intervention from government into health and nature and security. What once seemed like acts of god no longer do. But contention remains. Corporate spokespeople insist that the apparent warming of the environment is a natural fluctuation, so that government intervention into production processes is unwarranted. On the other hand, Christian fundamentalists insist that HIV spreads through human choices, not nature, so that victims can be blamed for their own illness; victims respond by insisting on the medicalization (or naturalization) of the problem.

The concept of responsibility, which accompanies a construction of blame, has two sides. Actors may be responsible for *causing* some threat or responsible for *fixing* it—and these responsibilities do not always fall on the same actors. In modern societies, especially, we hold government responsible for fixing a range of problems it did not cause, from crime to epidemics and recessions. We also hold it responsible for preventing a number of threats—for example by predicting bad storms or intercepting terrorists—and lack of prevention becomes a form of cause. And if nothing else, we expect governments to clean up afterwards. For this reason, various levels and branches and agencies of government are frequently the first targets of strategic action, the most important "third party" in many interactions (although they often metamorphose into opponents rather than remaining judges or keepers of the arenas).

When we hold government responsible for redressing a wrong, we add incapacity to the original threats we fear. Government, in a democratic nation, represents our power to control the world. So when it is not responsive to our pleas, we feel the additional threat of impotence. We can feel milder forms of the same frustration in dealing with other entities such as corporations, but our indignation is muted because we rarely view them as an instrument by which we control the world. When government agencies or elected officials must approve plans, we know exactly who is culpable. We can figure out where the proposal for a public housing project came from. There is an added dimension of outrage in these cases, as we usually expect governments to be democratic and accountable and thus protective of our interests (we forget that other groups have their interests too). We are more shocked when governments do not protect us than when corporations pursue their own interests. (The modern middle class, at least, usually expects government responsiveness. Poor and oppressed groups know better.)

In modern societies, gods and nature have receded as explanations for mishaps, and organizations loom larger. Allocating blame becomes more and more a strategic activity. As Anthony Giddens and others have pointed out, we rely increasingly on experts and the systems they create, since we cannot directly accomplish much for ourselves—whether in transportation, communication, production, or even government. "Instead," says sociologist William Freudenburg, "the expectation is that *someone* will be performing the necessary calculations, and doing so in a way that others can 'count on.' But it may be precisely this expectation that becomes increasingly problematic as the societal division of labor grows more complex."[41] Institutional failures have increased, he believes, but I would add that strategic conflict over whom to blame for those failures has also increased. (Corporations have become especially adept at dodging blame.)

The flip side of seeking someone else to blame is for strategic players to avoid being blamed themselves. Like the corporations that shift culpability for plant closings onto the "natural" processes of markets, bureaucracies seem to be designed as vast systems of organized irresponsibility (as C. Wright Mills put it). Corporate executives have usually moved on before their mistakes surface, leaving their successors as scapegoats.[42] In many arenas, such as courts, blame must be assigned for every possible failure. In strategic settings, considerable cultural work goes into allocating blame, as this in turn affects outcomes. National governments blame international agencies, and vice versa. Blame is a crucial part of creating "character types," especially victims and villains.

The rhetorical work that goes into denying or affixing blame affects action, whether it is accurate or not. The "real" causes are only a small referent in broader arguments. Interestingly, social scientists are more likely to attribute outcomes to impersonal causes—something like acts of god—than strategic players are. Strategists must mobilize allies and supporters by blaming individuals and other players for perceived threats, hiding the underlying market or other forces that share some of the blame. Even if they are wrong in their attribution, the effects of their framings are the same. As William Gamson puts it, "Concreteness in the target, even when it is misplaced and directed away from the real causes of hardship, is a necessary condition for an injustice frame."[43] Of course, concrete players often *are* to blame.

To blame someone is to insist that they acted intentionally—or should have acted intentionally and did not (as with negligence). Individuals vary considerably in the degree to which they attribute intention to others. At the extreme, paranoids see intention everywhere, even in behavior the rest of us would see as random, accidental, and unmotivated. As a result, paranoids are quick to see threats in the world around them. Because they expect others to act strategically, they get involved in a larger number of strategic interactions. They make more enemies because they see people as enemies quite readily. They are prepared for engagements, and they bring them on themselves partly as a result. (Chapter 4 treats the Paranoid Dilemma further.)

Several factors contribute to a person's willingness to blame another, thereby possibly initiating strategic interaction. According to sociologist Candace Clark, they include the other person's perceived causal responsibility, but also prior offenses, cultural capital, degree of contrition, punishment already suffered, as well as mitigating and extenuating circumstances and the closeness of the relationship between judger and judged.[44] The person's character matters as well as her actions. In contrast to Clark's finding that cultural capital makes someone less blameworthy, two other researchers found that those with hierarchical authority were more likely to be blamed. They also found some cultural differences between Americans and Japanese: The latter took the obligations of a person's role into greater account.[45]

Just as we face the Engagement Dilemma in deciding whether to initiate strategic action ourselves, we face it in deciding whether to respond to the actions of others. Even when we feel that an injustice has been committed, even when we can single out actors for blame, we may not think it is worth the effort to fight or protest. Fighting back will keep us reliving the affront, which may have been traumatic or stigmatizing. Like all strategic programs, our reaction is likely to be expensive, too. At the same time, retaliation is often satisfying and can become a goal in itself, regardless of any other initial goals—call this the Revenge Dilemma, a version of the Engagement Dilemma. "Anyone who thinks," said Machiavelli, "that recent benefits make great people forget old injuries is simply deluding himself."[46] In addition to the satisfying emotions that revenge entails, justice is one of our fundamental goals, worth considerable time and effort to attain.[47]

INTENTIONAL THREATS

Threats are often intentional moves by other players to get something from you. They are usually part of an ongoing engagement, but sometimes they are the opening move. Kidnappings and ransoms are the obvious example. But anything that we value can be held up to threat. Threats are a form of promise, or words, although the threat may promise much more than words. Just as another player's offer or contract commits them to doing something that you desire under defined conditions (usually an action on your part), a threat commits them to doing something you do not want. If you refuse an offer, you are no worse off; if you ignore a threat and it is carried out, you are.[48] You have a choice when threatened, but typically one option is extremely undesirable. Otherwise, it is "not much of a threat," as we say.

Stated threats come in different forms, and at the milder end of the continuum, they merge with warnings. Legal theorist Kent Greenawalt distinguishes four types, depending on whether the words are meant to induce action and whether they themselves change the situation of the player threatened. The mildest is a mere warning: I inform you that if you do something, harm will result, but I do not propose to cause the harm. Second, I may tell you I intend to harm you, perhaps for revenge, without trying to extract any change in action from you; I am not trying to coerce you. The third case, a warning threat, is trickier: I tell you I am going to do something to you, such as call the police if you do not clean up the rat-infested heap of trash in your yard. I want to induce action, but I am not changing your situation—since I already intend to call the police, and am offering you the opportunity to forestall this action. Finally, by a manipulative threat I create a new situation for you in saying that I will take an action (that I otherwise would not) if you do not do what I want. I create a problem for you that did not exist before. In the third case, I am responding to your own actions and situation, whereas in the fourth I am initiating some kind of engagement in pursuit of my own goals (blackmail is an example). In the absence of my ability to communicate with you, I would still act as I have threatened to in the third case, but probably not in the fourth.[49]

The structure of a threat—promising not to follow through if the victim complies—makes for interesting problems. If the victim of a threat refuses to comply, what does the other party do? She has lost her capacity to get what she really wants, compliance, and following through with her threat may be costly to her. But she gets the satisfaction of revenge and in some cases may enhance her reputation as a player to be taken seriously. Many threats are relatively secret, so that a reputation for how one deals with refused threats may be of limited use (but it is damaged if you fail to follow through). "If the victim refuses to give in to the threat," Goffman points out, "the blackmailer has nothing to gain from that particular victim by going through with the disclosure. . . . spite has no place in a well-conducted business—although the impression that one is spiteful does." A threat is only credible if your victim thinks you will follow through on it. In this case, concludes Goffman, "blackmailers must convincingly act as if they do not appreciate their dilemma."[50]

The dilemma to which Goffman refers is partly a variant of the Engagement Dilemma: the threat must be credible enough to arouse a strategic response from the threatened party. (Goffman does not address the possibility that the latter may react strategically but make a different move than paying the demands, such as going to the police or other powerful agents who might intervene.) Game theory has done a great deal to explain this problem of threat, beginning with Thomas Schelling's analysis of nuclear deterrence. Threats are not credible, he argued, if the costs of carrying them out are high and the threatening player is left in a worse position if he follows through on the threat. But this ignores the emotional dynamics, which can be self-destructive, as well as the concern for maintaining a certain reputation.

Game theory shows the interaction of possible moves, allowing players to compare alternatives. One way to make a threat credible even though the action would be costly—even irrational—is to make some kind of commitment that would be difficult or impossible to break. This has become known as the "grim trigger" strategy. Alas, few strategic players are willing—or even able—to bind their own futures in this way. If nothing else, threats are a form of communication that signals intentions and goals to others.[51] Intentional or not, they are the main moves or perceptions through which strategic interaction begins.

THE COMMITMENT DILEMMA → When you make a commitment, whether a promise of something positive or a threat of something negative, it reduces your strategic freedom. Others will not usually complain if you back off from your threat, but they will if you renege on a promise. A commitment makes certain strategic choices more costly: your reputation suffers if you do something you have promised not to or fail to do what you have promised. Commitments made to allies are frequently problematic, as when allies act in ways you deplore. And if your allies believe in your total commitment to the alliance, they can ignore your preferences in making decisions (something like this has happened to African Americans in the U.S. Democratic Party).[52]

✗

Some threats are strong or unfair enough to provoke strategic action; others are not. Perhaps the resources, opportunities, and arenas for a response are there, perhaps not. Maybe a player can be found to blame, maybe not. Nonetheless, a perception of threat seems the most common reason to enter strategic engagements. But to understand the full range of human values that can be threatened, and indeed the motives behind all strategic action, we need to examine the things humans desire—a diverse lot indeed. No simple model can do justice to them.

CHAPTER 3

GOALS

The greatest joy is to conquer one's enemies, to pursue them,
to seize their property, to see their families in tears, to ride their
horses and to possess their daughters and wives.
→ GENGHIS KHAN

Id quod est praestantissimum maximeque optabile omnibus sanis
et bonis et beatis, cum dignitate otium [What is desired the most,
by those who are healthy, good, and blessed, is leisure with honor].
→ CICERO

I have never been motivated by money in my entire life.
→ MICHAEL MILKEN, 1996

My last three years at New York University were taken up by an extended
battle over my tenure. I should have been leading the charge, of course, but
instead a large number of wonderful colleagues waged the battle on my behalf. I should admit that I am not especially gifted as a strategic actor (most
social scientists, I think, write about things that mystify them), so the fight
was better off in their hands. I had published twenty journal articles and
book chapters, was finishing my third book, and had a great reputation as a
teacher and contributor to the life of the department. I only had two official
votes against me, but that was an opening wedge for problems at higher levels. Some were fluke events, others reflected an inept administration, a couple were the acts of a dean who disliked the department and was reputedly
thinking of closing it, and some suggested surreptitious campaigning by

my departmental opponents. (Leading the charge against me was my wife's first husband, hardly an unbiased evaluator.) Among other odd events, a former dean of the New School for Social Research wrote a bizarre evaluation letter which, ignoring my work, pompously argued that anyone who studied social movements was more ideological than scholarly.

In brief, there were battles at every level until a corpulent dean of arts and sciences decided that—in the interest of being tough in the style of corporate managers—he could not pass such a controversial case no matter how personal the opposition. A national wave of angry letters to the university president caused him to send the decision back to the dean the following year, but the dean returned it to the same committee (with five of the same six members) that had already decided against me. When challenged, not surprisingly, they decided they had done nothing wrong! The same decision went back up, and this time the president went along (although he soon fired the dean for his ineptitude in mine and similar cases: it is harder to admit the system has erred than to get rid of the personnel who made the mistake). Two grievance committees found strongly and indignantly in my favor (several members wrote personal notes of outrage in addition to their joint report), but they were simply ignored.

Out of the many strategic aspects of this long battle, I want to concentrate on only one: my own complex mixture of motives in the midst of it all (in multifaceted strategic settings, introspection is often the most thorough research technique). At first I was angry at the negative votes in the department, especially since I knew they had nothing to do with my record. I wanted to stay to exact revenge, although part of my revenge fantasy was to stay and be perfectly forgiving in order to demonstrate that I was not the kind of person they apparently thought I was. The pleasure of conquering my enemies gave way to thoughts about my reputation and self-identity. Running through both, though, was a simple sense of indignation over injustice. You hate to see bullies win. Also, I knew that a stigma went with getting turned down for tenure, no matter what the circumstances (more people would know that I was turned down than would know why). Even more than these reasons, I wanted to stay because I enjoyed the work, the department, the location. I took enormous pleasure from it all. As the battle progressed, I developed an additional motive: appreciation for the hard work my colleagues were putting into their fight on my behalf (one of them told me that in the last six months she had written more words about my case than she had toward her own research). I fought harder so as not to let them down.

But almost from the start I developed contrary motives. The uncertainty of my academic future made me stop and ask—as moral shocks tend to do—what I really wanted to be doing with my life. The answer was, I wanted to write full time. I made endless financial calculations to convince myself (and my wife) that this was feasible, with the result that it was hard to work enthusiastically to win my tenure battle. Instead, I spent my time finishing *The Art of Moral Protest* and consulting for a large foundation. At that point, the job came to look like little more than a paycheck, which certainly had some value but not enough to make it worth suing over—not even enough to keep up the fight. My new goal came to dominate the rest.

THE DIVERSITY OF GOALS

The usual goals of human action are numerous but not infinite. The obvious ones include dignity, wealth, command over your own body, holding and exploiting positions, control over your personal life as well as more remote aspects of the world, understanding and respect from others, solidarity with groups, affective bonds with other individuals, compassion and altruism, voyeurism and exhibitionism, erotic and sensual contact (including altered states of consciousness), knowledge and understanding, spiritual purity and righteousness, creativity, beauty—and of course riding your enemies' horses (otherwise known as revenge or maybe sheer, cruel power). Providing all of these things for loved ones, especially your children, is another powerful goal.

Philosophers have argued over the purpose of human life, reaching little consensus. Some crave stability, comfort, and safety; others enjoy risk and change. Some want solidarity and sameness with those around them; others want to distinguish themselves. Cicero's honorable leisure—which he never quite attained—is a far cry from the Khan's passion for rape and revenge. The list of satisfactions is long, and only a case-by-case study of psychology and culture could explain how an individual or group selects from or ranks them.

The dream of moralists and political analysts has been to compare all human goals and motivations on the same metric, usually that of wealth or power. This is especially true of economic models, which depict politicians as maximizing votes or bureaucrats as maximizing the budgets of their agencies.[1] Such an approach seems necessary if humans are to choose easily between different payoffs in simple games, or if utilitarian policymakers are to maximize happiness in their societies through the one best decision. This kind of oversimplification should help us judge an action to be rational or irrational: it is rational if it maximizes our total utility, an aggregation of all our desired ends. Alas, such a utility function must remain a utopian fiction. Any model that posits one primary human goal—or even a set of comparable ones—is creating a straw man.[2]

Even in the simplified world of mathematical monetary payoffs, where outcomes are easily compared, there are different decision principles. In games that have no single dominant strategy, computer scientist Henry Hamburger lists four different ways of choosing. One is the optimistic principle of finding the highest payoff in the whole matrix of possible outcomes and working to reach it (in other words choosing the row [or column] containing that cell and hoping to manipulate the other players' choices)—known to game theorists as the "maximax" strategy. Another is the pessimistic principle of picking the row with the best worst outcome, that is, playing it safe—the "maximin" strategy (maximize the minimum you can get). This makes sense when we have no control over how other players will react to our opening choice. We might also pick a row where the possible outcomes average out to the highest return—reasonable if we thought other players were responding randomly. Finally, we might try to minimize our regret, choosing the row where none of the outcomes is very bad. "All of these principles," Hamburger observes, "are logically distinct since they all may lead to different choices in a matrix without a dominant strategy."[3] Other principles might include selecting the simplest moves, the moves chosen last time, or those that would give all the players—taken together—the greatest satisfaction. These choices reflect not only the Risk Dilemma but also efforts to look ahead to other games, as well as our varying guesses about what other players will do.[4]

You maximize in mathematical models, not the real world. There, you satisfice, settling for some acceptable level of satisfaction across many goals rather than constantly searching for some ideal maximum. The very concept of a maximum possible level of satisfaction is dubious for an individual, given the many activities and complex combinations open to most people. It is even less realistic for compound players, whose stated goals are rhetorical fictions. Satisficing can be a major or a minor amendment to economic models, depending on the criteria for "satisfactory"; Herbert Simon, who invented the concept, thinks that satisficing is not compatible with rational-choice explanations. Maximizing is a science; satisficing, an art.[5]

In theory, players may find systematic ways to satisfice, for example by developing a hierarchy of needs or goals. They first satisfy the most important one, which in many cases is survival, then address the next one, and so on. A government may be most concerned with clinging to power, concerning itself only secondarily with ideological agendas, and finally—having attained some satisfactory level of each—turning to material benefits for its citizens. Political scientist Richard Rosecrance calls such a hierarchy an "onion model," as one must deal with the outer layer before going on to the second.[6] But we can see how simplistic the onion model is when we consider the example of a state, which consists of thousands of subplayers pursuing innumerable goals simultaneously, not sequentially. An environmental ministry may relax some rules in a time of war, but it does not redirect itself entirely to the war effort (for which it would probably not be very useful). Most players, compound and simple, juggle a number of different projects at the same time.

Some satisfactions are subject to diminishing returns; others are not. With sensual pleasures, satiety sets in at some point for everyone, much as that point differs across individuals. People who care about fame or money, on the other hand, can never seem to accumulate enough, perhaps because the standards of what *is* enough are vague. Some accomplishments simply whet our appetites for more. It is not possible to say how much is enough.

Most students of strategic goals, from international relations to theories of the firm, have assumed that a player's survival always comes first in any hierarchy of priorities. Without the player there can be no pursuit of other goals. A moment's thought indicates that this cannot be right. It assumes a self-interested and unified player, something like an organism. Yet even organisms, including or especially humans, sometimes sacrifice themselves for broader teams or ideals. Compound players are often destroyed or disbanded for the sake of their component members. Protest groups that get what they want sometimes dissolve, and profitless businesses are sometimes shuttered. It is true that many of these organizations are *not* shut down when they should be, finding new purposes and organizational forms. But the possibility always exists as a dilemma.

SURVIVAL VERSUS SUCCESS → Being in a game and doing well in it are two different things. Normally, this is not a direct dilemma, as you must be in the game to do well. But mere survival may not be worth it without success. Survival may be necessary to success, but it is not sufficient. And we encounter occasional risks that combine the possibility of great success in the short run with extinction in the longer run. More commonly, withdrawal from one game (or the extinction of one player) allows greater success in other games and for other players. Corporate executives who milk their companies for their own gains, thereby weakening them in the long run, are a classic example. (Economists and sociologists have seized different horns of this dilemma in theories of firms: economists see them as pursuing profits, that is, success, and sociologists counter that they are actually interested in stability and survival.)[7]

THE BAD-MONEY DILEMMA → The tension between survival and success often leads players to dedicate time, attention, and resources to avoiding the loss of what has already been committed—throwing good money after bad. Ending the engagement means a certain loss, whereas continuing it leaves open some (usually small) chance of success—as well as the chance of even bigger losses. Vietnam posed this dilemma for the Johnson administration. Usually, the decision to persist in such a situation is simply a case of poor judgment, but it is sometimes a real dilemma, especially when devastating consequences would ensue from acknowledging the existing loss, with its symbolic and emotional ramifications. When your survival as a player is at stake, for instance, it may make sense to throw good money after bad for as long as you can.

Culturally based comparisons are crucial to satisficing: you may simply make choices that promise to improve your existing level of welfare, or you may instead strive to attain the apparent levels of some reference group. In the first case you probably have some normative impression of what kinds of satisfactions you deserve, which leaves you dissatisfied when you fall short. In the latter case you see others as a model for how you should live, comparing your accomplishments with theirs. In one case, you compare your situation with your own past and future; in the other, to that of other people or groups. Either way, cultural traditions affect our definitions of the term *satisfactory*.[8]

All the items on my list above are things that individuals may value, but a few are also possible goals for groups, collectivities, and organizations, especially wealth, reputation, and position. But even these depend, in the end, on the satisfaction that their possession or use gives to the individual members of the group. Organizations can have formally stated goals, but not motivations. And they cannot have satisfactions—only individuals can.

This is important for understanding the purposes of strategic action: we must always be wary when we speak of compound players, remembering that they always comprise simple players with their own motivations, able to defect from stated group goals.

Goals normally differ depending on whether you are initiating interaction or are responding to others. Initiators want to change the status quo; they see a prize they want, a new state of the world they hope to bring about. When you are reacting, especially to a perceived threat, you are usually trying to preserve the status quo in order to avoid something bad. If I was right in chapter 2 about basic human security, then preserving it will animate more activity than proactive campaigns, if for no other reason than the attention, planning, and resources that launching a stream of action demands. (Of course you may intend to change things in the short run in order to protect your position in the long run: various elites do this all the time by making concessions. In politics we call it reform.)

Max Weber, discussing strategic teams, pointed to the immense diversity of their goals. "All the way from provision for subsistence to the patronage of art, there is no conceivable end which *some* political association has not at some time pursued. And from the protection of personal security to the administration of justice, there is none which *all* have recognized."[9]

Is there at least some way to categorize so many goals? Historians have tried to do this with war. One traditional goal of war was glory, the ability to conquer others and prove yourself through combat; glory led to fame, making you the subject of legend and epic. Treasure was another draw, and in today's world of markets and materialism the control of resources is a standard theme of conflict. Wealth enhances reputations, allows sensual enjoyments, and yields a capacity to influence the world. In some cases, too, ideology has driven foreign interventions, although this too may be a form of glory—god's glory, in the case of the religious ideologies that have caused so much warfare (especially since the rise of ideological religions such as Christianity and Islam).[10] The point of an ideology is to shape the world according to some idea.

These goals fall crudely into three basic groups: *reputation* in the eyes of oneself and others; direct sensual *pleasures*, including loving and being loved; and the ability to have an *impact* on the world around one (honor, riches, and command, as Hobbes might have put it). I believe similar goals also drive smaller-scale projects. A study of burglars, for instance, found that they valued money most, followed by reputation (among their fellows) and the thrill of the activity itself.[11] But to these three classic goals, I would add a fourth, knowledge, overlooked because it rarely embroils a player in strategic interactions.

REPUTATION

"Reputation, reputation, reputation! O, I have lost my reputation! I have lost the immortal part of myself, and what remains is bestial." So proclaimed Cassio in *Othello*, showing how we especially value something we have just lost.[12] What do other people think of you? Throughout human history, in one fashion or another, this has been what people cared about most. It has been analyzed as glory and honor, status and prestige, respect and admiration, shame or pride, and many other terms. But they all add up to one's reputation among others both near and far. (Women through history have cared more about their near reputations; men, their extended reputations.) The term *reputation* traditionally captured the sweeping moral quality of these judgments (as opposed to *repute*, a more specific trait); it used to be said that someone was "of no reputation," as we still say, "He's of no account."

Our most basic sense of personal identity depends on recognition from others. It is hard to think of ourselves as tough, funny, or compassionate without some external confirmation. We belong to groups or categories that entail stigma or pride—such as an occupation with high status, the stuff of so many sociology articles. National pride has been the main cause of war in modern history, as one nation's leaders felt belittled in the eyes of others. Personal insults, similarly, have been the cause of every manner of strategic action. Once formed, any strategic team will develop a collective reputation, and its sensitivity to that reputation—as revealed (or imagined) in the words and actions of others—will affect its actions in turn. This is true regardless of the purpose for which the team was formed.

Respect and dignity are basic building blocks with which we craft an identity for ourselves as human beings, as members in full standing of a certain team, tribe, society, or community. It is often difficult for modern analysts, living in broadly utilitarian market societies, to appreciate the centrality of dignity as a goal. Much action is meant to establish dignity without "ulterior," namely, material, motives. It is one of the accepted "truths" of social movement research, for instance, that people do not join protests unless they think they can win, but protest itself—even in losing causes—can offer dignity to participants.[13] The Jews of the Warsaw uprising of 1943 did not really think they would overthrow the Nazis, but they chose a dignified death.

Dignity is a kind of "internal reputation": how you see yourself, as much as how others see you. Its opposite, shame, is similar: you can be ashamed of something you have done even if no one else knows about it. You imagine their reaction anyway. Philosopher Jon Elster, who sees reputational emotions like shame, guilt, and pride as the vehicles by which norms operate in social life, points out the fine line between shame and anger: if you think someone is intentionally *trying* to shame you, dignity demands that you respond with anger instead. Shaming someone works as a strategy only if it is seen as automatic and sincere rather than calculated and strategic. (This is an example of what I define in chapter 4 as the Sincerity Dilemma.)[14]

I group affection and attention, rather arbitrarily, under reputation, as they both have to do with other people's feelings about you. The desire to be loved (or to love) and to receive attention from others are basic human goals. The attention may be from strangers (fame) or from intimates (displays of love). "Attention must be paid," as Arthur Miller wrote of Willy Loman. Randall Collins speaks of a "social attention space, which has room for only a limited number of participants; hence there is an implicit struggle to position oneself within this attention space." The emotional energy generated in that space is a primary human goal, which Collins thinks drives compound players such as protest groups as well as simple players.[15]

Attention is a weak cousin of glory—a goal it is difficult for us to understand today. Although political leaders fret over how historians will judge them, premodern leaders cared as much about awe and majesty while they lived. Potlatches demonstrate a leader's wealth through his ability to treat others royally. In ancient Rome the wealthy and powerful (these were fused) sponsored public works and entertainments not merely to buy off the poor but to increase their own grandeur (although it is almost impossible for us today not to take the cynical view that political support and civil stability were their "real" goals).

Not all reputational goals are admirable. We compare ourselves frequently with others. We hope to arouse envy in them, and we are driven to action when we feel envy for them. Thorstein Veblen famously attributed the acquisition and conspicuous consumption of material possessions to our desire to arouse the envy as well as esteem of our fellows. In addition to showing off our own success, we also sometimes try to undermine that of others. Most often we simply take satisfaction from others' failures—seeing the mighty fall—but occasionally we take strategic action to bring that about. In some societies it is acceptable to try to harm others out of sheer malice, although in most modern societies we try to conceal such actions. (We often hide such motives even from ourselves.)

Like our interest in all goals, concern with reputation is a variable, not a constant. This is true of reputation as a goal in itself and as a capacity for further action. Concern varies, first, because one player may face a larger number of relevant audiences than a similar one, and must monitor its reputation with each. In addition, a player may simply care more about its reputation with one audience than with other audiences. Among simple players, a variety of personality traits affect the degree to which we care about our reputations. Corporations too differ enormously in the degree to which they cultivate their reputations in the form of their "brand," depending largely on whether they sell directly to consumers or only to other companies (or rather, their reputations with these companies have different sources). Firms like Ford, Nike, or Shell care about their good names—making them vulnerable, ironically, to protestors who wish to change their practices. Nastier firms are more likely to tell pressure groups to bug off.

I often joke that men do most of what they do in order to impress former or future lovers. In the former case they are concerned with their reputations; in the latter they also hope to derive sensual satisfaction from those reputations. But that gets us to another kind of goal.

SENSUALITY AND CONNECTION

Direct physical pleasures, those of touch and the other senses, come to us early and stick with us always. We do not require much cultural baggage or cognitive processing to enjoy them, although these may heighten them. Humans differ in the kinds of food and sex or sights and sounds they enjoy, but it would be a deprived person indeed who got no satisfaction from any of these. Pain is probably even more overpowering than pleasures. The ability to control our own bodies—not to be kidnapped, tortured, raped—is the most fundamental of human rights. Basic health and freedom from pain are elemental goals, and suffering and debility push other goals into the background. Fatigue, hunger, and lust easily crowd out other considerations in the present.[16] The body comes first in any hierarchy of needs.

The appreciation of beauty, in art and elsewhere, is far from the pleasures we can enjoy as infants, at the sublime end of the spectrum of pleasures we can obtain through our senses. All cultures have a sense of what is beautiful, of the abstract and sublimated enjoyment of the world. Often, a lot of cognitive work is required to appreciate it. For some people, contemplation of god or the universe is the ultimate in beauty.

The sense of connection with the world that worship usually suggests has a range of other sources. We have the same expansive feeling when we belong to a group, when we love another person, when we feel attached to a place. Such pleasures are not always directly physical, but they frequently feel *as if* they were. Attachments seem to cause sensations in our hearts, guts, or skins; the emotions they inspire feel quite physical.

Humans also have a sense of continuity, which I class under sensual pleasures because it can feel like a mystical union with all of life. They know that society will go on after they are dead. They know that if they are fired they will be replaced. If they divorce their mates, they know they are also likely be replaced. Such realizations are profound if not always pleasant. We know that the external world has laws of its own and will persist after we are gone. Death and eternity are mystical concepts that can grip us physically, as in religious rites. Narratives are satisfying partly because they have this sense of continuity. As Samuel Beckett would say, "I can't go on. I must go on." This feeling of continuity is difficult to achieve, but I think it is the central message and goal of all religions.

Our sensation of belonging is a goal in itself, but it also affects other goals, some of which are things we want for the group rather than directly for ourselves (even when we also benefit). Our goals shift because our group identifications change: we come to feel solidarity with a different group, defecting from an old one. Class solidarities are notoriously shifting in this way, strategically incorporating occupations that had been excluded and vice versa. As part of our family group, our ancestors and descendants also enter our calculations. Beyond the satisfaction of membership, we want reputation, pleasure, or control for the group. Collective identities can reshape all of our goals.

People work hard to avoid or repair ruptures in their social relations, which are perhaps the most frequent form of strategic threat. Neil Smelser captured this in his sense of strain: "The most obvious kind of strain results when membership (and rewards) are severed altogether, as in unemployment, disenfranchisement, expulsion or excommunication." Like unemployment, Smelser says, wage reductions or demotions shock us in part because they alter social relations, not just because they reduce income.[17]

Although I mentioned affection under reputation in order to get at others' feelings for us, our affection for others can entail such physical desire (as well as pleasure and pain) that it also belongs here. The sexual side of affection fits easily. But so does our love for our children. Their love for us never quite matches it—except perhaps at early ages when it is alloyed with dependence, again a sensual need for them and a pleasure (or pain) for us. Our love for our children is mostly about what we can do for them.

Protection and nurturance when they are young give way to furthering their goals and happiness in other ways—a goal that can crowd out all others. Politicians as different as Jesse Jackson, François Mitterand, and Jesse Helms have proved capable of setting up their children (legitimate and not) with jobs and investments and contacts in the most blatantly corrupt manner (in unabashed defections from their teams).

WHOSE GOALS? → Social connections raise important strategic choices. How inclusive should our goals be? Should we aim to satisfy our own individual goals? Those of our families as well? How about those of our community, region, nation, occupation? What about those of all humankind, or of all life on earth? Most people care about several different sets of interests, of vastly different scope. How we balance them depends greatly on personality and culture, and no doubt shifts according to circumstance. This kind of trade-off is at the heart of game theory in classic "social dilemma" games such as chicken, trust, and the prisoner's dilemma.[18] The usual formulation sees only two possibilities, contrasting a narrow rationality for the individual against a broader one that benefits a group. But groups come in all sizes. (Even the prisoner in the most famous game, the prisoner's dilemma, might consider other accomplices, other prisoners, his racial group, his family's reputation, and so on in his choices.) Thus simple trade-offs between an individual and a single group represent special cases of this broader dilemma of the scope of interests. To the extent that we feel part of a collective, its goals and what we perceive to be its interests become our goals and interests. The choice is not simply between individual and collective goals, but one of balancing the goals of many potential collectivities.[19]

IMPACT

Another basic category of things we humans value is the ability to affect the world around us. In many cases, the point is only to enhance your reputation or pleasure, but it is often an end in itself. Seeing the effects of some small task is satisfying; remaking the world according to some ideological blueprint is too. Improving the world may get you into heaven in some religions, but in the here and now it is also an end in itself.

Part of our pleasure in having an impact on the world lies in our sense of agency, the awareness of self, purpose, and action. I see several components to this sense of our own capabilities. *Creativity* is one. Humans are forever thinking up new ways to occupy themselves: new ways of communicating, new pleasures, new techniques for delivering old pleasures, new symbols and art works, new projects of every kind—the sheer capacity to make up stories and images and communicate them to others. Strategic action holds its own artful pleasures. *Projects* are another aspect of this sense of agency: we have some idea of how long we are likely to live and what that span may hold for us; we make plans. Some projects unfold over short periods, others take longer, and watching them unfold gives us pleasure. They involve specific programs of goals and sometimes means. A third aspect is *reflexivity*—an awkward word to mean that we pay attention to what we are doing, at least some of the time, and change it when we no longer enjoy it, or when we think it will not have the outcome we want. We think about our creativity and our progress. One form of reflexive monitoring is about our selves. We have a sense of who we are, as well as a sense of who we want to be. This sense of *identity* is complex and has many sources; for example, personal identity depends on all sorts of collective identities.

We may value our potential for affecting the world as much as what we actually accomplish with that potential. "Capabilities" and "freedoms" are the terms Amartya Sen uses for what humans care about doing. They are means but also ends: our ability to do things is what matters to us. Sen includes the ability to maintain health, to be free from torture or unfair imprisonment, as well as working, participating in politics, and so on. Some of these are wrapped up in the results, such as the ability to engage in close human relationships. But all are satisfying in and of themselves. It is important to be *able* to have good sex even when you refrain.[20]

Psychologists have stressed control as a basic human need. Whereas for Freud agency was important only as a means to acquire the satisfactions a person sought, later psychoanalysts saw an independent need for control. According to D. W. Winnicott, an infant experiences a subjective omnipotence which, even as it later must fade in the face of reality, shapes our interaction with the world. Heinz Kohut studied the centrality of creativity, functional harmony, and internal viability and coherence instead of following the traditional Freudian concern with sexual and aggressive drives. Human development means that we expand our ambitions and goals through life: each of us forms a self aimed at "the realization of its own specific program of action."[21] So strong is our desire for control that we frequently imagine it where it does not exist, as when we think we can influence the roll of dice or the hand we are dealt at cards.[22]

The human interest in control helps explain why games can become ends in themselves. The sense of flow and absorption can make a strategic interaction, despite the stress, enormously satisfying. Shop-floor machine operators, for instance, find ways to make their work interesting by viewing it as a game they are playing with management. Rather than trying to maximize their earnings, they are interested in control of their work pace and sticking it to their bosses—and to time-management consultants.[23] Any strategic interaction has its own satisfactions (and frustrations) that are unrelated to the supposed "ends."

KNOWLEDGE AND CURIOSITY

A final set of human goals fits poorly in my three-part scheme, and may represent a fourth category: knowledge, faith, and intellectual activity. Curiosity, the motivation behind them, has more to do with awareness than with agency, with the surprise of learning how things will turn out. At one level or another, almost everyone is curious about something. Some people enjoy learning about faraway cultures and customs, some enjoy cracking the laws and codes of the physical world. Others are more curious to see what cards they are dealt in gin rummy or what will happen in today's episode of *All My Children* (who will Erika Kane marry next?). Others are fanatical about political races, watching campaign strategies, mudslinging, poll results, and elections. Converting the unknown into the known seems a basic human goal, especially familiar to academics. But the term *curiosity* may sound too superficial. Edward Shils referred to a "cognitive passion" for the truth, which better expresses this activity's potential power.[24] Whatever we call it, I suspect it is less likely to draw us into strategic action than reputation, sensuality, or impact.

OBJECTIVES

We have, in addition to basic goals, objectives: intermediate goals that are valued as part of strategic interactions. They may yield some satisfaction in and of themselves, especially in the form of winning a game or a round of a game. But they usually also contribute, at least potentially, to the attainment of other, long-term goals. For some, making a lot of money is a goal, but for most it is an objective that moves them closer to other goals, such as driving a BMW or eating celebrity chef Jean-Georges Vongerichten's culinary delights. In war, taking a particular mountain or winning an important battle may be an objective, contributing to victory.

But we can distinguish goals and objectives only relative to each other, not in any intrinsic way. Objectives, once attained, are the means for reaching other goals. The difference between goals and objectives is like that between strategy and tactics. This is a handy distinction in the military, because it allocates activities by rank: generals work on strategy, while lower officers deal with tactics. In any hierarchy, what you do is strategic, while those below you pursue the objectives that will help your strategy succeed. Moves are tactics only within a broader strategy: "One person's strategy is another's tactics."[25] As Carl von Clausewitz pointed out, even winning a war may be a mere objective, subordinate to broader political goals like prosperity, trade, or even peace.[26] The distinction depends on your perspective.

All strategy can be broken down into tactics, or implementation. "Sports are not complicated in their objectives," says George Will in his book on baseball, "but in execution they have layers of complexities and nuances."[27] In sports, you must achieve "goals" to gain a point, and only the points determine winners—a simplicity that is misleading as a metaphor for most other areas of life. Even wars usually entail multiple goals. As Will suggests, sports goals are simple and arbitrary, and all the action is in what leads you to them. From one point of view, strategy is always about execution.

Like goals, objectives vary in how limited or open-ended they are. Capturing Poland is rather different from a general effort at world conquest; snatching a hostage is more limited than a drive for bargaining power. A player is rarely willing to admit to having unlimited objectives, as this is sure to frighten other players. But in turn, the others rarely believe a limited objective will suffice forever; they suspect grander ambitions. The more general the goal or objective, the harder it is to limit it convincingly. Why should I be satisfied with $50,000 in a divorce settlement when I know there is more? Gaining resources, as means to achieve most goals, is an especially difficult objective to satisfy. In addition, means can crowd out ends, and objectives can crowd out goals.

THE DILEMMA OF DIRTY HANDS → Many means are seen as necessary evils required to attain valued ends. At the extreme, we may perceive them as polluting those who deploy them, stigmatizing, for example, those who slaughter animals or behead condemned prisoners. Thus we often hire or allow others to do our "dirty work" for us. Informants, who are typically criminal insiders themselves, are an unsettling part of fighting crime (which is why prosecutors rarely ask them to testify in court). We need the information that former Nazis or Baathist officials can provide. When we must do the dirty work ourselves, we may try to split ourselves into two parts: the workaday drudge and the leisured weekend hobbyist, or the concentration-camp doctors who distanced themselves from their "Nazi selves."[28] Conversely, the most noble ends may only be attainable by those who have compromised with (and been compromised by) evil: those within a destructive system can do more to subvert it—should they choose to—than morally pure but powerless outsiders.[29] Weber would recognize this dilemma as a conflict between purposive and value rationalities.

The events of 9/11 required many choices related to the Dilemma of Dirty Hands, as a number of American liberties were severely undermined—in the name of liberty. In an especially urgent example, a handful of al-Qaeda operatives were captured who were thought to know something about additional planned attacks. Should Western police forces—normally controlled by laws forcing them to treat suspects with some civility—torture captives like these to get that information, especially if it might save lives? Defense lawyer Alan Dershowitz, calling this the "ticking bomb" scenario, argued that judges should be able to issue limited "torture warrants" in extreme cases. Most members of legal systems saw this as a "slippery slope" down which police would all too easily slide. This is an important observation about many dilemmas: once one choice has set a precedent, *it may be hard to reverse*, to climb back up the slope.

In a twist on the Dilemma of Dirty Hands, we may view some goals as becoming corrupted if too much attention is paid to means, even morally neutral means. Radicals can castigate moderates for "watering down" their goals in order to make them attainable, that is, adjusting them to available means. Sociologist Michael Young, writing of the radical abolitionists of the 1830s, says that they "sought a pervasive and permanent reformation of public sentiments regarding African-Americans through emotional conversions to repudiate racial hatred. Anything less smacked of expediency."[30] The means are not necessarily dirty, just distracting. At an extreme, when means become ends, we have what I call the Sorcerer's Apprentice Dilemma (see chapter 4).

Money is a nearly universal objective in modern society, a fact that utilitarian traditions have seized upon as a way to make their models mathematically precise. Although earning and accumulating money can become an end itself, especially for those who make and have a lot, most of us value money for what it can buy. It is the means for achieving many, many goals. In a monetarized economy, we all need it. At the same time, we know that "money cannot buy" certain things. Moreover, money seems to positively corrupt certain values, such as spiritual simplicity. When it does not corrupt us, it at least distracts us. Thus money never quite works as a universal measure of value.[31]

MONEY'S CURSE → Money is a special case of the Dirty Hands dilemma. Every institution in a monetary economy needs it. Schools, theaters, churches, hospitals, protest groups, armies, and individuals require funds to survive and fulfill their missions. Yet only one kind of player, the for-profit business, is recognized as being primarily and legitimately about the making of money. All the others run some risk, in their pursuit of money, of losing track of their main or "real" goals. An environmental group will lose its supporters if they begin to view it as nothing but a fund-raising operation. A person may lose family and friends if they think he cares only about money. Even an artist may have a certain taint if she makes too much money (and her concern for pleasing wealthy patrons may indeed ruin her art). Normally, money is supposed to be a means, not an end; if it becomes an end, it may crowd out other important goals. It is, as political theorist Michael Walzer put it, the "universal pander."[32] We examine these issues in more detail in chapter 4.

Those who hope to change the social structure of their society face the Dilemma of Dirty Hands, often because of Money's Curse. Feminists may need the power men have, and the working class may need the resources of business, in order to bring about desired transformations. Revolutionaries often need parliamentary democracies. The risk is that, by using the existing system, you reinforce it and undermine your main goal. To take one example, the activists who are trying to empower women in southern Africa in order to protect them against HIV infection find that they need to work through local chiefs—the very patriarchy they hope to shake up or destroy.[33]

RELATIONS AMONG GOALS

A friend who plays softball reports endless squabbles over who gets to play, especially who will pitch. In many cases, mediocre players are on the field, while better ones watch. In a setting like this, when the goal of the game—scoring more points than your opponents—is clear, you might think that the people with the best chance of achieving that goal would play. How naive! A good player brings his best friend, who is not so good. But if the friend does not play, the team may lose them both. More fundamentally, the teams in this league are sponsored by Broadway shows. So one of the hidden goals is to build camaraderie among those who work together, even when this means slighting talented outsiders. Winning isn't everything.

Human ends are related to one another in many different ways. As we saw earlier, some goals can be ranked in order of priority. Or, as in the world of economics, monetary values can be attached to them so that more of one can be "bought" or "traded" for less of another. Others may be positively related, so that more of one yields more of another. Still others simply cannot be compared or traded in any reasonable way, and people work out their own complex ways of pursuing them simultaneously. Broad objectives like money should help us attain many goals, although the Dirty Hands dilemma reveals some limits to this hope.

If conflicts among goals arise for an individual, far more are possible for a compound player. Just think of the numbers. If each person has ten primary goals, a group or organization of one hundred could have up to a thousand. Sure, there will be considerable overlap, especially since an organization's explicit mission is probably the basis on which these people have agreed to cooperate as a player. They agree to set aside other goals, although this does not mean that they do. Even if the collectivity is left with only twenty goals to balance, the hundred members will have an unmanageable number of different ways to rank-order them.

In his analysis of business strategy, economist Michael Porter suggests asking several questions to assess various kinds of consistency among goals and policies. Is there internal consistency? That is, are the goals compatible, do policies address them, are the policies compatible? Do the goals and policies fit realistically with the external environment and with the resources available to the company? Can they be communicated to and implemented by employees? For instance, "Is there enough congruence between the goals and policies and the values of the key implementers to insure commitment?" Much of this analysis is intended to uncover trade-offs that, if not addressed, could derail action.[34]

Because we have goals at different levels, with trade-offs among them, we also develop values regarding how to allocate attention among our goals. In the long run we want to be fit, but in the short run we would rather stay home and watch television than go to the gym. We even work out strategies for dealing with ourselves, or perhaps one part of us works out a strategy to coerce another part. I make a game out of aerobics class, comparing my performance with that of others. Or I reward myself with ice cream on the way home.

We may see some of the clashes as conflicts between superficial and "deeper" values, or between fleeting and long-term goals. Addiction, lust, and certain other "strong feelings" are especially satisfying to fulfill at the moment but in retrospect seem like mistakes. Rationalists such as Elster have analyzed the trade-off between short- and long-term goals in depth, seeing in it certain limits to rationality. People take a number of steps to reduce the trade-off, such as reshaping their own preferences through education or habit. They avoid situations that may lead them to do things they later regret, such as going off to an overnight meeting with a sexy coworker. They make public promises, such as quitting smoking, that are embarrassing to break later.[35] Below we encounter some of these steps in the dilemma I call Today or Tomorrow?

The diversity of goals shows how many different games you normally play at the same time. The game that makes you rich is rarely the one that increases your status (except to the extent that status comes from wealth) or the one which satisfies altruistic impulses—although you can take your gains and move them into a different game, giving to charity the money gained in business, perhaps overcoming your reputation for greed, as junk-bond impresario and convicted felon Michael Milken has tried to do. In some of these clashes, we hope for different rewards from different audiences. This is one reason that individuals can suddenly (or partially) defect from the team they have been playing for—substituting personal rewards for the collective goals the team is after.

CHANGING GOALS

With so many potential goals, it is easy to reorder priorities, switch attention from one to another, trade off more of one for less of another. This reworking of goals is a crucial part of strategy. One common move is to try to change *other* players' goals so that they are more compatible, if not identical, with your own. As later chapters show, we typically try to reveal to them their real but obscured goals, or help them reorder their priorities. Here I want to concentrate on the less obvious process by which players change their *own* goals. In strategic action, individuals and groups pursue many goals at the same time, usually with unclear or changing priorities. Goals and their relative salience change during—and as a result of—the interactions designed to attain them. Certain goals may be blocked during interaction, so that it seems prudent to concentrate on those that are easier to attain. Goals interact with opportunities.

THE DILEMMA OF SHIFTING GOALS → If strategy normally involves finding the right means to attain given goals, how do we know when to change goals instead, often by adapting them to our means? We may opportunistically abandon earlier goals so as to increase our strategic capacities instead of continuing to deploy them in fruitless pursuit of our original goals. Our means, in other words, take on an inherent value of their own, which we wish to enhance. Or we may elaborate, clarify, and interpret our goals. In doing so, we may remain loyal to basic goals, merely filling in some of the gaps, drawing some of their logical implications, or we may "reinterpret" them as altogether new goals, often hiding the fact that we are doing so. Hermeneutic processes can allow considerable mutual adjustment ("rationalization") between means and ends.

You can expand goals to increase gains or reduce them to cut losses. If a bully threatens me on the playground, my main goal is suddenly to avoid being struck. If a battle goes badly for my army, my main objective shrinks to survival. Severe deprivation, as in famines or concentration camps, also crowds out goals beyond immediate needs. Aggressive strategies that go badly can turn into desperate defensive ones. Contexts can also shift against you. French feminists fighting for sexual harassment codes had to curtail their demands drastically when, across the Atlantic, Anita Hill and Clarence Thomas reinforced widespread suspicions that this was a silly problem of American Puritanism; the feminists' full program was suddenly unrealistic.[36] From the defensive point of view, concessions are a way of keeping most of what you have while avoiding even greater losses. Unlike what an onion model of a hierarchy of goals suggests, different goals may come to the fore according to strategic circumstances, not merely according to what has been achieved.

Pragmatists go furthest in denying explicit goals, insisting that we are already embroiled in action before we develop our conscious words for goals. As Dewey put it, goals are milestones during the course of activity, not its purpose or starting point.[37] This is a sound warning against game models, with their clear endpoints that allow for tallying up scores. But it might be better to posit that we learn new goals as we go along, or learn to articulate them. Even routines can occasionally give us goals and hence purposive action. Emergent goals can redirect our actions.

THE PARADOX OF EDUCATION → At the individual level, a change in long-term goals is often associated with education or cultivation. We learn to appreciate more esoteric leisure pursuits or to seek more complex public policies. We become different people in the process. A person may be pushed out of an old role as well as pulled into a new one, like the downsized employee who learns the joys of consultancy.[38] Typically, an investment in education is hard to justify to the person without it. Only someone who has already benefited from the change in goals that it can bring can appreciate education as a means to those ends, because only she can savor the ends. How might we persuade a person with no musical education that it is worth learning about Beethoven's late quartets, which to that person sound awful? She may be curious why others like them—but they must be others whom she respects, not eggheads she thinks have been ruined by fancy learning. Either she trusts their tastes, or she has little choice but to comply with their suggestions. Education must be compulsory (socially or legally); otherwise most of us would not bother with it. As William Cowper wrote in "Table Talk,"

> Freedom has a thousand charms to show,
> That slaves, howe'er contented, never know.

There is no way to say that the long run is more important than the short; there is, as we will see, simply a trade-off between the two.[39]

A classic model in social science—"rising expectations"—explicitly relates goals to their chances of attainment. Alexis de Tocqueville argued, in counterintuitive fashion, that revolutions are more likely when conditions are improving rather than deteriorating: "The mere fact that certain abuses have been remedied draws attention to the others and they now appear more galling."[40] Aspirations may increase generally, or economic gains may not be matched by the political or status gains expected to accompany them. Moreover, new resources may become available for the pursuit of further goals.

Although I formulated the Dilemma of Shifting Goals as a tension between means and ends, another version pits players' identities against their goals. Goals can change even while players remain intact. Corporations reposition themselves, sometimes into new industries altogether. Foundations develop new eleemosynary programs. When compound players shift direction, some defections (official and unofficial) certainly occur, but the player's formal identity remains. Individuals too can change their minds. A spouse comes to realize that counseling is not really what she wanted; divorce is. And I came to see a full-time academic position as less desirable. Richard Scott expresses this dilemma as two conflicting definitions of a formal organization: one based on specified goals and one on formal structure—either of which can change.[41]

For a compound player, goals gain new prominence for both internal and external reasons. The former include new leaders or other organizational restructuring. New goals and programs may solve internal problems, such as distracting attention from a leader's poor performance or solidifying a new leader's or faction's position. (Bush II's 2003 invasion of Iraq served both purposes.) External circumstances can also force new priorities on a player, such as a sudden threat to survival or some other form of crisis. A player may also advance its interests externally—for instance, by differentiating itself from others—through a symbolic association with certain goals. Howard Dean became the Democratic presidential front-runner in 2003 by embracing peace more fully than the other major candidates. A distinctive goal made him a distinctive candidate.

Even if we know our current goals, we must decide whether to state them. You may think that letting other players know what you want will help you get it, or you may think that keeping it secret is the best approach. For instance "the power to declare war," according to Brien Hallett, "is emphatically not the power to initiate or start a war, as many believe it to be.

Rather, it is the power to compose a text, to draft a document, to write a denunciation."[42] Words are actions, which in this case define your goals for others to understand. If war were simply coercion, there would be no need to declare it, and a considerable advantage is gained by not doing so. But if war is seen as a multipronged strategy, there are reasons to articulate its intent. The declaration may avoid an actual war. It also allows one side to announce when it is over. But a formal declaration fixes the goals of a war in advance, discouraging flexible adjustment of ends to means, of goals to the potential for their attainment. An explicitly stated goal makes victory possible—but also defeat. There is little in between, less room for both sides to declare victory, to feel good about the outcome, to back down without losing face. Declarations of war, of course, are not the only public statements of strategic goals. We may file for divorce or sign a contract to deliver services. Even announcing a diet in front of others commits us to certain actions, albeit not necessarily strategic ones (although they may be strategic, if we enlist the aid of others).

Articulating your goals also makes you accountable to your own team, shaping their judgments of your success. American government policy after 9/11 reflected an effort to find a goal that could plausibly be attained. Bringing Osama bin Laden to justice gave way to toppling the Taliban, then creating a stable Afghan government, which in turn receded behind an invasion of Iraq. The rationale for that invasion shifted almost weekly, as Bush II tried to justify his plans to international and domestic audiences. To anyone paying attention, the constant shift in goals appeared hypocritical, but he finally hit on one that he could eventually say was accomplished. (In the meantime, the initial fight against terrorism had been reduced to the following three platitudes, presented in newspaper advertisements in April 2003: U.S. Secretary of Homeland Security Tom Ridge wrote, "You've probably wondered, 'Is there anything we can do to protect ourselves from the threat of terrorism?' Here's your answer: Step One: Make an Emergency Supply Kit . . . Step Two: Make a Family Communications Plan . . . Step Three: Be Informed.")[43]

THE ARTICULATION DILEMMA → Stating your goals clearly allows your team to know what they are working toward and when it has been achieved. It makes small defections more apparent. It may also advance negotiations with others, who can then decide what your aspirations will cost them. On the other hand, you may have goals that will outrage others or reduce the surprise of your actions. If others feel threatened, they may of course try to thwart you. Some goals are poorly understood even by those who pursue them. Only a few can be expressly stated and thus become subject to bargaining with others (international diplomacy would be much easier if all goals and objectives were on the table). Latent goals may pop up at inopportune moments, making others feel that they have been betrayed or misled. If you clearly state your goals, you may find it difficult to change them in the face of evolving circumstances.

The more precisely defined your goals, the more constrained the means you can use to pursue them. Taking advantage of opportunities can sometimes entail switching goals, pursuing those you think you have the best chance of attaining. Sometimes you scale back your aspirations, sometimes you inflate them. Hunter-gatherers demonstrate this kind of opportunism. A primitive hunter follows one track until he crosses a fresher (and hence more promising) one. If he happens unexpectedly upon a better find, such as a medicinal herb or honey tree, he stops and gathers that instead. With goals and means both shifting, a kind of emptiness may appear in much strategic action—what I called the vacant core—as though most strategic models left us nothing in particular to be strategic about. Thus in Erving Goffman's work it is hard to see a self with fixed goals at the center of all that strategic maneuvering and self-presentation.

Clear goals can hurt our strategic position partly by offering objectives to our opponents. Whatever we want, our enemies will be tempted to block; whomever we love, they can take hostage. This may be quite literal, when ransom is demanded. When one spouse in the middle of an argument picks up the other's favorite vase and threatens to dash it against the wall, that is also a form of ransom. The process may be more subtle, as when our adversaries befriend those we love—entangling their interests so that if we hurt our enemies we also hurt those we love. Between these extremes, the threat may be merely implicit, like that of the Tokugawa shoguns, who required the daimyos (Japan's most powerful aristocrats) to live half of each year in the capital—and during the other half to leave their wives and children there. As Sun Tzu advised, when things look grim for your army, "[s]eize something that [your enemies] love for then they will listen to you." The key here is that when we come to value some things and people more than others value them, they are more willing to destroy them than we are. They gain an advantage through this difference.

The goals of compound players are especially knotty. Different players and factions have their own opinions of what the larger group should be doing, and they interact with each other to influence the broader policies. Public announcements of goals, for this reason, may be intended to rally the whole team to work together as much as to signal intentions to outsiders. Even after goals have been publicly embraced, blocs who disagree often pursue their own pet goals instead—a serious coordination challenge. As different blocs gain control, a player's goals may undergo additional shifts.

I need to qualify this discussion slightly: goals are not infinitely pliable. We often do have priorities among them. Survival is usually basic. In addition, arenas partly impose goals on us. We normally start a business to make money or enter a campaign to win an election. But we must emphasize "partly" and "normally": you may run for office to make a point (see Ralph Nader), start a company to employ your family, and so on. It is better to discern fundamental goals through empirical research than to build them into our models as assumptions.

ACTS AND CONSEQUENCES

Certain actions are satisfying in and of themselves, regardless of the consequences. Some of these are moral acts, which fall under Weber's "ethic of ultimate ends," a deontological category in which acts are simply right or wrong. One does not kill another human, even if that person will grow up to be Adolph Hitler, or even if that person is already brain-dead. (Obviously, such principles rarely command total allegiance in a society.)

Other directly satisfying actions are those we usually think of as driven by "passion." We strike the bully who has been tormenting us, even though we know we will suffer for it later (he is, after all, a bully). We set lawyers on an estranged spouse mercilessly, knowing that nothing will be left for either of us after a long legal battle. We declare war to preserve the honor of our country—even though it destroys our economy and may result in another defeat. We join a revolution, even though rebels usually end up with their heads on pikes. Usually, such acts feel emotionally and morally satisfying at the same time.

A third category of actions are simply pleasurable in themselves, so that actions that look like means are in fact ends in themselves. Humans may derive reputational, sensual, and effective pleasures from their daily activities, which are rarely pure means to an end. (Zen Buddhism makes an art of this enjoyment.) Yet most scholarly models view work and politics as instrumental action aimed at payoffs. The classical game theorists' human is a drudge, working and doing other unpleasant things for some payoff at the end, without any feeling of pleasure in the activities themselves. This is a hedonist of a most unusual kind: willing to face unpleasant activities all day in order to eat well at night! Political-process theorists of social movements similarly assume that to be included in the polity is the primary motive of those who are excluded, implying that the exercise of power is the key motivation (although that power may also be seen as the means to accumulation); related theorists of the state see government bureaucrats as similarly driven by their strivings to accumulate power. When journalist James Fallows criticizes the news media for covering politics as though it were simply a horserace, ignoring the "real" implications of policies, he displays a one-dimensional view of human activity in trying to get at the "true" purpose of politics beneath the appearances.[44]

Pleasure taken in the game—as opposed to its outcome—may be a case of caring about the act rather than (or in addition to) its consequences. The pleasures of playing and of winning may combine a sense of curiosity about outcomes with a sense of mastery and sometimes a sensual delight as well. (They do not fit comfortably into my scheme of ends, I admit, even though I linked them to a sense of control before.) A taste for novelty similarly blurs means and ends. From a rational-choice perspective, this has apparently perverse consequences, as Jon Elster points out: "After a few choices, the person may have less of all goods than when he started."[45] If bargaining itself is a pleasure, he may even be happier at the end of the day, despite having less wealth. Utilities partly reside in activities themselves, aside from their effects on the distribution of wealth or power.

Many of these satisfying actions are normally perceived as costs or even as irrational, in that they go against our "long-run" interests. (Although the more morally based actions—which are more admired—are sometimes called "nonrational," while we pejoratively dismiss the more obviously emotional ones as "irrational.") But this frequently only means that the commentator disagrees with or misunderstands the priorities of the actor.

Some basic values are so important to us that they tend to override all other goals. Religious salvation, for some, functions in this way. Martyrs have basic values of some kind for which they are willing to give their lives. The philosopher Charles Taylor has called these "hypergoods." They tend to derail culturally accepted calculations of interest, to surprise opponents who cannot accept that anyone would believe so deeply in "that." Such beliefs generate morally immediate actions that curtail long-run calculations.

Many of our deepest desires are hard to fit into formal games, even though many gamesters insist that rational-choice theory applies only to means, not ends. In some cases, it makes little sense to separate means from ends. We all know the pleasures of anticipation and the disappointments of attainment. Indeed, the more humanly central a project is, the more important the striving is: writing a book or sailing in a race provides intrinsic pleasures, compared to which the publication or the crossing of the finish line may or may not seem important. Alasdair MacIntyre describes the class of activities—he calls them "practices"—that we pursue for their intrinsic pleasures: "[A]ny coherent and complex form of socially established cooperative human activity through which goods internal to that form of activity are realised in the course of trying to achieve those standards of excellence which are appropriate to, and partially definitive of, that form of activity, with the result that human powers to achieve excellence, and human conceptions of the ends and goods involved, are systematically extended."[46] Chess and painting are examples. In such cases, no simple conception of an "end" captures the intrinsic pleasures or the extension of human capacities involved in the pursuit itself.

Many act/consequence problems reflect the trade-offs we all face between the present and the future. A thousand dollars is worth more to us today than ten years from now, not only because of inflation but because of the chance that we will be dead in ten years and unable to enjoy it. As economists put it, the uncertainties of the future encourage us to "discount" it by some percentage. Just how high our discount rate is will affect our choices when one option gives us more now and the other later. (How much we put aside in savings is a good example.) We face the same trade-off between actions that feel good right now and those that will feel good later. When, in ten years, we have no savings, we may regret having sought revenge on an ex-spouse by devoting all our money to legal proceedings. But the vendetta felt good enough at the time that we were willing to discount the future enormously for the pleasure.

What affects our discount rate? Some factors have to do with the future: life expectancy, fatalistic attitudes, the facing of real dangers (as in wartime), other options that might arise (perhaps an expected inheritance). Other factors have to do with our attitudes toward the present, often embodied in our personalities: the power of our indignation or anger, the centrality of revenge in our culture, a sense of honor that must be upheld at all costs, value commitments so strong we are willing to die for them. To the extent that actions in the present appear morally or emotionally important, we are willing to discount distant consequences. An action, in this way, becomes a kind of goal, satisfying in and of itself without much regard to consequences. This is simply a dilemma to which there is no "right" answer.

TODAY OR TOMORROW? → Thinking about immediate objectives and thinking about distant goals often involve different processes, as do the actions taken to pursue each. This is a classic dilemma of economics: pleasures today may prevent pleasures tomorrow, the obvious case being the need for saving and investment summed up in the fable of the ant and the grasshopper. Despite that story, it is impossible to prove that long-run rationality is superior to short-run rationality; they are simply different. The short run is not necessarily an "irrational" time frame, and some immediate gratifications are worth the inattention to the long run. To put it in a different light, think of the short run as consisting of the routines that get things done. "Daily routine drives out planning," said James March and Herbert Simon, formulating a "Gresham's law of planning."[47] But daily routines can also get the *right* things done.

Individuals and organizations both negotiate this trade-off by developing rules about when to give in to short-run impulses, and when (and how) not to. Our identities are wrapped up in these rules, partly because we interpret our past actions as clues to what kind of people we are. But our rules can take on a compulsive rigidity, preventing us from making further judgments about how to balance short- and long-term goals. We become misers or workaholics. As we will see in the Sorcerer's Apprentice Dilemma in chapter 4, means can crowd out the end they were meant to serve.[48]

⚒

Not everyone views riding the horses of their enemies as the greatest joy, as Genghis Khan did. But what else to expect from a man who lived on his horse, sleeping every night in a tent? While he lived to conquer, his own grandson Kublai Khan (1215–1294), famed for building the palace of

Shang-tu, or Xanadu, was known for his ability to spend the riches amassed by his grandfather. What a contrast in their goals!

"There is no substitute for victory," General Douglas MacArthur told the U.S. Congress after returning from Korea in 1951. But victory is not always easy to define. Many outcomes can be declared as successes depending on one's goals, which are usually multiple and shifting. We cannot understand strategic action, much less judge its success, without knowing the players' goals. Having seen some of the situations that might lead us into strategic interaction, as well as the many flexible goals we might wish to pursue, we can turn to the capabilities that allow us to maneuver against others. And bear in mind that we often modify our goals to fit the means available to us.

APPENDIX: TERMS OF DESIRE

I treat values, motivations, and goals as roughly similar, or at least closely related, despite endless philosophical debates about the differences. They are the things that people want from life and, when possible, strive to attain. Not all actions are motivated by a particular goal in sight, but most strategic actions are—and if not by a goal in the sense of something desired and valued, then by shorter-term objectives that might ultimately enable us to reach our goals. Values are what we define as good in life, and we usually try to have more rather than less of the good. Goals are what we carve out as specific embodiments of what is valuable, and we can pursue them through strategic action. If we value political power, election to high office is an appropriate goal. Motives and motivations are what spur us into action oriented to these goals and values: the desire to attain them gives us energy.

I prefer the term *goal*. Its etymology is obscure, but its original meaning in old-English usage was probably much like its contemporary meaning: a line or place on a game field, reaching which is the point of the game. A goal is also, in many games today, the name for "a point." More generally, it is something we try to reach, a well-defined positive outcome. Working toward goals is how we operationalize our basic values; we can give reasons for our pursuit of them. In a game, all agree upon the goals. Not all goals are as well defined and agreed upon as the word implies (and, except for literal games, parties to an engagement may have different goals), but I think the term is the best we have for the "ends" of action. Most strategic arenas are associated with goals, even though we may also pursue unofficial ones.

The language of motive and motivation gives a different twist to the idea of goals (although my dictionary gives "goal" as one definition of "motive").

If a goal draws you toward it, a motive pushes you along: one is more external; the other, internal. Motives, a word with French and Latin roots in the concept of motion, are not far from Freudian drives that emanate from human nature. We speak of ulterior or hidden motives, as though we ourselves might not be aware of them. We do not speak of goals in the same way: they are explicit, spoken, even formal. We can state our goals more easily or appropriately than our motives. If lust is a motive, sex is the goal. Curiosity is a motive, knowledge the goal. Motives remind us that psychological mechanisms intervene in our pursuit of our goals. An actor might speak of her character's "motivation," as though she should have one dominant impulse, like the hubris of a tragic figure. But here fiction diverges from reality: fictional characters are more compelling and recognizable if they are self-propelled by a dominant trait (lust, jealousy, gluttony). Real people are rarely like that, although some make themselves into living caricatures. I largely stick to the language of goals, although I recognize that people also have obscure urges that move them to action but cannot always be easily stated.

"Desires" mediate somewhat between inside and out. We feel inside us desire for an object or goal outside us. To desire something is to wish, request, long for it. Like motivations, desires can compel us, operating at times through our bodies and against our will. Compared to desires, goals are well defined, often by the arena of interaction. Goals are more clearly (potential) endpoints of action, which ceases when we reach them. At the extreme, desires are "strong feelings," such as lust, that almost propel us in spite of ourselves.[49] *Desire* is the most general term, because it collapses interior motives and external goals, but it is vague for that very reason.[50]

The term *interest* implies something that is objectively good for us, contributing to our "welfare," whether we realize it or not. Originally interest denoted a legal, and somewhat later a pecuniary, stake in some property. Animals have an interest in decent treatment even though they are not "interested" in it (these two uses show the evolution of the word). Interests are useful to structuralists or certain game theorists who want to avoid any consideration of actors' points of view. It is suspicious that analysts usually claim to know people's interests better than the people themselves do.

Preferences, the term favored by economists, incorporate actors' perspectives. The term normally implies a comparison among imaginable options and, ultimately, a rank-ordering of several possibilities. It works well for material goods, each of which has a price, so that they can be reduced to the same metric. This is why economists favor the term. They can describe trade-offs among them, add them up, and posit some maximization. But many goals cannot be compared, except in the most contrived way.

If motives are murky, "interests" and "preferences" suggest too much objectivity or clarity. The term *goal* implies no particular relationships among the outcomes we desire; they can be quite random; to prefer something, however, is to choose it over others. But the term presumes too much. Most of my goals have little or nothing to do with each other. Some situations may force me to choose between them, as in allocating money or time, but this is not always the case. I want my daughter to be happy, and I want a new Lexus. I may be able to pursue several goals at the same time: making money, having fun, showing off for my buddies, and helping a Democrat get elected, for instance. In many cases it is senseless to ask if goals are compatible or incompatible. My basic categories of reputation, pleasure, impact, and knowledge already suggest how disparate our goals are.

All these terms have some utility. In particular it is useful to consider motives and goals, the push and the pull. These are crucial for strategic action and for human freedom. As Sartre put it, "[T]he reason, the motive, and the end are three indissoluble terms of a free and living consciousness which projects itself toward its possibilities and defines itself by these possibilities."[51] Situationalists highlight routine actions that have neither motivation nor goal, or, rather, they reduce both to the setting, just as choice cultists see all action as intentional.[52] Neither form of action is a good paradigm for the other.

If gamesters are too narrow in the goals they recognize, in order to make their calculations easier, situationalists barely recognize goals at all. Christian Smith, for one, has complained that sociologists have abandoned any attention to motivation. But he reduces motivation to morality and, worse, tries to revive Parsonian values as the model of morality.[53] Motivation is too important an issue for social science to be satisfied with crude oversimplifications about it.

CHAPTER 4

CAPACITIES

Gold is most excellent; of gold there is formed treasure and with it whoever has it may do what he wishes in this world and bring souls into Paradise. → CHRISTOPHER COLUMBUS

[Sherry] illumineth the face, which, as a beacon, gives warning to all the rest of this little kingdom, man, to arms; and then the vital commoners and inland petty spirits muster me all to their captain, the heart, who, great and puffed up with this retinue, doth any deed of courage; and this valour comes of sherris. So that skill in the weapon is nothing without sack, for that sets it a-work; and learning, a mere hoard of gold kept by a devil till sack commences it and sets it in act and use. → SHAKESPEARE, *HENRY IV, PART 2*

The American civil rights movement was born with the Montgomery bus boycott that began with Rosa Parks's famous decision on December 1, 1955. As secretary of the local NAACP chapter, she knew the implications of refusing to give up her seat in the middle of the bus, an area not preassigned to either race, but in which blacks were expected to give their seats to any whites standing. Another African American woman had been arrested for a similar offence only weeks earlier, and another the previous spring. But local civil rights activists saw in Parks, a woman of quiet dignity and impeccable character, the test case they had been waiting for. Any journalist who interviewed her would be sympathetic.[1]

Montgomery's black community was poor in 1955, but through strategic words and actions, the new Montgomery Improvement Association (MIA) was able to attract the resources it needed. In the twelve-month boycott that ensued, the local white power structure tried to reduce the value of each new wave of resources the MIA obtained. First, the boycotters relied on black taxi drivers offering heavy discounts. The police commissioner responded by threatening to arrest them for charging less than the legal fare. So the MIA developed a private carpool system. The city responded by trumping up charges against drivers and boycott leaders—who promptly turned this setback into a victory when their hearings attracted more than one hundred reporters from around the world. This in turn helped the MIA to get new resources, as sympathetic citizens sent donations from around the country. But when the group used them to buy several cars of its own, the city got a state injunction against them for operating an unlicensed municipal transportation system. Finally, they turned to their last resource: their own feet. Virtually all of Montgomery's African Americans walked to work each day for five weeks until their eventual triumph.

The MIA attracted physical and financial resources partly because of the personal traits of two of its members. Parks perfectly symbolized an unfairly victimized American, a churchgoing seamstress who only wanted to rest her feet on the ride home. (That she was asked to relinquish her seat to a man flew in the face of widespread ideas of chivalry as well.) The other was an obscure newcomer, the twenty-six-year-old preacher the MIA chose as its leader, Martin Luther King Jr., whose ascent to stardom was so great that he appeared on the cover of *Time* after the boycott succeeded. He came to embody, for all Americans, the polite but determined spirit of the civil rights movement.

King and his fellow protestors had what we might call "moral charm": they moved national audiences through their moral character, the justice of their cause, and their patent victimization. They could use these various kinds of charm to attract resources. Personal traits and intelligent strategic choices substituted for—or attracted—the tangible resources that the civil rights movement initially lacked. Physical resources on the one hand and charm, skill, and intelligence on the other: together these are the basic capacities necessary for strategic action.

MEANS OF ACTION

There are two great families of strategies, one based on physical resources, the other on intelligence. Coercion and payment involve resources; persuasion is a form of intelligence. Resources are a form of raw muscle: you are bigger and stronger than the other kids on the playground; you have the money to buy what you need to win; you have a larger military with better arms. "Nine-hundred-pound gorillas don't need strategies," says Steven Kelman, meaning careful plans, or intelligence.[2] The alternative—if you don't weigh nine hundred pounds—is to be clever, to outflank the larger army, to outwit the giant in the fairy tale, to surprise and confuse opponents with novel or unexpected moves. It is the old conflict of David and Goliath. For the Greeks, the paradigm was Odysseus and Achilles; for the Norse, it was clever Odin and dimwitted Thor, son of the earth (they chose Odin as their god of war). Among boys, this distinction begins early, as smaller lads learn to be clever or funny in order to avoid punches from the larger. Most of the time, those with superior physical resources—*power*, as I use the word—win.[3]

But power can breed complacency, even stupidity, leaving some opening for those who are smart and skilled. "He who possesses strength," said Nietzsche, "divests himself of mind. . . . Power makes stupid." Commenting on this, Bent Flyvbjerg claims that "rational argument is one of the few forms of power that those without much influence still possess; rationality is part of the power of the weak."[4] If intelligence did not occasionally beat resources, underdogs would never win, smaller armies would never enter the field, and elites would always reproduce themselves. I could have formulated resources versus intelligence as a dilemma, but I think it is rarely a choice: you use whatever you have or can attract. As Napoleon recognized, "When an army is inferior in number, inferior in cavalry, and in artillery, it is essential to avoid a general action. The first deficiency should be supplied by rapidity of movement; the want of artillery by the nature of manoeuvres; and the inferiority in cavalry by the choice of positions. In such circumstances the *morale* of the soldier does much."[5]

In theories of war, Sun Tzu was the great theorist of intelligence, focusing on surprise and deception, while Carl von Clausewitz was the theorist of brute power. In some ways they continue to represent Eastern and Western forms of warfare. Overwhelming force has been the "Western way of war" since the Greek hoplites, at least according to historian Victor Hanson.[6] Even a great commander like Douglas MacArthur was taken by surprise during the Korean War when Chinese troops marched long distances along mountain ridges, totally unseen, to appear suddenly on all sides of the American and South Korean forces. There, clever deception fought brute force to a standstill that has lasted fifty years.

Some resources and skills serve all purposes, while others are specific to an arena or kind of strategy. Money is notoriously general as a resource; it provides access to almost any other physical capacity available for sale. Knowledge about human nature is transferable knowledge, while that about the rules of an arena is less so. Most of the time, *general capacities provide flexibility, while specific ones yield efficiency.*[7] Edward Luttwak sees a trade-off between narrow and broad techniques of war, for instance. Very specific weapons may leave open a vulnerability, but broad resources can usually close one. He cites as an example small torpedo boats, which one hundred years ago managed to take deadly advantage of the fact that battleships had extensive armor above the water and little below. But the wide-ranging resources aboard battleships were partly diverted to deal with the new threat: searchlights to see the torpedo boats coming, small-caliber guns to destroy them, and steel nets in which the torpedoes would explode at a safe distance from hulls. Narrow resources, and presumably narrow skills, can be a great advantage for short periods, but *broad ones tend to win out in the long run.*[8]

Both skills and resources can also be divided into those that exist prior to the start of strategic action and those acquired during (often through) that action. Typically, your recognized capacities shape the actions you undertake, and they may even affect whether you launch a strategic action in the first place. Poor people can less easily afford the lawyer's fees to file for divorce or hire a family counselor, or the time off from work to organize a protest movement to advance their interests.[9] Those with considerable resources or skills usually feel more comfortable launching programs of action, even though they may have less of a "need" to do so. Their cushion of resources also protects them if things go badly, shielding them somewhat from the Risk Dilemma.

The distribution of both kinds of capacities changes during the course of strategic interaction. You gain new intelligence from experience, you purchase or produce new resources—or invent them. Ingenious new skills or resources can render old ones obsolete, as surely as tanks replaced cavalry (and made trenches obsolete as a defense). Most of all, though, strategic interaction can itself redistribute capacities. Part of that interaction entails efforts to mobilize capacities by calling in favors, signing up allies, or—best of all—capturing the capacities of opponents (a more straightforward matter with resources than with human intelligence, admittedly).

The lack of a particular resource or skill is a vulnerability that your opponents may try to exploit. Much strategy consists of searching for these weak spots and figuring out how to take advantage of them. (The other main kind of vulnerability arises from strategic mistakes, which do not always reflect a lack of intelligence.)

The contrast between resources and intelligence is not as stark as it sounds. Most resources require competence in their use—otherwise they sit in storage, like advanced fighter jets sold to a country with poorly trained pilots. Conversely, skills do not lie inertly in people's brains; they must be put into action, which usually requires resources. A brilliant idea for a flanking maneuver cannot be implemented without infantry, cavalry, or tanks to put in motion. Resources and competencies can to some degree be exchanged for one another: those with resources can sell them to hire those with needed skills, just as those with skills can use them to accumulate necessary resources—as the MIA did in Montgomery. The distinction between resources and intelligence is partly an analytic one between two different aspects of reality—but only partly: many strategic moves depend more heavily on one than the other.

Arenas differ in the scope they offer for resources or intelligence. In his analysis of China's communist insurgency as a twenty-two-year version of the ancient game of go, Scott Boorman says that games are influenced by physical power or dexterity, strategic choices, and chance. But some games, like go or chess, eliminate the role of chance (unlike card games) and of physical capacities (unlike tennis).[10] A legal system aims at eliminating the same two factors, but it fails because prosecutors have varying amounts of resources for investigations, and defendants have varying amounts to hire lawyers. In the competition among entrepreneurs, Max Weber thought that resources (capital) usually defeated skills—although he recognized both as sources of strength.[11] Formal games are unusual in having such restrictive rules.

RESOURCES

Resources are the tools and raw materials we use in our strategic interactions, the physical capacities to do things—along with the money to purchase them. Resources have to do with the material dimension of life, even when they carry cultural messages and affect other dimensions. If there is one regular source of power, it is resources, especially if we remain true to power's underlying energy metaphor. I include both coercion (direct physical force) and money (the capacity to buy needed materials) under resources. Kingsley Davis once said that the potential military and diplomatic power of a nation was a function of its population times its productive efficiency: what material resources it could produce.[12]

In war, humans themselves become resources, often no different from the horses they ride or the guns they fire. To decision makers, they are sometimes nothing more than a physical capacity. You expect your front line in football to block, your soldiers to stand their ground and fire. Of course, they may fail, just as technologies do. (Soldiers probably have the same failure rate as their technologies, freezing up or fleeing—just as rifles occasionally jam.) Of course, this is an idealized image, allowing commanders to overlook the fact that soldiers are also strategic actors who have capacities for resistance and defection. *People can be treated like resources, but they never fully act like them.*

THE FODDER DILEMMA → Leaders at various levels may be torn between viewing followers as resources or as players: a physical force to be deployed as needed, or strategic actors with whom to interact. This is too stark a dichotomy, of course, as neither extreme is common. Leaders may switch from one attitude to the other and back. The same general who sends division upon division into a hopeless battle, knowing most will die, may also try to give a rousing speech to his troops beforehand. When you treat humans instrumentally as resources, they have a way of reminding you they are more than that. As for your opponent's rank and file, you normally prefer to reduce them to cannon fodder and do so when you can. You would like to reduce their strategic choices, but they too have a way of fooling you. (Sometimes, on the other hand, you appeal to their strategic sense, encouraging them to defect from their *own* leaders.)[13]

One example of the Fodder trade-off is the use of stimulants in warfare, from Shakespeare's sack to the amphetamines liberally handed out to "forces" in every war since World War II, especially pilots. Shakespeare notwithstanding, uppers are much more effective than alcohol, which is not only a depressant but impairs motor coordination. Amphetamines give men and women more physical energy and aggressiveness but sometimes undermine their decision making by hiding their real fatigue. Like sack, in other words, Dexedrine is good for cannon fodder, not for decision makers.

Your available resources restrict the strategies and arenas you can choose. In some cases, a lack of resources discourages or prevents you from initiating or even reacting with strategic action at all, pushing toward one horn of the Engagement Dilemma. In many arenas, you need certain resources in order to play the game. If you are rich in some resources relative to your opponents (say, your neighborhood group has little money but includes several lawyers willing to give free advice), you naturally try to shift interactions to arenas where those resources are worth the most. Corporations, rich in cash but poor in persuasive moral rhetoric, prefer behind-the-scenes lobbying and campaign contributions, if not outright bribes, over direct public debate.

Resources may be physical equipment, but cultural meanings and know-how are necessary in order to use them. Not only must you be able to read the instructions to operate your new fax machine, but you also need to be able to write effective letters, know other people's fax numbers, have networks of allies to send messages, and so on. You have to know how to spend the money you raise: how to hire a good tort lawyer or maintain the kind of diary that will help you win a lawsuit. Resources are necessary, but knowing how to use them matters as well.

Resources are also symbols. Parades of missiles through Red Square demonstrated the USSR's might and modernity, a samurai's sword proved his status. Law firms' libraries are useful but symbolic as well. Many resources are for show; indeed, their dominant use is probably to intimidate or reassure—and only when these functions fail are they actually used. It is one thing to have tanks, another to send them into the streets (although sending them into the streets is also a display, far short of letting them fire). In a Bangladeshi village, anthropologist Beth Roy was surprised to find that many peasants had swords and shields, normally used in festivals as a reminder of earlier days when their ancestors had served as soldiers for local chiefs—but also available when real conflict arose.[14]

It also requires intelligence to invent and test new resources. You want guns that do not jam—or at least you want to know how often they jam. Aware of this problem, the U.S. Army opened its first "proving ground" in 1861. The history of technology includes notorious failures. For example, tanks tested for cold conditions by driving them straight into and then out of special chambers proved unable to turn in cold weather. When you go into court with a new kind of forensic evidence, you want to know its vulnerabilities to cross-examination (so as to know whether to conceal them or raise them yourself).

Physical traits of players are sometimes resources. A boy's size may give him an advantage in fistfights. An island nation's boundaries may protect it from invasion. Advantages like these are resources in that they influence what you or your opponent can do physically. Size matters, even in sports like baseball, where it matters indirectly at best. According to sports lore, "Little Poison" Waner of the Pirates watched the legendary Yankees warming up before the 1927 World Series. "Jesus, they're big," he wailed. The Pirates proceeded to lose four straight games. Size is not crucial in baseball, or in most arenas outside sports, but it can certainly burnish a myth of superplayers. Size can matter for compound players, too: giant corporate monopolies and big countries intimidate others. Resources can threaten without being put to use. (The *potential* versus *actual* use of resources returns us to the Engagement Dilemma: one of the risks of engagement is the destruction of resources, such as all those shiny tanks and planes the commanders love.)

Most resources are specific to the kind of interaction in which they are used. A boy's strength will help him in a fistfight but not in verbal repartee; the best knife is no help in a gunfight. The money to hire a smooth-talking lawyer helps little when you are sued in a small-claims court that bars lawyers. Over time, humans have shifted many of their engagements to less violent arenas. In a general way, money has replaced force as the key resource across many arenas—part of the modern world's civilizing process. Money really can do anything if, as Columbus thought, it can bring souls into paradise. Short of that, it is a good multipurpose resource but it is not infinitely applicable—as we saw with the Dilemma of Dirty Hands.

Resources should not be confused with rules and other aspects of arenas—even when these favor one side over the other. One company may have a legal monopoly in a market. Men have advantages over women in some property courts. Some types of terrain favor defenders over attackers. Resources interact with rules in a number of ways. In U.S. criminal court, if both sides lack the resources, including people, to do convincing research that would enable each side to poke holes in the other's case, responsible juries must return verdicts of "not guilty" due to reasonable doubt: generalized bumbling favors the defense. Resources are a form of property, furthermore, and modern societies have thick webs of rules (laws) governing the use and transfer of private property: about trusteeship, nonprofit organizations, and tax-deductible contributions. Resources receive their value from arenas and cultural uses, but they are not the same as arenas or meanings.[15]

As we saw with tanks, there is a difference between having a resource (a structural factor), showing it off (a strategic choice, as in a threat), and actually using it for its intended purpose (a coercive action). The last may reduce humans to their physical dimensions: guns can kill them or chemicals immobilize them. Anthony Giddens is getting at this idea when he says that the "materiality" of such resources "does not affect the fact that such phenomena become resources . . . only when incorporated within processes of structuration";[16] that is, their value as resources depends on how they are used and understood.

Although initial resource distributions affect strategic action, much of this action consists of gathering the right resources. You procure watches, tape recorders, electronic bugs, aircraft carriers, neutron bombs, or whatever you think you need. If you discover you need a fax machine to coordinate a letter-writing campaign, you raise the funds to buy one. In the end, money allows you to get the physical capacities you need, and no one has an infinite supply of money. Even governments are constrained in their ability to raise taxes. They must use the same strategic tools we all do to mobilize resources: rhetorical persuasion, reliance on allies, the demonization of enemies, promises and threats, and so on. FDR used all these in trying to push his country toward involvement in World War II, but he succeeded only after the emotional reaction to the attack on Pearl Harbor.

As you try to increase your resources, you also try to decrease those of your opponents. Direct destruction is one route; even better is to seize them for your own use. A less direct approach is to reduce the value of your opponents' resources. A common wartime tactic, for instance, is to forge your opponents' currency, depreciating and destabilizing it through inflation. The United States used this trick against Saddam Hussein in 1991 and against the Taliban ten years later. The Nazis tried it against the British in World War II, employing counterfeiters in prison camps and managing to create pound notes that were rumored to be more perfect than the genuine versions.

THE SCORCHED-EARTH DILEMMA → Do you preserve or destroy resources that opponents may be able to seize but that you might otherwise use? This is the focus of the Scorched-Earth Dilemma. The choice no doubt depends on which side you think is more likely to control them and what each could do with such control. The resources may be crucial or marginal to the team. (This is one of the dimensions of the Home-Turf Dilemma, crossed with the Today or Tomorrow? dilemma.)

THE GOOSE DILEMMA → The control of a resource flow (when it is not threatened by immediate seizure, as in the Scorched-Earth Dilemma), poses the Goose Dilemma (after the goose that laid the golden eggs). You can overexploit a resource for short-term gains, perhaps destroying it in the process, or you can cultivate it to sustain the flow indefinitely. As historian William McNeill comments, "Very early in civilized history, successful raiders became conquerors, . . . [that is, they] learned how to rob agriculturalists in such a way as to take from them some but not all of the harvest."[17] No doubt they discovered techniques of social control that made this patient choice more attractive.

An advantage in resources is especially crucial to winning so-called *wars of attrition*, when each engagement results in roughly equal losses on both sides, so that those who can keep replacing those losses longest will win. If you have a large enough advantage in resources, you can afford to lose more than your opponent in each battle—Ulysses Grant relied on this method for winning the U.S. Civil War. Employers often turn strikes into wars of attrition, if they can better afford the costs than strikers.[18]

In some long-lasting, low-level conflicts, victory goes not to those with more resources but to those who can build the interaction into their daily lives more fully. Thus, in the Vietnam War, the United States had more resources, but Vietnam's liberation fighters could sustain a longer fight by making it part of their lives. Of course, if we think of humans as resources, the U.S. forces were badly outnumbered (the American military fought against most of the Vietnamese civilian population). As conservative Rambos claim, the United States was unwilling to make this into a true war of attrition, matching deaths one for one.

So far I have been speaking of resources that help a player engage in strategic actions, but you may also use resources as a kind of ransom or payoff to get others to do what you wish. If you control anything that others desire—any of the sources of satisfaction mentioned in chapter 3—you have leverage. You can pay them, help their offspring, withhold affection or praise. For every goal a player has, others can offer a corresponding incentive. I think only the physical incentives should be called resources. The others—like helping someone's family—are strategic actions.

THE SORCERER'S APPRENTICE DILEMMA → You need resources and skills, the power of which comes from getting known outputs from your inputs. You expect familiar results from familiar routines. I may know how to slow down a construction project by filing a lawsuit or how to blow up a building with jet fuel and fertilizer and a van. But as I come to rely more and more on the means I have available, they begin to shape the way I think about ends: I pursue the ends that I can attain with my means. My vision of means also narrows. I become less likely to think about other paths of action, other means that could be available with a little extra effort. I stick to the ones I know. I grow overly proud of my surveillance satellites and stop hiring informants on the ground. The use of experts provides an example: once you hire lawyers, they push you to employ legal strategies that are familiar to them but which may not be the most effective ones. As in the original tale, the power of my tools means that I cannot always control them.

In addition to restricting what we can do, our means often *become ends themselves*: we act to protect our resources, develop our technologies, or expand our organizations—since Heidegger, this has been criticized as the triumph of "instrumental reason." (In this second version, the Sorcerer's Apprentice Dilemma is a variation on the Dilemma of Shifting Goals.) For one thing, your means may become valued symbols of success.[19] In other cases your means may literally take over when they are embodied in strategic actors. Civilian leaders, for instance, run grave risks when they turn to the military to retain their positions.[20] Or your investment in your means may simply undermine the goals you are hoping to pursue, as when a military buildup frightens other nations and ends up undermining your own security. Political scientist Barry Buzan refers to this as the "defense dilemma."[21]

Another possibility is that your team may not put the effort into the game that you require of them. This is a problem of principals and agents, which we might also dub the "do-it-yourself dilemma." You cannot do everything yourself, but you lose some control when you hire or persuade others to carry out your plans. You may need to divert more and more resources to surveillance and control of your own team.

For compound teams, resources are never a straightforward capacity. In addition to all the challenges of coordination involved in using them, there is the problem of their control. The team as a whole rarely controls them; subunits do. In many cases control of resources becomes another arena for conflict—an internal one. Each soldier controls her rifle; each teacher, her classroom. This is another way in which "resources"—one's "fodder"—can take over.

INTELLIGENCE

Intelligence comes in many forms. *Strategic* intelligence is the ability to come up with winning moves, to surprise or trick opponents, to win over third parties. *Expert* intelligence consists of knowledge about the world around us, based on scientific observation: resources can usually buy such intelligence. Part of what experts do is categorize information and events usefully, to recognize what is most relevant. A third form of intelligence, the ability to *express* your inner sensibilities or to empathize with those of others, can often contribute to strategic success, especially in persuading others. All three contribute to an *organizing* intelligence, which helps you use your resources efficiently, allowing you to get more than others can out of the same inputs. Resourcefulness, far from meaning "full of resources," is closer to the opposite: making do with few resources, or doing a lot with those you have. It is an important skill to be able to rally your followers, attract volunteers, "motivate" others—to have the kind of charm that Martin Luther King Jr. had. Resource-rich players, like nine-hundred-pound gorillas, need not be so charming. Other forms of intelligence, such as the ability to do math or music, or to write powerful poetry, are less obviously relevant to strategy. (In the military, intelligence simply means information.)

Other skills seem derived from these forms of intelligence. One is *empathy*, the ability to see things from another's point of view, which is extremely useful in anticipating how others will think, feel, and act. A related skill is the ability to *process information*, often of different types and quality and from different sources. Much relevant information is vague rather than neatly measured, making it hard to deal with. Both these skills increase your ability to *avoid mistakes*. There is also *creativity*, the ability to thwart opponents' expectations or to craft more effective ways of doing things. *Rhetorical powers* to persuade others are another important dimension of strategic intelligence, partly the result of empathy, creativity, and information processing.

In many resource-rich settings, intelligence is a suspect capacity, as it is in warrior cultures that idolize pure physical strength. Clever Odysseus was not popular among his fellows, although they happily turned to him at key moments as the only man who could get certain unsavory things done (cajoling bitter Philoctetes into rejoining the army, for example). Modern corporations are apparently similar. "One of the most damaging things that can be said about a manager," observes Robert Jackall, "is that he is brilliant. This almost invariably signals a judgment that the person has publicly asserted his intelligence and is perceived as a threat to others."[22] Many of his fellow generals grumbled about Wesley Clark in the same way—as just too clever. Smart players frequently disconcert other members of their own team because of the possibility that they will partly defect to pursue their individual goals.

The business example shows that suspicion of intelligence is not simply based on a preference for brute strength. Many cultures perceive that intelligence erodes basic human loyalties, making individuals more likely to defect. They appear untrustworthy if they are always calculating, always thinking of new ways to do things, perhaps contemplating new allies and partners. It seems more difficult to control and coordinate the actions of clever people. (In the following section I distinguish two desirable traits in allies: good intentions, and the capacity to follow through on them. Smart people are better at the latter.) Warned Machiavelli, "The man who makes another powerful ruins himself. The reason is that he gets power either by shrewdness or by strength, and both qualities are suspect to the man who has been given the power."[23]

Even when those who have them do not defect outright, particular skills—like particular resources—have their own logics. This is their strength, after all: that they enable us to accomplish certain feats. As we saw in the Sorcerer's Apprentice Dilemma, these logics can sometimes clash with the strategic logic that players otherwise wish to follow.

INDIVIDUAL COMPETENCIES

Some people are better than others at getting what they want. How are they different? Erving Goffman listed several traits that help individuals in face-to-face strategic interactions: emotional self-control, intellectual self-control, and technical knowledge about mechanisms for getting information.[24] Mastery of your emotions not only prevents information from slipping out inadvertently, but may allow you to feign emotions and mislead interrogators and observers. Through intellectual control, you may, for instance, avoid getting caught in a lie by contradicting earlier testimony. But knowledge and self-control hardly exhaust the personal traits useful in strategic interaction.

Charm is a vague quality that we often use in an effort to sum up what allows some people to get what they want. (The sociological term *charisma* gets at the same traits, equally vaguely.)[25] They may simply, by their own example, inspire others to act differently, without having to articulate demands. They tap into broader cultural values, or simply capture others' imaginations. They embody what others would like to be. In 1527 Castiglione described his ideal courtier as "endowed by nature not only with talent and beauty of countenance and person, but with that certain grace which we call an 'air,' which shall make him at first sight pleasing and lovable to all who see him."[26] Goffman refers to "poise" as "the capacity to suppress and conceal any tendency to become shamefaced during encounters with others," an equally circular description.[27]

What are the components of personal charm? *Physical attractiveness*, for one: we pay more attention, of every sort, to those we enjoy looking at (penetrating eyes are especially important).[28] The timbre, volume, and resonance of one's *speaking voice* all matter as well: we like listening to certain people. *Engagement* and *sincerity* are other components: we want to spend time with a person who seems to care about us, pays attention to us, likes us, or understands us—someone who leans forward when we talk, makes eye contact, has his shoulders squared toward us. Of course, the opposite of this engagement sometimes works, since a kind of vagueness or distance can be a blank slate on which people project their own fantasies. Wit can make you like someone more, but it may also undercut their (or your) sense of moral purpose. A kind of simplicity or sincerity may work better for those who rely on their moral charm to get things done (recall the suspicion of intelligence mentioned above).

Finally, we have Dale Carnegie's "six ways to make people like you": "Become genuinely interested in other people. Smile. Remember that a man's name is to him the sweetest and most important sound in the English language. Be a good listener. Talk in terms of the other man's interest. Make the other person feel important—and do it sincerely."[29] Sincerity is an obvious problem if you are trying to get people to like you for purposes of strategic advantage:

THE SINCERITY DILEMMA → Appearances are crucial. You may wish to have a certain kind of reputation—for being nice, competent, trustworthy (or sometimes for being ruthless, violent, or inept). But you do not necessarily have to be or act that way. You can shape others' perceptions and expectations by a good public relations effort. You can even obtain some startling effects by letting down the facade occasionally to let someone see a different you. As the disenchanted Rochefoucauld put it, "The really astute pretend all through their lives to eschew intrigue in order to resort to it on some special occasion and for some great purpose." But it is usually easiest to maintain a reputation if it accurately reflects who you are, since you need to devote less effort to PR work.[30]

A related dilemma pits good intentions against strategic intentions, which are widely viewed as being at odds. As the legendary acquisitions editor Doug Mitchell describes his job, "The editor has to have the gift of friendship, cementing bonds of trust with people who put their careers and intellectual labor in your hands. If you try to use the authors for your own advantage or gain, they'll find you out. The bond should be almost for its own sake, for the honor of collaborating in good conversation and publishing good books. . . . Don't be a mere flatterer, bonding for ulterior gain, and don't be obsequious, just to make people feel good."[31] The editor needs to get books from his authors, but strategic manipulation beyond that shatters his charm. Recall that paralyzing shame turns into righteous anger if we think someone is trying strategically to shame us rather than being sincerely horrified by what we have done.

Truly charming people are probably less likely to act strategically, refusing to put their charm to strategic "use." (This adds to the Engagement Dilemma: launching strategic action may undermine some of your capacities for doing so, such as good will.) "Bad" reputations pose only the first aspect of the Sincerity Dilemma: you do not need to be as bad as your reputation. People who are patently strategic are not so charming. A frequent ingredient in charm is shyness, an unwillingness to interfere with other people's lives, a curiosity about them, and an interest in leaving them as they are. To the extent that you appear to want something from them, to be *trying* to charm them for some purpose—instead of simply being charming as part of your personality—you undermine your own charm. Charm should not be too aggressive or goal-oriented. You cannot use it strategically too often, and it may be strongest if you are altogether unaware of it, although this renders you incapable of putting it to strategic use. Perhaps it is better to infect others with your enthusiasm, sweep them along with your projects, rather than trying to engage them in specific tasks. And yet, alas, I suspect that aggressively strategic people get more of what they want, despite their lack of charm.

THE CHARM DILEMMA → Transparently good intentions are part of charm, but they may undercut strategic effectiveness. The tension between innocence and power, after all, is a staple of legend and art. The most charming people are usually enthusiastic about what others want for themselves, helping them attain their own goals. This means they are less likely to achieve their own. But the more they focus on their own purposes, the less charming and persuasive they usually are to others. We have all met people who seem intent on pleasing, but leave the uneasy feeling that they want something from us. It's a tough balancing act for a strategic-minded person.[32]

Passive-aggressive individuals are caught on the horns of the Charm Dilemma. They engage others strategically (the aggressive part), but they try to hide this in order to retain the charm of nonengagement (the passive part). As long as they can use the charm to hide their strategic intentions, they can avoid being seen as passive-aggressive. But as soon as the epithet is applied, it effectively destroys the facade of charm.

A number of cultures have terms that get at the Charm Dilemma's pitting of inwardness and outwardness, which is related in turn to the Engagement Dilemma. Islamic *jihad,* or struggle, can either be an effort at inward self-control or an aggressive holy war. The Hindu concept of *swaraj,* or self-rule, can also refer to self-control or to national autonomy. The dilemma requires us to choose passivity or aggression, either in alternation or combination.

You do not need to charm people if you can convince them that you share their goals. If your interests coincide, they will try to put up with you even though you are anything but charming—making for "strange bedfellows." But of course one part of being charming is to project a feeling of shared interests, identities, and other common bonds.

People distinctly lacking in charm have a hard time engaging others in their projects. Some people make you feel uneasy (they give off a sense of ulterior motives, or they lack candor); some have disturbing physical habits (although sometimes, as with Rasputin's greasy hair and body odor, this can add to their aura!); some make you feel bad about yourself. They are usually less able to enlist others for their strategic projects.

Yet the opposite of charm can sometimes work, for instance when you scare or intimidate people rather than charming them. Most people, especially those in the middle class, are accustomed to dealing with others who exert considerable control over their emotions, who put on a pleasant facade even when they feel hostile, who avoid conflict and especially physical coercion. Few of us know how to respond when someone stops acting this way, even for a moment. We don't know the surly body language that is effective in tough neighborhoods, for example, and are thus vulnerable to those who do. In the short term, coercion often works.

THE PARANOID DILEMMA → If charmers are reticent to engage others strategically, paranoids expect to. They scan the horizon for aggressive moves by others, seeing them where they are not intended. They mistrust and test their closest team members and allies. They look for slights in offhand remarks. They never forget or forgive perceived insults. They are more prepared for strategic engagements, but their very preparation makes such engagements more likely. By expecting others to be enemies, and treating them that way, paranoids create more enemies for themselves. Some extremely clever strategists, such as Lyndon Johnson and Richard Nixon, have had paranoid streaks. Religious beliefs represent an extreme: you are more likely to see Satan's hand everywhere if you believe in Satan. Paranoids lack charm, but it may be useful to have some on your team, always scanning the horizon for danger, as long as you can prevent them from dominating the team.[33]

Empathy contributes to strategic abilities—up to a point. The benefits come from cognitive empathy, the ability to get inside the heads of others, to understand and predict how they will feel and respond. But the emotional dimension of empathy, the ability to *feel* what they feel, is likely to breed sympathy, which leads you to take others seriously as ends in themselves, or at least to value their ends more. You find it harder to use them purely as means to your own ends. In a word, you become charming. A number of emotions create bonds of obligation between people: love and affection, gratitude, trust and respect, and of course sympathy. We perceive those we are bound to as ends in themselves.[34]

Some people have low levels of these "normal" human emotions. The "antisocial personality disorder" of contemporary psychiatry (common among politicians and con artists, it turns out, who depend on understanding others without necessarily sympathizing with them) involves some opposite traits, such as deceitfulness, aggression, and a lack of remorse. Antisocial personalities can be charming for long periods, so that their strategic moves, when they inevitably come, are more devastatingly effective—as Rochefoucauld would appreciate. Whatever our labels for them, certain personality traits enable players to engage in strategic action more fully and enthusiastically.[35]

Inspiring trust in others is an important asset for both individuals and organizations (even if it becomes necessary to abuse that trust!). Trust may operate at the level of ends or of means. The first is *moral*: we trust someone to have the right impulses, to want to do the right thing, to be a good person. This is a kind of moral charm that people like Martin Luther King Jr. exude (and that wit, cynicism, or irony often undermines). On the second level, we trust someone who has an aura of *competence*. Others believe that such a person knows how to accomplish their shared goals, has the intelligence or resources to get things done. These two forms of trust may conflict with each other: balancing competence against good intentions is a version of the Charm Dilemma. When we look for allies, we judge their intentions *and* their abilities.

Motivation is crucial to strategic success as well as other kinds. It involves concentrated attention, effort, and persistence. People who pay more attention to their strategic engagements are likely to do better at them. But motivation can backfire, as with the Charm Dilemma. If others see you as trying too hard to win, they may feel threatened. Or in certain settings they may find your enthusiasm misplaced, even creepy. You want to try hard without seeming to: "Don't let them see you sweat." You may wish to work hard not only at your strategy, but also at hiding your efforts. And if you pretend not to care, you cannot be judged harshly if you fail.[36] Exceptions arise, of course, as when you make a show of your strategic efforts in order to impress allies.

Determination is a valuable trait. Those who see your determination will expect you to continue an engagement even when many others would tire and drop out, even when it no longer seems rational—in terms of what is to be gained—to keep going. If you convince others that winning matters more to you than anything else (and more than it does to anyone else), they may decide not to compete. They will often let you win. This was the key to Rome's military success: Romans recognized no middle ground between victory and annihilation. This intransigence frustrated their greatest opponent, Hannibal, who could never translate his victories on the field into the end of the conflict.[37] Such determination, whether personal or collective, is a clear signal about character and goals. It can also provide a supreme sense of confidence.

Our bodies, to pull together several threads of the discussion, are an important part of strategic action. Our bodies convey all sorts of signals. They are not only resources capable of force or charm, but also the medium through which we express words and feelings. Sometimes they help us hide our true emotions; at other times, they give them away. Occasionally, they simply give out: fatigue is a factor in more arenas than war. The stress of many interactions is just too much, as minds and bodies both give way. Dexedrine has its limits.

REPUTATIONS

Reputation, as we saw in chapter 3, is a basic human goal. It is also a powerful strategic tool for individuals and collectivities. We rarely know as much as we would like about the people we interact with, so we use their reputations to help us predict what they will do. Reputations amount to stereotyped images that others have of us (and that we have of ourselves), and one of the interesting features of stereotypes is their tendency to link traits together. Evidence of an individual's or organization's credibility in one situation leads people to assume that credibility in other situations. They will attribute other positive traits to that player, sometimes without justification. Through most of recorded history, a man's confidence and aura—his potency—arose from intertwined performances in bed, in battle, and with the bottle.[38] Evidence of wrongdoing, in similar fashion, taints the entire person or organization.

Like resources and skills, reputations are often the result of strategic action. The most accurate predictor of how you will behave in a strategic game is how you have behaved before. Prior performance conveys a lot of information to other players—perhaps more than you would wish. Other aspects of your past may lead others to make assumptions about you that are often unwarranted. You are assumed to be wise because you have traveled a lot, or—also implausibly—because you have suffered some great victimization. We have an emotional resonance because of what has happened *to* us, which is quite different from what we have actively *done*.

We have reputations whether we want to or not (this is the basis of the theory of symbolic interactionism). Even when no opponents or allies are trying to shape our images, people with whom we interact inevitably fill in the blanks to attribute all sorts of personality traits to us. In any given culture, certain facts or traits are thought to imply other ones, so we build elaborate impressions of others on the basis of very little knowledge—an apparently universal cognitive error. This has been called "implicit personality theory."[39] We tend to "characterize" people according to clusters of traits that correspond, for instance, to hero, villain, and victim.

Reputations are fragile. A single serious blunder can ruin your standing forever, especially if you have enemies interested in crafting their own persona for you. Often, the result is a kind of caution: nothing ventured, nothing lost. A corporate executive with a promising future can only blow it by initiating risky ventures (one of the risks of engagement discussed in chapter 1).

Reputations may be either good or bad, and each has its strategic uses. Good ones are usually superior, since they inspire trust. A reputation for honesty and credibility make it easier to find allies who are confident you will not defect in the middle of a game. But a reputation for bad behavior also has advantages, laying the groundwork for a strategy of intimidation, for example. Those who are seen as nice cannot make credible threats as easily as those who are seen as ruthless. Even a reputation for incompetence, which usually undermines alliances and promises because others believe you are incapable of following through on them, is occasionally an advantage. Academics, for example, see this in colleagues who are so inept that they are never asked to assume administrative responsibilities, which frees their time for other things (although not usually strategic pursuits).

NAUGHTY OR NICE? → You can get others to do what you want through intimidation or loyalty, fear or love. Machiavelli suggested that a Prince should inspire both fear and love, and most rulers try to punish enemies and reward friends. But it is difficult to maintain such a mixed reputation. More often, we go one way or the other. Our choice depends partly on our own tastes and personality and partly on what we want from others. Long-term cooperation on a range of fronts may require love and loyalty, especially if the other player is not under our direct supervision and control. Fear is especially effective in limited engagements, although it may be so over long periods as well.[40] Specific actions and our broad reputations both fall under the Naughty or Nice dilemma.

You may want a nasty reputation among competitors but a nice one with other types of players. A company that is known to spend huge sums to drive out competitors will discourage startups in its industry, even if there is room for them. It may have to sell below cost to do so, but what it loses in the short run, it hopes to gain in the long run by scaring off other potential entrants. It only has to win a couple of nasty fights before others stop challenging it. But none of this need damage the company's reputation with customers or suppliers.

There are probably no traits, no aspects of a reputation, that are universally useful. The effects of your reputation depend on your audiences, the form of strategic interaction, your past actions and hence others' expectations, and no doubt much more. There is no such thing as a reputation in general, only reputations with specific audiences. We may fantasize a "generalized other" to sum up our representations, but when it comes to serious strategic thinking, we always distinguish how specific players feel about us. It is often part of our strategy to cultivate different reputations with different players, especially friends and foes.

Naughty actions—those of which most players disapprove—pay off if you can obtain a quick and irreversible victory, but if such engagements are prolonged, your reputation will suffer. The fear you arouse in others may lead them into quick concessions. The risk is that some powerful player or alliance will decide to punish your transgressions.

Players work hard at their reputations, whatever kind they cultivate. A credible and persuasive public-relations effort is vital, especially during crises or attacks on reputations. If rumors circulate about a leader's health, he will try to appear on television, jogging or swimming in the Yangtze (as Mao did even when confined to a wheelchair). Corporate spokespersons must appear immediately after an industrial accident to salvage their company's credibility and manage public impressions. "Spin" is important for all strategic actors, even if their audience is not the national public but only their mother-in-law. Their work can be more subtle in normal times, when the attention of bystanders is not focused on them. "Successful political leaders," observes Stephen Skowronek, "do not necessarily do more than other leaders; successful leaders control the political definition of their actions, the terms in which their places in history are understood."[41]

CONFIDENCE AND AGENCY

George Bernard Shaw had it right: "To be in hell is to drift; to be in heaven is to steer." A player who expects to win has confidence. This often derives from reputation, since you are more likely to think you will win if others do too. Indeed, the more confidence your opponents have in you, the less they have in themselves. Confidence encourages you to try a broader range of things or to be more enthusiastic about them in anticipation of success. It kindles action. Warriors who believe they are invincible because of a magic charm will be more aggressive. If you can shape everyone's expectations in your favor, they can be self-fulfilling. (As we saw in chapter 2, many threats stimulate reaction, but not those from an actor perceived to be unstoppable.)

Fatalism or timidity, at the opposite extreme, can paralyze you, limiting your range of actions. Fatalistic assumptions suggest that your actions cannot influence outcomes—although, reassuringly, you also doubt the efficacy of other players. Timidity can keep you from pursuing what you may cognitively recognize as opportunities: you leave such actions to others. Fatalism is an impersonal lack of confidence; timidity is a personal one. A lack of confidence can obliterate your chances of success, if for no other reason than that you devote less time and resources to pursuing your goals. You avoid engagement, you remain passive.

Although deep-rooted factors like personality and culture affect a player's confidence, the strongest influence is experience. Winning builds confidence, and losing reduces it. Short of those outcomes, doing something, acting at all, at least reassures you that you can act. Action spawns agency. A new CEO reorganizes her corporation just to show to investors, employees, and herself that she can—as well as to develop a take-charge reputation. A quarterback throws a few short passes as "confidence builders" early in the football game. The results of such actions are more important as means for future ends than as immediate payoffs. They build momentum through small accomplishments.[42] At the opposite extreme, we can also learn to be helpless, with devastating consequences for our ability to act.[43]

The probabilistic nature of strategic interaction means we should never be completely sure of any outcome. But *our assessment of the odds changes those odds.* We act differently if we are confident, and so the outcome may differ. Take a college athlete who aspires to become a professional. She knows the odds are against her, but every tough academic course that would give her a serious education to fall back on as an alternative takes time away from her training and decreases her odds of turning pro. Although not strictly a strategic choice, how she resolves the Basket Dilemma (see chapter 6) depends not only on how highly she values that small chance but also on her own confidence.

The confident player spins a sense of *inevitability* about his actions, making his plans seem like the path of least resistance. Thus Bush II, in the months before and the month after the 2000 election, talked as though victory was naturally his. If Gore had won, he would then have appeared to have somehow stolen the race—even though something closer to the opposite happened. The mystery is how Bush convinced the media that his victory was inevitable. Sometimes this momentum is defined in terms of power: one side is growing in power, is invincible, while the other side is portrayed as weak, vacillating, fearful. Hitler managed to present himself to the world in the former terms in the late 1930s. Alexander the Great had such a powerful reputation that many walled cities simply opened their gates when he arrived (hoping for better treatment as a result). Another way to feel and appear invincible is to have a narrative of history that puts you on the side of change. Communism had this advantage (and few others) for decades. For this reason every small battle in the Cold War was interpreted as a sign of historical momentum. A confident player may close off alternatives, such as the possibility of retreat—forcing his team to play more fiercely. Cortés did this in burning his boats after landing on the Mexican mainland, and some generals have done the equivalent by lining up their armies with a cliff or river behind them.

Luck—not in the sense of sheer accident, but as an abiding personal attribute—can be an element of confidence. Although strategic players generally attribute their successes to skill, others often view them as lucky. We all want to be with "lucky" people, in the same way we want to have effective lucky charms. An example from recent history is Bill Clinton, who managed to survive a number of scandals largely through his own personal charisma. Large numbers of people simply liked him and sympathized with him. Clinton managed to convey luck through his gestures, facial expressions, and words—alongside more sympathetic traits such as humility and enthusiasm. Some people just seem to embody luck, which illustrates another way in which we craft reputations through attribution.[44]

Confidence gives you a sense of *agency*, a belief that the world responds to your actions, that you are in control of events. Recall Machiavelli's counsel: if you are about to be forced to do something painful, do it to yourself first. If your girlfriend is about to dump you, call her and be the one to break up first. You retain a sense of control, dignity, and agency, and avoid the role of victim. This sense of competence, as we saw in chapter 3, is a basic human good, but also a necessary prerequisite to action. Developmental psychologists have traced it to very young ages, as an infant learns (in Erik Erikson's words) "to let the mother out of sight without undue anxiety or rage because she has become an inner certainty as well as an outer predictability."[45] The world slowly becomes predictable and manageable.

Many of those who carry on stressful interactions—professional sports or war, for example—use superstitious rituals and magical charms to give them confidence. In some cases it is hard to know where magic ends and rational information and learning start. The elaborate data that professional baseball managers collect is an example, covering batting, fielding, and pitching styles for all the players in the league. Some doubt that it makes much difference to winning, compared for instance to players' natural abilities. It may instead have the effect of calming players' (and coaches') nerves, like a lucky charm that gives them an aura of control. They can focus on how to pitch to each batter, how to field him. Certainly if other teams gather such information, your confidence requires that yours should too. (If every team does it, it appears to make no difference; but it might if one team stopped doing it.)[46] We can use all sorts of objects and activities to reassure ourselves in this way. Jon Elster speaks of his smoking as "a ritual that served to highlight salient aspects of experience and to impose structure on what would otherwise have been a confusing morass of events. . . . It helped me to achieve a feeling of mastery, a feeling that I was in charge of events rather than submitting to them."[47]

Baseball coaches with their statistics show something else, too: the need for leaders to display confidence to the rest of the team. According to legend, Alexander the Great slept so soundly the night before Gaugamela, his decisive confrontation with Darius, that he could barely be awakened, demonstrating his insouciant self-assurance. Through sufficient confidence, according to Edward Gonzalez, Fidel Castro managed to overcome a number of organizational inadequacies and succeed with his revolution.[48] His approach demonstrated the rebellious individualism of the *caudillo*, a kind of heroism that denied obstacles, risks, and realities—as well as the need for planning, organization, and coordination. Clever leaders can even turn bad luck into good. In a famous incident during Rome's civil wars, Julius Caesar tripped when disembarking in Africa, falling flat on his face. He brilliantly spread out his arms to embrace the earth in a symbol of conquest, transforming an omen of failure into one of victory—which he went on to achieve.[49]

Playing a strategic game strengthens you in all sorts of ways that are helpful for future interactions—and not just future rounds of the same game. In addition to the obvious development of skills and intuition, engagement creates in players a sense of themselves *as players*, a collective identity as actors. By conducting war and diplomacy, early modern states vitally polished their reputations with their own populations, who bore so much of the burden of these campaigns. The states became actors, crafting new national identities in which citizens could take pride. Greater internal mobilization thus became possible.[50]

A central benefit of confidence is increased *energy*, a sheer level of activity that is higher than it otherwise would be. The reverse is a kind of *fatigue*, either a literal bodily exhaustion or a more figurative weariness with current lines of action. The latter can be a sort of boredom that hobbles action. More frequently, it is a form—mild or severe—of depression.

Confidence can mold your assessment of your skills and resources too much, leading you to overestimate yours and underestimate your opponent's. (A lack of confidence leads to the opposite distortions.) Those magic amulets, in the end, do not protect warriors with spears from Gatling guns. The problem of *over*confidence is serious, leading to reckless actions that may succeed because of their audacity but may fail because they are just too difficult. We may tend to have too much confidence in our own knowledge, a failing especially of the professional middle class. Their special training leads them to think they know how to solve any problems in their area of expertise, whether they are risk analysts, engineers, surgeons, or military advisors. They make the widespread "attribution error" of thinking that the world is under their control—an especially bad assumption in strategic settings where the other side has all the skills and knowledge that you do.[51] "The surest way to be taken in," observed Rochefoucauld, "is to think oneself craftier than others."

In strategic interaction, part of the world is trying very hard *not* to fall under your control. The greater the number of players vying for control, the smaller the part of the world that is likely to be under the sway of any *one* of them. Take a strategic conflict with six distinct teams, one of them much stronger than the others. If only 30 percent of what happens is out of anyone's control, and five of the players each control 10 percent of what happens, that leaves the dominant team—which has every right to think it controls the situation—with influence over only 20 percent of what happens.

THE TITAN'S HUBRIS → The stronger we are in either resources or personnel, the more confidence we have. But the same confidence may encourage us to let our guard down a bit; in other words, it may turn into overconfidence. If we are sailing on the best ship ever built, we figure we do not need lifeboats for everyone. Or we wait passively behind deep moats and thick walls. Our very strength may become a weakness—the "disease of the strong."[52] Many armies have been defeated when they saw their enemies appear suddenly through an "impassable" thicket or mountain range. This is a risk more than a dilemma. When we are successful, we have little incentive to examine our procedures for flaws, to change what we are doing. As Edward Luttwak says, "Victory misleads, defeat educates."[53] What is worse, our very strength may lead others to mobilize against us out of fear or envy. Hubris, after all, refers to pride in our very real strength. Titans are rarely modest.

Our own leaders can create titanic hubris by shielding us from knowledge of our vulnerabilities and defeats and exaggerating our strengths and victories. The result is that we do not take steps to protect ourselves. The Japanese were quite unprepared for surrender in 1945, having listened for years to upbeat radio reports about their nation's glorious victories. Upward flows of twisted information—due to efforts to please superiors—can have the same result as downward distortions.

For better or worse, our emotions shape our thoughts about our actions. Morale can be good or bad, high or low, giving us hope or taking it away. Either way, it affects our assessments of our chances of success; it filters the information we gather. We may have a psychological bias toward hope, toward the illusion of control, which only memorable defeats can destroy. Only the depressed seem to be free of this illusion of control in their assessments—at the same time that they lack any motivation to act, strategically or otherwise.[54] To act in the world is to care about it, and the resulting play of emotions colors what we think and do.

ORGANIZATIONAL CAPACITIES

The skills of individuals may be the most important capacity a formal organization has, since individuals think up and carry out strategic moves as well as representing the group to others. But there are other capacities. Resources are most obvious, as they can be accumulated, owned, and controlled by organizations as well as by individuals. We can think of organizations as collections of individuals, resources, know-how, and expectations about how an organization acts—all constrained by legal rules. Because we understand their explicit purposes, we can easily see organizations as compound players trying to fulfill them. (The mistake is to view them as similar to simple players, thereby exaggerating their unity and attributing intention to them.) Coordination among individuals is obviously a trait of groups, not individuals. Organizations both *have* and *are* capacities.

A number of important competencies held by individuals can also be sustained by organizations, so that individuals can be replaced and new ones trained. To the extent that know-how can be formalized and made explicit, it can be written down and taught to newcomers. Intelligence is a trait of individuals, but certain organizational structures are better able to encourage it than others. Some settings encourage more unconstrained discussion than others. Effort and determination are emotional quantities that ultimately reside in individuals, but organizational settings can be better or worse at inspiring them. Typically, the more resources an organization controls, the less it works to develop its intelligence.

In general, organizations enhance their intelligence by bringing diverse sources of ideas together: by mixing insiders and outsiders, those with personal and vocational commitments; by relying on both strong and weak network ties; by trying various repertoires. They mix these diverse individuals and their ideas together through regular and open deliberation, by listening to different constituencies, and by remaining accountable to those constituencies. They also work hard at monitoring what is working and what is not. Organizations with the flexibility to adjust quickly according to empirical results can concentrate on the most successful tactics. They try many things, and go with what seems to work best in a given time and place.[55]

Formal organizations do not exhaust all forms of social organization. Social networks are crucial for strategic action: who can be mobilized to act supportively? The affective commitments of allies are as important as shared interests—and both are sources of loyalty and dependability that must be cultivated over time. Persuasion is necessary, as others will be trying to "turn" your allies against you with the same persuasive techniques you use to keep them in line.

Just as skilled individuals are assets to an organization, positions in formal organizations can be assets for individuals, who can divert the resources, reputation, and contacts derived from their positions to their own personal ends. Organizations give them added capacities, no matter whose goals they pursue with them. But organizations have their own routines that, as with resources, also constrain or subvert the individual goals of those working within them. Preservation of the organization may even crowd out the purposes for which it was originally founded, a form of the Sorcerer's Apprentice Dilemma.

GO-SANJŌ'S DILEMMA → Tension frequently arises between using formal positions and rules to get what you want and using personal traits and informal social networks instead—the position or the person. Individuals can have a lot of role distance or a little. They can inspire cooperation through their human attributes or through the trappings and resources of their position. Some people fight against their official roles; others are almost absorbed by them. A priest, for instance, can rely on his personal charisma or on the rituals of the church in going about his duties and dealing with his congregation. (Note that this dimension is mostly independent of the relative robustness of the role, the routinization of which Weber described so eloquently: the role of parish priest is well defined even if practitioners distance themselves from it.) The most effective players probably combine the two methods, but they can interfere with each other. The classic example is the eleventh-century Japanese emperor, Go-Sanjō, who abdicated in 1072 to become a monk but continued to exercise power unofficially—the beginning of decades of "cloistered" government. Former emperors had considerable room to maneuver, but at the same time they lacked the official position and symbolism of the throne. They switched the key arena from a formal to an informal one—and were eventually subdued by a young emperor who managed to switch it back.[56] This is a dilemma for individuals whether they are pursuing the organization's goals or their own (the issue concerns means not ends).

Indispensability is based on this dilemma. It is a reasonable strategy for a person to try to make herself indispensable to her group or organization. Even the most formal organizations contain enormous stores of local, informal knowledge lodged in the heads of people who take much of it with them when they leave. Individuals try to hoard knowledge and resources to make themselves indispensable and hence more valued. In New York, some divorce lawyers have been accused of this: they demand enormous fees just before going to trial, when they have become familiar with a case, and threaten to quit without it. Organizations therefore try to preclude the indispensability that individuals seek, hoping to keep people replaceable because formal rules govern what they are to do.

BEING THERE

Carl Gilbert, Nixon's special trade representative from 1969 to 1971, had a heart attack early in his term. But his staff, concerned about the already limited influence of their office, hid the extent of Gilbert's incapacity by signing his name to letters and generally continuing as if he were still very much in charge. They knew that a leaderless office was a moribund office, especially in the personalistic politics of the Nixon White House. As Woody Allen once quipped, 80 percent of success is simply showing up.

As every military leader knows, what matters is not having the most resources, but getting them to the right place at the right time. In wars, the speed with which a country can call up its reserves, if it has them, can be vital. Many of the great innovations of modern warfare have moved troops with greater speed, with trains and now aircraft. Filing a legal brief by the deadline, showing up in court on the right day, getting a squad car to a crime while it is still in progress—all these are cases of "being there." How many individuals have been taken out of strategic engagements because they got drunk and showed up late (by hours or days)?

Availability applies to people as well as other resources. Leaders must be there to make decisions and inspire confidence. Heads of state are usually toppled when they are traveling abroad, not while they are on the throne or in military headquarters. Spokespersons for public players must also be available at all times in this age of instant news, ready to interpret events. After the nuclear accident at Three Mile Island in 1979, local antinuclear activists in Harrisburg, expecting the worst, evacuated. It took the news media several days to find them. This was sound protection from radiation, had there been any, but not good strategy. No one heard their side of the story.

One of history's most famous lessons in the importance of being there was the vacuum left after Julius Caesar's murder on March 15, 44 BCE. Cicero encouraged Brutus and Cassius, the senior officeholders on the scene, to call a Senate meeting for the following morning. They, sticklers for procedure, insisted on sending a delegation to find the Consul, who had the highest authority. They underestimated their opponent, Mark Antony, who now had time to secure his position, cajole Caesar's will and a good chunk of money out of Caesar's widow, and secure his famous role in delivering the funeral oration several days later. With this, he made Caesar's assassins even less welcome in Rome, and most fled to their country estates, leaving Antony a free hand to maneuver.

Official positions are another form of being there. As part of your daily routine, you watch the action unfold and are called upon to participate. Placing your agents on other teams, where they remain your agents, is a common strategy. I saw this with the French national electric company, EdF, which managed to get multiple representatives on each important energy-planning commission in France. They were not spies, as everyone knew their affiliation (although they of course reported back if trouble loomed). But they were there. Most of these commissions ended up adopting positions that favored EdF. (Being there was not enough, of course: they also had to outmaneuver other players when conflict arose.) In the "iron triangle" pattern, businesses are especially eager to have representatives (official or unofficial) on any committees that affect them. Such agents are frequently the most diligent participants because they have the most to lose or gain (as well as plentiful resources).[57]

Being there or being absent is symbolic as well. Politicians attend funerals, go to disaster sites, and meet countless representatives of other compound players. Events and places have emotional resonances that rub off on players. Absence can also send symbolic messages. In a 2003 Iowa debate, Democratic presidential hopefuls Kerry and Edwards joined only by satellite. They remained in Washington as part of an effort to block the Republican Medicare "reform." The message: they had important things to do, such as running the country and standing up to the Republicans.

Physical deprivation is one way to ensure that players are no longer fully "there." Utter exhaustion or torture drives people within themselves so deeply that survival crowds out other concerns. At the extreme, a kind of apathetic fatalism sets in. As anthropologist F. G. Bailey says of the effects of famine, "[P]eople presumably once endowed with the normal amount of altruism descend through theft and betrayal of their comrades into the stupor of resignation and helplessness: a total loss of will."[58] Depression too may leave you unable to act or decide.

Short of these extremes, simply not paying attention is a way of absenting yourself from interactions. In 1945 studio executive David Selznick was absorbed by Vidor's *Duel in the Sun*, a problem film that starred Selznick's new girlfriend Jennifer Jones; his inattention allowed Alfred Hitchcock to make the innovative film *Notorious*, including a long embrace/kiss between Cary Grant and Ingrid Bergman that flaunted the censorship rules of the time. According to Erving Goffman, a player can also "flood out" of an interaction through distracting emotions, including sadness, amusement, and especially embarrassment (which he thought the most common form).[59] Such emotions can range from mild and brief distraction to crippling shame or depression.

Those who care the most about an interaction pay the most attention, devote the most energy, and usually get what they want. On the other hand, according to exchange theory's "principle of least interest," those who care the least have considerable power because they can threaten to abandon the interaction altogether. There are many forms of being there and not being there.

TASTES IN TACTICS

Resources and competencies are not simply neutral means to various ends. We make cognitive investments in learning how to use resources and how to pull off certain tactics, but we also have moral and emotional attachments that influence our choice of tactics. Some tactics are really part of a group's goals: nonviolence is an end in itself, and so is participatory democracy for many groups. But all tactics can be subject to milder forms of loyalty. If I develop a reputation for candor in interpersonal dealings, I am likely to think that candor is a good trait in all strategic settings. Conversely, if I am willing to be deceitful, I am likely to have rationalizations to excuse that (hard decisions have to be made; the ends justify the means). In both cases I develop not only skills but also a fondness for certain ways of acting.

They become part of my identity as well as my skills. It would rattle me a bit to abandon them. I want to believe they will work, given my moral and emotional commitments, so I am never entirely ruthless in assessing their efficacy.

All tactics have some emotional and moral valence for those who choose them. They may detest certain tactics, using them only as a last resort or not at all. They may enjoy others, or see them as important moral statements. Still others may be relatively neutral. One way to think of tactical tastes is that your tactics have different audiences: internal audiences (your allies and team members) may be drawn to certain ones, but your opponents may be more influenced by others—this is the Janus Dilemma of reaching in versus reaching out that we examine in chapter 5. (If means are partly an end in themselves, by the way, game theory cannot accurately define the payoffs it needs for its models.) The Sorcerer's Apprentice Dilemma suggests that we are tied to our capabilities not only as a practical investment but also out of moral and emotional commitments.

Teams and alliances often fracture over issues of tactics. Agreed on basic goals, they prefer different kinds of moves: shocking or traditional, legal or illegal, democratic or hierarchic, and so on. Different tactics "feel right." For compound players, what kind of organization to form is a basic issue around which different tastes arise. All sorts of dilemmas about leaders, hierarchy, and control can lead to different responses, often fervently held. Successive cohorts of a team, distinguished by the period in which they joined it (and often, correspondingly, by their reasons for joining), frequently exhibit different tastes in tactics.[60] When factions disagree over tactics, it is frequently because they have different primary audiences in mind for their actions.

※

Skills and resources are lodged in both simple and compound players. For this reason, strategic interactions depend crucially on how the various players line up. Who is engaged? Who is on your team, who is an ally, an opponent, a bystander? The lines of contention and cooperation shift again and again. We turn now to the players, whom we will think of especially as audiences for words and actions, to emphasize the cultural interpretation and emotional reactions at the heart of all strategic action.

CHAPTER 5

PLAYERS AS AUDIENCES

I speak for no one: I have enough difficulty speaking for myself.
→ ALBERT CAMUS

The other day I chaired a meeting of our local neighborhood association. We had a complex group that night, with several invited guests in addition to about thirty neighbors. Our member of the New York City Council and her assistant were scheduled to be there, but had not arrived at seven o'clock when we began. The assistant manager of an enormous office building, source of perennial noise and congestion problems, had bravely shown up, no doubt only because he had been told to. (Anger about the building was so great that this man's predecessor had come to one meeting but refused to tell us his name, I suppose fearing that we would start calling him at home.) The local precinct had sent a sergeant, whose good will was vaguely important to us.

There were many "audiences" at the meeting, and I had different aspirations for each. Even my neighbors differed considerably in their attitudes toward the building, the city council member, and the degree of confrontation they thought we should exhibit in our tactics. Most had come to scream at the building manager about a recently installed bank of noisy exhaust fans. (No one comes to these meetings unless they have complaints.) I let them go at him for a while. I thought it was good for him to hear just how upset people were about this new development. Moreover, these managers seem to be replaced every year or two, so I had little incentive to establish a good working relationship with him. I also hoped everyone would vent their strongest feelings before our council member arrived, so that with her we could turn to practical remedies.

I nonetheless intervened with an occasional joke to deflect the nastiest comments, in the hope that he would be more willing to deal with our comparatively calm executive committee if he saw us as the moderates of the neighborhood. (I sent him a sympathetic note after the meeting to reinforce this image.) It is always energizing for a group to have an "enemy," but with the enemy in the room it was difficult to demonize him entirely. The poor man squirmed, sweated, and tried hard to exonerate himself. In deflecting the blame, he gave us useful information about the building's owners and the tenant who had installed the fans—in violation of the building's rules (now we could play managers, owners, and tenants off against each other).

When our council member arrived, I tried to keep the conversation focused on practical measures that her office might help us to enforce despite managerial turnover at the building. A written letter of agreement and intentions was my goal. She actually took over this part of the conversation, nicely parrying some of the more vituperative comments still aimed at the building manager. But I also did not want her to think that we only cared about our little neighborhood, so I raised a couple questions about more general policies and issues, a direction that did not interest most of our association's members. I wanted her to have a good time at our meeting, to have a chance to act as policymaking politician rather than just conflict mediator, and so to carry away positive feelings toward our block. (I also had a couple of general political points I wanted to convey.) This could only help us in the future.

My neighbors were themselves divided over the proper emotional tone for the meeting. One would roll his eyes at me when someone else went on repetitively; another was visibly disturbed when anyone's voice rose toward shouting range. Two others did nothing *but* shout. I had to be careful not to alienate anyone, the group being small enough already. It was hard to mediate between those who thought shouting was the best tactic and those who wanted to pin down specific proposals. I found myself being more conciliatory toward those I knew better, my ongoing affective ties with them being as important as any strategic considerations at the meeting (of course these bonds helped strategically as well). Yet in some cases, I felt I could rely on those long-standing bonds to allow me to ignore someone's raised hand or cut someone off: I trusted that I could explain and cajole them back into good humor later. Fortunately, I was free from one worry that leaders often have: that they will be ousted by a disgruntled faction. I knew no one else had any interest in running these meetings.

I thanked the building manager after an hour and let him escape, so that we could have a more candid discussion of strategy. Part was aimed at getting the police officer (head of our precinct's community policing effort) to feel he was on our side, so we might get better enforcement of city regulations. Part was about the additional pressure our council member could apply. After the formal meeting ended, several of us discussed how best to get these two city officials to follow through. Finally, I went off to sooth several upset neighbors, assuring them of our shared goals. These conversations paralleled several I had had before the meeting, asking various members to raise certain points in public.

I propose that we view strategic players *as audiences watching and listening* to each other's actions and words. The point is to emphasize attentiveness and interpretation. Strategic engagement focuses players' attention. In addition, they actively interpret whatever happens, including their own actions. Strategic action is thoroughly cultural. Only at the rare extreme can one player reduce others to mere physical objects whose conscious awareness is irrelevant. Almost always, we engage their minds. Rhetoric, the art of persuasion, is at the core of strategy.

MULTIPLE PLAYERS

A decision maker must always balance several audiences. Some are internal to her team: her own rivals, disaffected factions, those who desire more radical tactics, those who desire less radical ones, those who simply want different tactics, those who are bored or afraid or angry, and so on. There may be disagreements between paid and unpaid team members, between those with official leadership positions and the rank and file. No compound player is a fully unified actor, but a collection of individuals and blocs who always have some power to defect partly or fully. External audiences are even more complex: in addition to explicit opponents (themselves often a composite of actors who can be played off against one another), there are allies, potential allies, potential recruits, the media, and a long list of state agencies (police and military, elected officials, legal courts, regulatory bureaucracies, and so on). Even the most personal interaction—lovers squabbling for example— is open to state interference. If they behave badly enough, private players become public ones. We cannot always predict which audience will receive the most attention—the focus of attention shifts during engagements. Different moves are typically aimed at different audiences.[1]

Much of the time, full separation of audiences is impossible. A head of state who addresses the UN General Assembly knows his voters back home can read his speech and that domestic news media will comment. As an official in the Bush II administration candidly observed after his president's pugnacious UN address in September 2003, "There's a feeling that you have to assert that the United States is still in control [in Iraq], if nothing else for domestic concerns. . . . We're going into an election year and the president has to project an image of power and authority."[2] Or take a real estate developer, who must sell her project to neighbors, local politicians, banks, and investors, as well as those who will occupy the buildings. The architectural renderings used in these presentations are vital propaganda, which often have little to do with the final result.

Although formal game theory and most literal games feature two sides arrayed against one another, real-world strategic interaction usually involves a host of additional players. Even two individuals engaged in strategic interaction may turn to other players if they think that will help them. Although theatrical and sporting metaphors suggest a distinction between players on the stage (or field) and audiences in the seats (or bleachers), this is misleading. If bystanders were truly inert, they would be irrelevant to strategic calculations. If they matter, it is because they are *potential players*. (Even in theaters, audiences are never entirely passive.)[3] If nothing else, they actively interpret each other's words and actions, waiting to do more if necessary. If all players are audiences, all audiences are potential players.

The opinions of initially neutral "bystander" publics that are not organized to act directly, may sometimes help sway other players such as elected officials. Such publics can range from schoolmates to global media audiences. In personal interactions, such as divorce, you worry about what mutual friends will think. In modern electoral politics, bystander publics have become crucial forces, at least rhetorically. American presidents appeal to them over the heads of Congress; lobbying groups mobilize them to call, fax, and e-mail elected officials.[4] They are relevant players because, if nothing else, they can affect more organized players (or more accurately, organized players can refer to their "opinions" as needed). It is more useful to distinguish between more and less organized players than between audiences and players.

The range of players in any interaction is affected by the interaction itself. As part of my strategy, I may try to interest additional players in the interaction. I may seek to interest government regulators in my grievances against a local company. I may take a departmental squabble to the dean. Of course, any of these players may enter the fray on their own if they see their own interests at stake, feel compassion or outrage, or see this as part of their role (say, as a good manager). Each player will have a different cluster of goals, ranked in different ways.

Almost always, additional potential entrants are watching who may decide to join the fray. These bystanders must make a variety of calculations. Engagement carries risks, the most obvious being the costs of conflict. Before they get involved, potential participants must feel threatened, be confident of victory (if entering the conflict brings victory to their side, they can expect big rewards), or see opportunities for gain whichever side wins. In the latter case, the newcomer may gain victory in a minor arena while attention is largely focused on the main arena of conflict. In almost every engagement, potential players are watching.

THE BYSTANDER DILEMMA → By definition bystanders do no more than watch an interaction, but they usually have the potential to become more actively involved. They face the Engagement Dilemma. Those who are already players face another dilemma in deciding whether to encourage the bystanders to get involved. You may think you know what they will do to or for you, but you can never be sure. The interaction itself may change their goals and capacities. The sheer addition of players also changes the nature of the interaction in ways that are hard to predict. The Bystander Dilemma is what to do *about* bystanders, not what they must decide. Do you encourage them to join?

Some bystanders are meant to be just that: observers only. The media are professional bystanders, although of course they affect the interactions in that their own biases and selections shape the information flowing to others. Peacekeeping forces are meant to watch, with the idea that world attention may calm local conflicts, although they sometimes intervene to prevent certain kinds of actions. The "blue helmets" of the United Nations, however, are frequently so weak that they must align themselves with the most powerful local faction. According to some observers, they keep a conflict going rather than letting it run its course, primarily by protecting weak groups who would otherwise negotiate more urgently for peace.[5]

A player can even act as an audience for her own actions. She watches what she does, evaluates her own performance, thinks of ways she might have done things differently, takes measures to compensate for inadequacies. She is pleased or displeased, thinks differently about herself as a result ("I didn't know I had it in me"), and gains or loses resolve. Most of all, she tries to learn from her experiences. This image of the player as an audience fits well with situationalist images of action: the actor is just part of the setting, like everyone else, helping to interpret and define the flow of action. The "situation" dominates the action. This is part of the story, but only part. The actor who makes a move also has advance knowledge of that move and may see the action differently, as part of a broader strategy. She has a unique context, unavailable to the other audiences, in which to place and interpret her own moves. Each audience has a different point of view, or "partly obstructed" seats. Seeing each player as an audience for her own actions gets at the insight of Camus (and many others) into the fragmented nature even of simple players. Each of us has several ways of viewing an action simultaneously.

In special cases you are the most important audience for your own action. Sometimes you are the only audience, as when you privately rehearse a speech. In the case of "venting," which many of my neighbors were doing at that meeting, the strongest effect may be your own sense of emotional satisfaction, not a change in other players. Complaining and telling your story are important satisfactions, as is expressing your emotions. Sometimes this feels sufficient. Many protest groups turn inward, building a sense of community that is deeply satisfying to participants, but giving up efforts to transform the external world. Large, compound players sometimes communicate internally when different units or factions watch how the others interact with outsiders. In this way they interpret the goals and moods of other parts of their own team at least as accurately as through direct communication.

The most important distinction among audiences is probably that between insiders and outsiders. The boundary can apply either to arenas or to players. Especially for the latter, the distinction is relative: allies are outsiders from one vantage point, insiders from another. (At our neighborhood meeting, we embraced our council member as part of our team for some communications and confronted her as a distinct, external player for others.) The boundary also shifts, frequently as the result of strategic action. Corporations must satisfy employees but also please investors and consumers; university administrators must run their institutions but also raise funds from the outside. Religious groups, Max Weber pointed out, feel the Janus Dilemma in an acute form.[6]

THE JANUS DILEMMA → Some strategies are designed to reach out to outsiders, while others are aimed at insiders (a third category aims at those who are potential recruits). These are very different audiences. Outsiders may need to be educated about a team's identity, interests, and purposes more than insiders do (although such things are often debated internally as well). Insiders may favor a more radical self-image than it is wise to project to outsiders. Celebrities and experts often mediate between the two audiences, a representative or bridging activity that does not always sit well with insiders. When you must rely on the fervor of your team members, you must usually spend more time reaching in than when you have the resources simply to pay them—one reason that protest groups often turn inward and become sects. Foreign policy, too, is often derailed (or wars begun) by the need for a government to win domestic elections. When this happens, a much sharper sense of friends and foes (or insiders and outsiders) can develop, and perhaps must develop to keep the group together. Maintaining team solidarity, in other words, may conflict with pursuing your team's external goals.[7] As Janus, god of thresholds as well as new beginnings, suggests, it is possible either to look in or to look out—but it is hard to do both at the same time.[8]

Distinguishing among audiences helps us to recast a number of scholarly debates as ongoing dilemmas. For instance, do formal organizations spend more time pursuing their substantive purposes, such as producing commodities, or more time bolstering their legitimacy through rituals and symbols? Do corporations pursue the former, nonprofits the latter?[9] In fact, organizations pursue both, with different audiences in mind, neither of which can be ignored. Many structural constraints can be reinterpreted as strategic trade-offs.

CREATING PLAYERS

We have already seen several ways that people and groups become players in strategic engagements. For compound players to persist, they must put a great deal of work into creating and sustaining their identities as players. An explosion of research in the last two decades has examined collective identities in politics, including that on nationalism. Compound players must foster a *myth of unity* that underlies the obvious differences among individuals. Nation-builders fabricate nostalgic images of shared histories and tightly knit communities. Families joke about their idiosyncrasies. Political parties find issues on which to distinguish themselves. In a recent annual report, we read statements such as "Nokia believes . . ." and "At Nokia, one of our top priorities . . ." At some level *all compound players are fictions*, which is why people must work so hard to create and sustain them.

Individuals seem to be natural strategic players, as it is easy to think of them as having interests that may diverge from those of others. But they must still learn to think about those interests, to feel they have the right to pursue them, and to discover ways of pursuing them. And it is rare for a person to have no one else on her "team"—at some point we usually feel shared interests with our family, if not our village, nation, school, or occupation. This depends on the scope of the interaction: we may feel solidarity with our family compared to the rest of the village, or with our village compared to the rest of the nation. We saw this with Whose Goals? in chapter 3.

Just as you create players when you engage in strategic action, one of the moves available during an interaction is to try to change the roster of those involved. You try to engage a local politician, or the police, as my neighborhood group did. This is a *social escalation* of an interaction, as opposed to the *psychological escalation* of the emotions of existing players.[10] You hope to expand your team and to sideline some of your opponents and their allies (making them into bystanders or even your own allies). Changing the players often involves shifting the arenas of the conflict (see chapter 6). Many arenas come with their own gatekeepers and judges who enforce formal and informal rules. Some players are left behind in these shifts. One group may not have standing in court; the media may be shut out when a family or organization takes its squabble private (or tries to: it is easier to expand audiences than to exclude them once they are involved).[11]

"Behind closed doors" is where a lot of strategic decisions are made, for good reason. The greater the number of players present, the more distinct audiences must be served. Two people can have a more direct and candid conversation than three. As soon as you introduce a third person, each conversant begins to think about the distinct effects of what she says on each of the others. The original pair now have an audience for their actions, another potential player with a variety of interests and reactions and possible effects. "Third parties" can mediate conflicts between the other two, extort considerable compensation for aligning with one, or simply benefit from their conflict.[12] Even more effects arise with further players. Restricting the players simplifies an interaction, making agreement easier, but those excluded can always cause trouble later if they think their goals were not considered.

The definition of who is a player is often subject to elaborate strategic action, as in the case of who has legal standing in court cases. Stephen Wilson, reporting on Corsican feuds, found that when a feud began, a family "would let it be known to what degree of kinship the hostilities would extend." Such agreements were hardly ironclad, and violations and intentional misunderstandings were common. In one case, "'the relatives of the victims resolved to take reprisals and in order to achieve this they declared emphatically that they wished only to punish the killer himself and not members of his family. Tricked by this deceitful declaration, the latter took no precautions,' and two of them were ambushed shortly afterwards."[13] In this case "rules of standing" were literally made to be broken.

Players are frequently transformed by their own involvement in strategic action, which increases their sense of identity and agency. They see who they are by observing how they act, who their friends and enemies are, what arenas they enter. My neighbors felt more engaged after complaining indignantly to the building manager. But action can rarely build identity from scratch; it mostly adds content to vessels already available—we were already neighbors, after all. As Roger Gould put it, "If events increase the likelihood of collective action, it is because they crystallize collective self-understandings—not by forging new ones but by attaching new significance to old ones."[14] Nonetheless, enough events over time can create new identities. And a single event that is dramatic enough, like a war or revolution, may create a new world for us, especially if it establishes new institutions. It can suggest new players as well. Wars are especially good at creating nations.[15] But any moral shock can transform a player's world.

THE EXTENSION DILEMMA → The further you reach out to expand your team or alliance, the more diverse it will be and the less unified—in goals, resources, skills, and contacts. You gain breadth but lose depth. A more focused identity may concentrate enthusiasm for your cause but generate less power to pursue it. A wider identity will likely incorporate a number of goals at the same time, and yours may not get priority. You want another MRI machine at your hospital, but when you enlist the aid of the Radiology Department to deal with administrators, it turns out they have been hoping for several other devices as much or more than an MRI machine. In the end, they may be treacherous allies. (This is the converse of the dilemma of Whose Goals? from chapter 3, which dealt with a player's identification with broader groupings; here, the point is that they may not reciprocate.) In addition, homogeneity of goals may go along with homogeneity (and hence a narrowing) of relevant skills and contacts with other players. Broader definitions, in contrast, may gain diversity at the expense of focus. For instance, how heavily should an army rely on conscripts, who are more numerous but less trained than professionals?[16] Efficiency is another dimension of the Extension Dilemma: larger players gain efficiencies of scale while losing some coordination and control.[17] Theories of corporations seem to flip back and forth every few years between favoring conglomerates or streamlined businesses, caught forever on the horns of the Extension Dilemma. A player's own internal expansion can bring on the Extension Dilemma, if growth brings specialization and differentiation.[18] This is the Janus Dilemma applied to constructing a team.

Georg Simmel links extension to a sense of threat: "Evidently, the more numerous and varied are the elements which associate, the smaller is the number of interests in which they coincide—in the extreme case, the number is reduced to the most primitive urge, the defense of one's existence."[19] This is the solidarity, much remarked upon, of nations at war. The causation can probably work either way: great extension leads teams to shed nonessential goals, while pointed threats encourage extension. Just as the emotions of threat were at the core of engagement, so they are fundamental to extension.

Religious leaders face the Extension Dilemma in choosing between strict rules about who can be a member of the faith versus universal proselytizing. The costs are high for groups that choose the former, such as the celibate Shakers, or the Parsis (Zoroastrians) in India, whose numbers have dwindled so in recent years that they have been dubbed the "sparsees."[20] Just as dilemmas arise over addressing insiders versus outsiders, a dilemma arises over distinguishing among them. Friedrich Engels recognized the problem of overextension in his scathing criticism of the Knights of Labor: "An immense association spread over an immense extent of the country in innumerable 'assemblies,' representing all shades of individual and local opinion within the working class; the whole of them sheltered under a platform of corresponding indistinctness and held together much less by their impracticable constitution than by the instinctive feeling that the very fact of clubbing together for their common cause makes them a very great power in the country."[21]

Powerful allies pose a crucial extension challenge. As we saw, you want allies to be both *reliable*—to honor your goals—and *effective*—to accomplish what you need them to. But the more powerful they are, the less reliable they are. They will pursue their own projects. This is the problem of feudalism, analyzed by Max Weber and others, which Eiko Ikegami sums up nicely in her study of the origins of the samurai: "The more effective a warrior—for instance, the greater his fighting skills or the more money he had to mobilize a large military force—the more likely it was that he would not prove reliable; that is, he could be sufficiently independent to find a more lucrative source of patronage."[22] The ideology of samurai honor and fidelity helped ameliorate the Extension Dilemma—but only partly (samurai were not always as loyal as the cultural ideal suggests).

In contemporary politics, celebrities are powerful allies for public players. In showing how politicians publicized and yet distorted the message of the nuclear freeze in the early 1980s, David Meyer referred to their "smothering embrace"; powerful allies watered down the freeze message. Senator Ted Kennedy "deliberately wrote his freeze proposal in vague language to attract moderate support, perhaps considering the right wing of the Democratic Party."[23] News media can also be powerful allies for public players by getting their message to broad audiences, but they are likely to distort it in doing so. They tend to favor colorful individuals and photogenic tactics, and to create celebrities rather than recognize real leaders (more precisely, they force the Janus Dilemma, cultivating leaders who are good at reaching out rather than those who reach in).[24] Like allies, donors, and celebrities, the media are a useful but treacherous tool.

I suspect that most players favor reliability over efficacy in putting together a team or alliance, that loyalty probably dominates most processes of building compound players. Entrepreneurial teams, for instance, are frequently composed of similar individuals rather than people with diverse, complementary skills.[25] In part we simply reach out to those we already know, even though our team may lack practical skills—solidarity is often a goal in itself.

THE UNIVERSALISM DILEMMA → You are special in some way, different from other individuals or groups, and thus you deserve unusual protections, powers, authority, or respect. Or you are merely speaking for everyone, which increases your appeal but makes it unclear why you should be followed or obeyed. The Universalism Dilemma is not just one of group formation but also of leadership styles. Basil Bernstein pointed to this dilemma of rhetoric in parenting styles: "because I am your father" is an entirely different rationale for a command than "because children should not set their siblings' hair on fire." One is based on the authority of position; the other, on universal rules of behavior. The Universalism Dilemma appears in both the grounds of rhetorical appeals and the basis for group memberships. In the latter case it is a version of the Extension Dilemma.

Risks and opportunities arise from shifts in attention by various audiences. A small conflict may attract the attention of bigger players, who see a chance for gain at the expense of the parties initially involved. A new audience always shifts your potential costs and benefits. According to most historians of the American civil rights movement, for example, the federal government began to take protestors' demands more seriously because other nations expected moral leadership—not hypocrisy—in the "fight for freedom" of the Cold War.[26] In addition, when protestors attracted national media attention, they added a sympathetic audience to the mix (as we saw in chapter 4's opening vignette about the Montgomery bus boycott). Viewers from around the country, outraged by the brutal repression, contributed time and funds.

You often want to make another player think there is an audience watching what they do. Lobbying legislators is about more than expressing your group's opinions: it shows them how salient an issue is to you. You and your members are watching. At the same time, you may want to signal your awareness without letting opponents know about your activities, by implying, for instance, that thousands of individuals care enough to write letters on their own without prodding by an organization (although this prodding is hard to hide). In addition to targeting third parties and opponents, lobbying activities can also be directed at your own team, to scare or rouse them to action or simply to inform them about your activities. You may have all these audiences in mind at the same time. Good rhetoric has multiple effects.

You want to gain the attention of potential team members and allies, to form a coherent team with shared goals. But above the level of individuals, when the players are organizations or groups, the sociological issues are pervasive and complex. How does a group come to feel it has an interest to pursue? How does it learn to coordinate personnel, resources, and technologies in order to engage others? What level of trust is necessary within a group? What kind of boundary must be perceived between your team and other teams?[27] These are rhetorical issues involved in persuading potential players, including yourself.

SEGREGATING AUDIENCES

Ideally, you would craft different strategies and rhetorics for each important audience, corresponding to the different objectives you have for each. Radical talk for your radical flank, moderate messages for the rest. You could demonize outsiders to insiders, but reassure outsiders to their face. Alas, it is not always possible to segregate actions or words. In trying to do so, compound players often use a kind of onion strategy (to recycle the satisficing metaphor), adding or peeling audiences as new layers for different kinds of actions and discussions. This is what my neighborhood group did in successively shedding outsiders, so that we could then talk about each one in more strategic terms. The larger and more complex the player, the harder this is to do. There are more layers and fewer ways to keep them apart.

Stealth is one of the best ways to segregate audiences. If you are sure of your collaborators—especially their ability to keep secrets—then you can do a lot of work behind the scenes before your opponents know what is happening, perhaps before they even know that a strategic game is underway. Secrets help define teams, drawing lines between insiders and outsiders. Erving Goffman identified *dark secrets* incompatible with the team's image, *strategic secrets* about what the team will do, *inside secrets* that define membership, *entrusted secrets* that are badges of trustworthiness, and *free secrets* which can be disclosed without harm.[28] Preventing certain players from becoming part of your audience, in other words, can be crucial to your success and to your identity as a compound player. Similarly, you may use deception in conveying a misleading message to a specific audience, causing them to act in a way that advances your plan.

For the same reason you want to segregate your audiences, your opponents will try to convey your messages to the wrong ones. Opponents and the police send spies to supposedly internal meetings; a message designed for your supporters may get into the media and so reach other actors as well. The point of doing this is to capture you in a contradiction, which might indicate some deception. They imply that your "real" intentions differ from the stated ones. A protest group may wish to appear radical to activists and supporters, but moderate to the public—a balancing act made even harder if opponents are eager to point out the discrepancies.

THE AUDIENCE-SEGREGATION DILEMMA → It is extremely useful to get different messages to different audiences, but doing so brings the risk of appearing duplicitous—especially when your opponents package these contrasting messages to make you look bad. In the modern world, the boundaries of audiences are treacherously permeable. If you try to segregate audiences, you cannot be sloppy about it, and no matter how much care you take, it may still backfire. This dilemma lies at the intersection of the Sincerity and Articulation Dilemmas, as well as being a form of the Naughty or Nice? dilemma.

Codes are one tool for segregating audiences, in that each of them may take a different message from the same communication. Literal codes are crucial in wartime for coordinating activities. Code-breaking then becomes equally important, especially in modern wars that make use of multiple and complex technologies for communication. If you break your opponents' code, and they do not know it, you can anticipate their actions. But if they learn you have broken it, and you are unaware that they know this, they can feed you devastating misinformation. It is advantageous to know who your audiences are for any given word or action and what it will mean to them. Osama bin Laden—a clever strategist whatever else we think of him—is thought to send hidden messages to his operatives through publicly broadcast speeches.

At the looser end of the spectrum, coded language may mean different things to different subcultures. In American politics of the 1970s and 1980s, racist demagogues like George Wallace and Ronald Reagan perfected an elaborate coded speech. To audiences who shared their views of the world, phrases like "welfare queens" or "special interests" had clear meanings and a strong emotional charge, while to others they made (at first) little sense at all. At this point, *code* is not the right word. We are simply talking about cultural meanings and resonances that differ across groups.[29]

Another possibility is to send a message that needs further interpretation. You may signal to one audience that they should discount your message in some way or read between the lines. Hostages forced to read messages to be broadcast may speak in a sullen or sarcastic tone of voice, for instance, if compelled to praise their captors. Audiences who know them well will recognize that they are constrained in some way.[30] Alternatively, you may send an ambiguous message that requires local assistance in interpretation. The foreign ministry makes an announcement, but local ambassadors "interpret" it (sometimes literally) for their host nations. Of course, if the ambiguity is patent, it will arouse suspicions. (This possibility crosses the Audience-Segregation Dilemma with the Articulation Dilemma.)

A player may feed different messages to groups that communicate little with one another. The best case is when they speak different languages. Yasir Arafat was often said to denounce the Palestinian intifada's martyrs more strongly in English (of course, those who said this were attacking him for duplicity). One hundred years ago, many American companies faced industrial work forces divided by national origins and languages, with their own newspapers and residential neighborhoods. It was easy to feed different information to each of them, especially about the treacherous actions of the others. Mutual suspicions had to exist to start with, and it no doubt helped to bribe an editor or two. The trump card, of course, was the threat of African-American strikebreakers. It was hard for a unified working class "player" to emerge.

Imagine an Army colonel who writes articles and makes speeches about the future needs of the American military. He worries about his reputation among his peers as well as among the scholars who write about the future of warfare—in the academy as well as in the services. He also wants to praise and support his own "warfighting community" within the army; perhaps he is a believer in unmanned tanks. But he also feels he must represent the interests of the army, when the navy wants a greater portion of the defense budget or the marines insist on a role for amphibious landings in every war. He may also think about the military as a whole, arguing for increased defense budgets when he has Congress or the American public in mind as an audience. Audiences do not entirely line up with potential arenas of conflict. In this last case, with the public as an audience, our colonel may have two different games in mind: the competition for government funds and the potential conflict between the United States and future opponents in wars. He carefully crafts his words for his specific audiences.

As this example shows, we often do no more than approximate our chosen audiences. The colonel may publish in different kinds of journals, intending each article to be read mostly by the kind of people he hopes to reach. Yet he is also aware of *seepage*: others have access to that journal, even if they are not regular subscribers. Someone looking to discredit his claims—one of those darned marines perhaps—will search for inconsistencies. Several social-structural factors affect how easy it is to segregate audiences. The modern news media, always looking for a new trend or colorful dissent, intrude everywhere, broadcasting messages nationally or, increasingly, globally. How cohesive your group is, how dense its network ties, will also affect your ability to keep messages within that group alone.

Actions have rhetorical force as much as words do, but because they lack a "literal" import, they are open to looser processes of interpretation. On the one hand, it may be hard to prevent unfavorable interpretations of your actions. On the other, you can supplement the actions with words—your own interpretations. These may be directed privately to different audiences: top managers issue new rules to give workers a voice in how things are run, while privately assuring shop-floor managers that they will continue to support their authority despite the new rules. Or you may make your interpretations public through the media: a group has set off a bomb and needs to say why (this works best when the relevant public is already sympathetic). Sometimes what we *say* we are doing is as important as what we *are* doing, especially if our words and actions are directed at different players. We interpret our own actions for others.

Even if you can isolate an audience, as in a private tête-à-tête (or the note I sent the manager after our association meeting), that audience may develop an interest in sharing what you have told her. Information has value, after all. Even allies may spill secrets, but opponents are understandably treacherous. For instance, in a private conversation, Khrushchev chided Kennedy that the United States was surely less threatened by tiny Cuba than the USSR was by the Shah of Iran, America's ally. Kennedy distanced himself from the Shah, insisting that he would not be a friend of the United States for long if he did not begin to treat his own people better. His offhand statement was soon leaked, no doubt in exaggerated form, to the Shah, who began to fear a CIA coup against him.[31]

If you can segregate audiences, you can also manipulate them. One trick is to put your own side surreptitiously in the role of the audience, to show people how they should respond. A good cop/bad cop team can manipulate a suspect, who sees the good cop express fear that his partner really will follow through on his threats. The good cop pretends to be audience, not player, and the suspect is swept up in emotional contagion and grows more afraid. In other cases, you may present yourself to a naive audience as a different kind of player than you are. Agents provocateurs can push a group in a radical or mistaken direction that will undermine their credibility with outside audiences or bring on official repression. An audience that is assumed to be one sort of strategic player (or nonplayer) may turn out to be a very different sort of player, perhaps even an opponent.

DIVERSE AUDIENCES AND ALLIANCES

Audiences vary in size. When numbers grow large, you can no longer interact separately with every other player. A business may have hundreds of competitors. For many public players, the audience of "bystanders," amplified through the mass media, can easily be in the thousands or millions. In cases like this a strategic actor obviously cannot get inside the head of each of these others or anticipate their individual actions. Instead, she models the typical action or range of actions that are likely. This is the classic economic model of a competitive market, where relevant information about competitors is reduced to spare signals such as the price (and sometimes quality) of its products. With large numbers, strategic action takes on the character of planning, much as one would plan against famine or drought. Audiences can then appear similar to forces of nature rather than strategic actors: we can make predictions about them more easily when we aggregate across so many players. In such cases plans are more likely to involve the accumulation of resources and capacities and structures that could support a number of actions, and less likely to have the interactive feel of a game. Strategy can become manipulation, when you do not see the others as strategic actors responding to you. Advertising is meant to affect those who see it without making them aware that they are being manipulated.

In addition to size, the diversity of each audience's components is significant. Each compound player may consist of many individuals, networks, or organizations with distinct goals or tastes in tactics that continually threaten the team's unity. Energy and attention are always shifting among engagements at different levels, often derailing or halting action at one level as they do. Every complex audience can, by definition, be broken—or can break itself—into a number of smaller audiences. *Every compound player is an arena as well as a player.*

This problem of diversity is especially severe with alliances: groups of players who agree to cooperate for particular purposes, often for limited periods, and usually governed by some contract. In some cases, especially in international relations, where the players are the most compound of all, we may speak instead of *alignments*. Less formal than alliances, these include those who cooperate with one side in a conflict, sometimes in a tacit way. They are effectively allies, without legal treaties to support that status. Most formal alliances are specific to an arena. A military alliance does not concern itself with trade, and vice versa. Some alliances, though, are defined by their shared goal, which may cut across arenas. An industrial lobby may use the media, courts, and elected officials to pursue its interests. But if diversity poses a weakness for your team or alliance, it probably does for your opponents too. Each side tries to exploit the diversity of the other, looking for potential defectors—issues for later discussion. Logically, the basic challenges of alliances and alignments are those of the Extension Dilemma.

THE BANDWAGON DILEMMA → If one player or alliance grows in power, other players must decide whether to join and take advantage of that power or to resist in order to help limit it. In international relations, realists argue that nations usually try to counterbalance any nascent hegemony, knowing that a concentration of power will eventually be used against them. But if they can become part of that power center, they may well be the ones using it rather than being on the receiving end. In an organized system, you may be able to protect yourself from the hegemon rather than fearing it, and so jump on the bandwagon. It all depends on how you expect the great power to act.[32] In response to Bush II's Iraq invasion of 2003, different countries made different calculations about their relationship with the hegemon. This is a form of the Extension Dilemma, a special problem of having one powerful ally.[33]

Temporary coalitions can form for specific actions without much formal or lasting association. The creation of welfare states, one of the most important legislative developments of the last century, was the work of varying coalitions. In Scandinavia, social policy depended on an alliance of workers and farmers; in the United States, Britain, and Canada, old-age pensions depended on an alliance of workers and policy experts. Further legislation in the United States New Deal was the work of a more formal alliance among Northern Democrats in Congress, aided especially by the labor movement.[34] Situationalists tend to portray such coalitions as *structural conditions rather than strategic accomplishments*. But a lot of work goes into them. Even *coalition* is sometimes too strong a term. In many cases the players who cooperate to achieve something do not think of themselves as a grouping at all. They are disparate players who work momentarily for a shared objective or goal. Far from a structure, there is nothing more than momentary cooperation—although that cooperation may create the knowledge and good will that enables joint efforts in the future.

Some arenas come with their own patterns of alliances. Electoral politics has its political parties, which have characteristic lines of conflict and styles of interacting with one another. Traditional lines of ideological cleavage can be so strong as to prevent new political ideas from entering the arena, just as there are barriers to the entry of new players. When I studied the politics of nuclear energy, for example, I was surprised to find that national debates were twisted by preexisting ideological cleavages among national parties in France, Sweden, and the United States. Instead of straightforward arguments over costs, risks, and benefits, Republicans and Democrats tended to see an issue of government interference in markets, French politicians saw a battle between the interests of labor and capital, and Swedes saw a question of Social-Democratic hegemony. Arenas and their ongoing alliances can reframe issues.[35] Only a few arenas formally impose alliances, which usually emerge from the conflicts that the arenas structure.

In addition to this cognitive framing of issues, existing alliances of friends and foes frequently impose affective frames on new strategic initiatives. You trust proposals by those you like; you are suspicious of enemies' efforts—even when the proposals have little or nothing to do with the reasons the affective patterns arose. In local politics, residents often battle against the large organizations they live near—corporations or government bureaucracies or even universities. After years of conflict, they develop a gut dislike and mistrust of the large player. In many cases, basic scientific research has been loudly opposed simply because it is being done by a bully of a university—by people who on demographic, occupational, and other grounds would not be expected to oppose such research.[36]

These cognitive and emotional dynamics suggest the extent to which alliances are cultural accomplishments as much as calculated creatures of necessity. As a result, informal alliances based on inchoate solidarities can be as powerful as those formed through explicit treaties.

THE SECURITY DILEMMA → In arenas of great conflict, where power is relative, the strengthening of one player entails the weakening of others. A move that a player feels is defensive may be seen by others as offensive. In the realist view of the international system, this is a common occurrence, often leading to hostile spirals. Other players move to defend themselves, the first player interprets these moves as offensive, and so on. As Robert Jervis put it, "[M]any of the means by which a state tries to increase its security decrease the security of others."[37] In many arenas, the growth of one player threatens others and may trigger unwanted engagements.

✕

The image of players as audiences, watching and listening to each other and themselves, suggests a rhetorical approach to words and actions. Rhetoric, with its 2,400-year history, is the oldest continuous body of thought about the intersection of culture and strategy. Because rhetoric deals with the interaction between speaker and audience, it is especially useful to a strategic framework. We can examine the emotional reactions of audiences, for instance, as well as the construction of frames and symbols that resonate with various audiences. We can assimilate several other approaches to culture into a rhetorical framework, including those that model culture on language (the "semiotic model"), on dialogue, on narrative, or on identity. As long as we do not reify the roles of speaker and audience, but instead realize that everyone can be an audience, and every player a "speaker," we can adapt rhetoric to strategy. I put "speaker" in quotation marks because it is not just words, and certainly not just spoken words, that form rhetoric. We also convey messages through our actions, our body language, our clothes. Often we are most eloquent when silent.

Strategy is thoroughly cultural. We filter information through our cognitive biases and emotional states. Our mistakes frequently reflect our cultures and personalities. Our goals emerge from culture and emotional bonds. Players use cultural tools to make their choices, and deploy rhetoric in interacting with others. We persuade and mobilize by arousing emotions in our many audiences. Even the most cultural creatures still make decisions.

From a structural perspective, the main things we need to know to predict the outcome of a conflict are the alliances and the capabilities of each player. Yet the cast of players does not remain stable any more than their capacities do. Otherwise, strategic choices would not matter. But on top of this, we have another variable that can shift during strategic interaction: the arena or arenas in which the action unfolds, to which we turn in the next chapter. Arenas impose many constraints, which is why we try to change the arenas even as we are maneuvering within them. You always try to find arenas in which you have advantages.

CHAPTER 6

ARENAS

When you think about the defence of England you no longer think of the chalk cliffs of Dover. You think of the Rhine. That is where our frontier lies today. → STANLEY BALDWIN, M.P. (1934)

In my first serious social research, back when Jimmy Carter was president, I looked at grievance procedures in two traditional industrial factories in Massachusetts. Here was a formal system, demanded in both cases by the United Auto Workers (UAW), to enforce contracts and protect its members from arbitrary action by management. The employers grudgingly came to tolerate grievances as a way of dealing with petty nuisances. At times, the procedures did what they were formally supposed to: allow workers to get a fair hearing about a perceived infraction of the elaborate rules. They were designed to remove certain issues from the strategic struggles between labor and capital. At other times, they were used quite differently. Instead of depoliticizing complaints, they became part of the broader conflict between employers and unions. The form was still there, but the substance beneath it changed. The stakes were new.

At one plant, where two thousand workers assembled automobiles, grievances would proliferate in the months before contract negotiations. As part of those talks, union leaders would offer to make most of the claims "go away." The grievances became a political bargaining chip. As the timing suggests, even the workers who filed them saw the grievances that way. At the other plant, where two hundred workers made hi-tech parts for the aerospace industry, the substance of the grievance procedure was different. The number of grievances filed had been falling steadily for years, largely because an aggressive personnel manager was weeding out those who filed them as troublemakers. The union was weak, and heading for decertification. In one case the union used the grievance mechanism for its own ends, in the other the personnel manager did. In both cases there was a sharp contrast between the explicit and implicit uses of grievances.

This contrast between form and content is only one way in which strategic actors try to switch the game, hoping to find one more favorable to them. Sometimes the letter of the law favors them, as when workers slow their pace by "working to the rules." At other times, the spirit of the law helps them advance their goals. Few strategic conflicts unfold in only one arena. To stick with industrial relations for a moment, these struggles spill across National Labor Relations Board charges, elections, and even appointments, across Congress and state legislatures, across contract negotiations, grievances, informal behavior on the job, the media, and public opinion. Different players become relevant to each setting. In some, the local is the salient player; in others, the UAW; in still others, organized labor as a whole along with its allies.

The aggressive personnel manager admitted to fiddling with other formal mechanisms as well. Advancement from one job classification to the next usually required a written exam, at which a management and a union representative were both present. If the personnel department wanted the employee promoted, their proctor would leave the room during the test— to smoke or urinate, say—knowing that the union agent would feed the test taker any needed answers. (Union reps presumably played the same game, giving better answers to those they liked.) No rules are hard and fast.

An arena is an open-ended bundle of rules and resources that allows certain kinds of interactions to proceed, leading to outcomes that may be formal or quite casual. Some arenas strictly demarcate who the players are; others are more open. They need not be legal or formal, operating instead according to customs and habits. By constraining their behavior, arenas place some limits on what contestants can expect from each other—which is why it is often a clever move to break out of the arena altogether. In arenas, as in literal games, if you push the normal rules too far, you are really moving into a different arena (if you move your rook diagonally, you aren't playing chess).

KINDS OF ARENAS

The term *arena* has a useful ambiguity: it was originally the pit of an amphitheater, the place where the action occurred (it originally meant sand, strewn around to absorb blood), but it came to include the spectators as well. All engagements have potential audiences who are, although in a different way from the direct combatants, part of the arena. *Field* has been used as a similar metaphor, although I find it more vague.[1] They both differ from a conflict, which can spill across arenas. *Arenas are defined by actions and stakes; conflicts, by the players involved.*[2]

Arenas differ on a number of dimensions, shaping interactions accordingly. One is simply *scope* or *size*: how many actors and actions must be coordinated over how extensive an area. Arenas range from a couple in bed (he wants sex, she wants a backrub) to global alignments of national governments negotiating the colonization of space. Variations in physical size require different technologies of communication and coordination; increases in the number of people produce complexities of social dynamics. Shrinking or enlarging an arena—or a conflict across arenas—is usually an option for players.

Most arenas have rules or traditions that define who can play in them. The number of people and their form of interaction both affect the degree to which the players are personally *familiar* with one another and thus have a history of personal trust and affection (although familiarity does not always breed either). Families have complex affective bonds and neurotic subtleties. We even feel some bonds with neighbors, and certainly with friends. But as we move away from face-to-face arenas, we usually lose two dimensions: the body language and facial expressions of personal interaction, and the direct knowledge of interactions across a range of games that have been played over time. Information about other players becomes less direct and often more formal—in part because we also move from simple to compound players.

Some arenas have physical characteristics that, along with rules and expectations, affect what players can do in them—their "horizons of opportunity." Are antagonists forced to remain face to face, or are there places to escape and cool off? How many bystanders can be present as an audience—both directly and through the media? In war, the terrain obviously affects what kinds of weapons, vehicles, communications, and so on are most effective; fighting in jungles differs from that in deserts, towns, or trenches.

Physical characteristics affect the flow and relevance of information, the value of resources, and the available moves.

Arenas' boundaries—usually physical traits along with rules and customs—vary in how rigid or permeable they are. For instance, in the arenas of traditional political action, the boundaries are normally clear, corresponding to the structure and functioning of territorial political systems. In the United States, you can lobby or elect sympathetic legislators or executives, pursue favorable court rulings, and switch from federal to state to local levels (or move back up). In most democratic regimes, you can also try to affect public opinion through the media, build political coalitions (with financial support or logrolling of votes and backing), and sometimes initiate referenda. Legal arenas and their procedures are also usually well defined. Many other arenas are not. Goffman referred poetically to the "interaction membrane" through which the outside world affects the game at hand.[3]

The density of rules within arenas also varies. Some settings are extremely routinized, while others have little bureaucracy. Over time, as Max Weber knew so well, almost all arenas develop more rules, inasmuch as solved problems become future precedents. Arenas with few rules, such as families, may develop implicit customs instead of formal arrangements— although many of these begin as explicit bargains. But no rules or customs are so sacrosanct that they can never be challenged, broken, or twisted. For the most part they are only as strong as the players who enforce them.

THE DILEMMA OF FORMAL PARTICIPATION → Echoing the Engagement and Go-Sanjō's Dilemmas, players must decide whether to enter an arena as formal participants or to act through informal, indirect (and often stealthy) channels. Instead of being a plaintiff in a lawsuit, for instance, they might file an *amicus curiae* brief or secretly fund one of the parties. (Go-Sanjō is about the means players actually use, whether or not they formally belong in the game—but of course they cannot use formal positions unless they formally belong.) This is a dilemma for gatekeepers, too, of whether to grant formal standing to a player or force it into less formal channels. Formal standing brings both rights and controls. More players bring with them additional points of view, and unrepresented interests can later derail agreements. Sometimes, however, it is better to narrow down the players to a manageable number in order to reach that agreement.

Typically, it is better to *know* all the interests in play but harder to *address* so many.[4]

Arenas differ as well in the goals, objectives, and motives with which we enter them. From any given arena, we can expect some things but not others; we need to attain some objectives along the way but not others. We do not usually initiate legal proceedings to make friends and allies. The "stakes" are a crucial element defining an arena, distinguishing it from other arenas.

Arenas also vary in the norms of behavior that are accepted or considered deviant, for these also help define the arena. When we bribe a judge, we are stepping outside the legal arena into a private interaction between two individuals. Disputes over proper behavior in an arena are common means of pursuing a conflict. They may involve an effort to exclude a player from an arena or to damage that player (through fines and other penalties or through injury to its reputation).

Arenas also differ in the ease with which they can be avoided. We can simply ignore many challenges, such as the neighbor with a barking dog, rather than engaging in some kind of strategic response. Sometimes we can quit a job when the strategic games are too onerous. Other games are unavoidable. A spouse files for divorce, or someone sues us. We are drafted for war. We are unemployed and must do what it takes to find a new job. In between are semivoluntary engagements, or perhaps linked engagements, which offer complex combinations of costs and rewards. We often put up with the games, when, as in the case of a job, there are rewards we want despite the games.

Different actors can play in different arenas. When a conflict spills into a new arena, new players have a chance at involvement. When the Bush-Gore election battle in 2000 unexpectedly came down to a few Florida counties, local election board members and state officials had a chance to fight for their candidates anew, battling it out over "hanging chads." Some new players are officially associated with certain arenas, like World Trade Organization officials in trade disputes; others are allies with skills or resources especially helpful in the new arena.

Different kinds of resources and skills are necessary for playing (or playing competently) in various arenas—some of which pose high barriers to entry. The resources required might include the capacity to build a factory in order to enter an industry, the money or conscription to build an army, or the cash to enter a high-stakes poker game. Skills usually involve a certain kind of expertise. You cannot go to court without lawyers or testify at Nuclear Regulatory Commission hearings without engineers and scientists. Other barriers to entry are organizational and legal: it is hard to expand your nonprofit organization without incorporating so that contributions can be deducted from taxes—these are some of the rules of the arena.

As discussed in chapter 4, some resources and competencies are useful in almost all arenas, while others are specific to certain ones. At the extreme, some personal attributes—in the form of roles—are entirely a function of the arena. At meetings of the Fraternal Order of the Elks, a high official wears elaborate headgear; elsewhere, he is just a friendly geek trying to sell used cars. "Pecking orders" are arena-specific. Boys fight with one another until a pecking order is established, so that fights are mostly unnecessary. But a boy who moves to a new school must find his place again. A girl's "popularity" is probably a similar commodity, a local reputation that may not travel well. On an international scale, many if not most wars arise because the pecking order is not clear. Two nations have different impressions of their relative power, or one nation thinks it is not being accorded sufficient respect, or a nation's reputation differs across arenas (it has more military repute than economic, for example).

Bringing resources or capabilities into an arena that is unaccustomed to them is sometimes useful. We are surprised when a fellow member of the middle class assumes a threatening demeanor, when a panelist at a professional conference pushes his chair back and threatens to punch us, or when a neighbor puts his face three inches from ours, close enough to smell alcohol on his breath, and says in a barely controlled rage, "Don't fuck with me on this." Most members of the middle class cringe at bullies, whose only resource is bodily strength and the apparent willingness to use it to inflict physical harm. The bodily intimidation of the schoolyard belongs primarily to the world of young men, but there are less physical forms of intimidation as well. Many bullies—individuals and organizations—pick fights in order to develop a reputation for being tough, so that they won't *have* to get into fights to prove themselves. They want to be the kind of player no one "fucks with."

Some arenas eventually boil a conflict down to a single definitive decision, which players may or may not be able to appeal. Others (probably a majority) feature a series of smaller decisions. Sometimes a single person makes the determination. As an individual, she is playing multiple games, thinking about several audiences, feeling a number of pressures. The CEO of a tuna company may find it easy to stand up to boycotting consumers but not to his twelve-year-old daughter—and a wife who is proud of her daughter's burgeoning autonomy. In public arenas, you usually have allies as well as opponents, so that isolation is rare. But in private, your family can gang up on you.

RELATIONS AMONG ARENAS

At one point during their 1944 campaign, Tom Dewey decided to attack the incumbent Franklin Roosevelt for having ignored secret decryptions warning of the attack on Pearl Harbor. When George Marshall, the army's top general, learned of this, he immediately wrote to Dewey to inform him that the United States still gained valuable information from deciphering the same diplomatic codes, which the Japanese—amazingly—still did not know had been broken. Dewey's plan to advance his campaign would cost the United States its best source of Pacific intelligence. Dewey backed off. Goals in the international arena—and the solidarity that furthered them—trumped those of domestic politics. (I'm not sure today's candidates would make the same choice.)[5]

Most strategic interactions are waged simultaneously in more than one arena, just as a number of fronts add up to a war. Within each arena, successive engagements may occur, like a series of battles on the same front. Because any victory may help, or lead directly to another victory in a subsequent engagement, many strategists play in all the arenas they have the resources for. Sometimes, on the other hand, a concentration of risk in just one, if it is crucial one, may be the right strategy.

THE BASKET DILEMMA → One strategic approach is to try to narrow the contest down to one arena, or even one decision, in an all-or-nothing bet, putting "all your eggs in one basket." If you think you can win it, entering a "decisive engagement" makes sense. If you are not sure, it may be wiser to spread the conflict out over a number of arenas, no single one of which will then be decisive. If you can coordinate your activities well on multiple fronts, this may be appealing. Your choice may depend on what kind of resources you have. In a guerrilla war, a large number of dispersed units without many resources can beat an adversary with extensive resources by forcing them to disperse those resources (or by catching them when they are dispersed). On the other hand, wars of attrition usually favor those with more resources. A decisive engagement is normally less attractive if you have committed a large proportion of your total resources to it—so that a loss may put you out of the game (or any other game) altogether. You rarely risk all your resources if you can't replace them or when survival is at stake.[6] Like "crucial experiments" in science, decisive engagements are often recognized only in retrospect. The Basket Dilemma is obviously related to the Risk and Engagement Dilemmas.

Another version of the Basket Dilemma concerns moves or tactics rather than engagements. A player can concentrate on doing one thing well, for instance on using a particular weapon in war or using a specific tactic in a single arena. Or a player can retain flexibility through some familiarity and skill with diverse weapons—even at the cost of being less skilled at each. Concentration involves economies of scale, whether in learning skills or producing resources. But in strategic interaction, others will try to find ways to block precisely the tactic you have concentrated on. If you can win with that move quickly, fine. But over time, it is likely to be rendered less valuable. (For this reason, Edward Luttwak claims that concentration—or "homogeneity," as he calls it—is fine for internal operations but not for direct engagement.)[7] Furthermore, diverse strategies may allow you to locate unexpected weak spots in opponents. Concentration is another risk associated with the Sorcerer's Apprentice Dilemma.

Engagements can seem to be decisive when they are not. Often they merely signal other kinds of change. Instead of determining the outcome, they reveal other trends that are the real causal forces. For example, an engagement may demonstrate that a new technology or symbol is particularly powerful. The easy victory of Hitler's tanks over the Polish cavalry may serve as an example. Or engagements may show that the balance of power between two sides is shifting. In the American Civil War, for instance, Gettysburg partly showed that the North was finally gearing up its industrial production and draft apparatus in a way that assured its eventual victory. The battle was a turning point in that it revealed underlying forces at play, not because its outcome directly decided the broader conflict. The ancient Greek battle of Marathon, on the other hand, was probably decisive. It could easily have gone the other way, and if it had, the whole war would probably have gone with it.

A player, as I have said, normally avoids the all-or-nothing option in the Basket Dilemma when survival is at stake. Many theories of the firm and of international relations assume survival to be the overriding goal. But as we saw, it is not the only one, and players are sometimes willing to extinguish themselves in pursuit of other goals. In addition, the all-or-nothing choice can be forced on you, if your chances of survival or success in the risk-spreading option look slim. A low probability of winning is better than even lower ones. Sometimes, on the other hand, you cannot choose the all-or-nothing option because people will defect from the team in the face of threats to their survival. Most warfare in history, for instance, has consisted of warriors with spears running away, coming back, dancing in and out of harm's way; casualties are minimized. (Much to the annoyance of better-armed adversaries. Ancient Greek and Roman commanders constantly complained of their adversaries' guerrilla style, which they interpreted as cowardice.)

The Basket Dilemma demands that you compare how your team will act when it is concentrated or divided versus how other teams will, for they must usually concentrate or spread their moves in response. By opening many battlefronts, you weaken yourself, but you may weaken them more. In war, for example, you may wish to take advantage of your opponent's separation into two distinct armies, inserting yourself between them. But cutting them in two can also be understood as your being surrounded. The move may work if you can fight one army at a time, but not if they close in on you. (Debates in eighteenth-century military theory revolved around finding the single right solution to this problem of "internal lines," as though it were a problem of geometry rather than an ongoing dilemma.)[8]

Part of the Basket Dilemma involves how to position yourself for future play should the engagement prove indecisive (as it usually does). A smaller effort at this time may translate into strength later, especially if it conserves resources or credibility. Surprisingly, John Kerry left $14 million unspent at the time of the 2004 election—saving it for possible legal challenges later. That same year, the U.S. Supreme Court ruled that a defense lawyer could concede her client's guilt without consulting him, in order to set up a credible argument at the later, sentencing stage. Confidence in victory in the current round can prove disastrous if you fall short. Ruth Benedict observed this in Japanese prisoners in World War II. "Unlike Western soldiers, prisoners had not been instructed about what to say and what to keep silent about when captured, and their responses on all subjects were strikingly unregimented. This failure to indoctrinate was of course due to Japan's no-surrender policy." Prisoners cooperated fully with their American captors. "Old Army hands and long-time extreme nationalists located ammunition dumps, carefully explained the disposition of Japanese forces, wrote our propaganda, and flew with our bombing pilots to guide them to military targets."[9]

One strategic move, then, is to force another player to look ahead to the next round or another arena. Often you try to frighten an opponent into diverting resources from the current engagement—as Kerry felt forced to do. In other cases, anticipating the next round may lead a player to devote *more* resources to current play, for instance, if this engagement is a test or proxy for another. For example, if I need to hire a contractor for a big job, I may hire him for a little job first to see how he does. If I want a real gauge of his normal craftsmanship, I will not tell him about the bigger job. I can manipulate his work differently if I frame the current job as a test for the later one, getting better work out of him now but not knowing how he will perform later. (For contractors reading this, I swear it is only hypothetical.)

Arenas vary in their autonomy. None are entirely independent, but some are especially influenced by others, often because conflicts spill across arenas, just as local, state, and national politics in the United States pit the same parties against each other. The broader the scale of a conflict, the more arenas it can affect. A divorcing couple may appeal to the courts, to friends and family, perhaps to the media if they are famous or flamboyantly nasty. But a political battle has virtually every arena open to it, including that of international pressures and personal interactions (between friends or between leaders of different sides).

PLAYERS OR PRIZES? → A strategic interaction can focus on the players or the arenas. You are interested in defeating opponents, or helping friends, and this goal spills across different arenas. Or you focus on attaining certain prizes from arenas: getting some money, seizing a territory, winning a job (this has usually been dubbed competition, as opposed to conflict).[10] When you focus on an arena to gain a prize, the players with whom you interact are less important, and may change. You probably do not care what happens to them as long as you get the prize. You usually restrict your action to the arena that contains that prize, entering others only in a subsidiary way. In sum, you may want to win against a particular player or to win a particular game: relative gains in one case, absolute in the other.[11] When you care most about the players, you may even be willing to ruin all available prizes just to keep opponents from getting them. Player-centered rivalries usually spill across arenas, and prize-centered ones mix up the players. More complexly, you may pursue strategies that carry you back and forth between player and prize orientations.

Player-based and prize-based engagements can overlap. In addition to one engagement that sprawls across arenas, many other types of engagement are often occurring at the same time. One player may be involved in several. Thus Indian nationalists pressed their claims for independence especially hard when Britain was distracted by the two World Wars. With British attention so desperately needed elsewhere, it was reasonable for Indians to assume they might pull off a victory in their subarena, although it was just as likely that the British saw every front as important. But even if British attention were there, their resources might not be. It is better to hope that your strong opponent is defeated in a different conflict, leaving it weakened for your own.

Ongoing patterns of friends and foes, as I discussed, can make the players themselves into the issue. In particular, mutual hostilities can crowd out an engagement's origins, perhaps in ideology or interests. Hurting your opponents becomes more important than your own gains and losses. This polarization is not restricted to partisan politics. I have observed the same phenomenon in local politics, especially in towns with one large player, such as a corporation or university. Cleavages come to revolve around the expansion or undue influence of the big player. You are either part of its alliance or against it, with little middle ground. This kind of polarization arises from hostilities among players rather than over issues.[12]

Big, complex arenas have become increasingly linked in modern market societies. Spies report on economic as well as military capacities, as war has come to depend heavily on industrial production. Politics also reflects concern about the economy, as leaders are judged according to measures such as unemployment and inflation rates. The legal system is also a regular arena for any number of strategic interactions that once escaped it. The interdependence of arenas reflects not only the increasing need for money as a resource in strategic action but also the ever-increasing dominance of formal organizations in social life—a development mapped well in systems theory.[13]

Some arenas are parts of a broader one: we can call them *subarenas* to denote their subsidiary relationship. Sometimes the full arena is nothing more than an *aggregation* of decisions in the subarenas. When a strategic balance is relatively even, so that interaction is stalemated in an arena, an obscure subarena may be thrust into prominence. In 2000, the Gore-Bush election suddenly turned on several Florida counties, on butterfly ballots and hanging chads, on manual recounts and court challenges. We saw a large—and disturbing—amount of information about voting systems and the laws covering them. For more than a month, the presidential election was contested primarily in several tiny subarenas.

Some arenas are related to each other in a *hierarchy*, allowing upward appeals for the losers. You do not get what you want from colleagues, so you go to your department chair; when she says no, you might go to an assistant dean, or even higher—especially if you have personal connections with those in higher positions. Some of these appeals are formal, as with the courts—which are also a kind of super-arena over many others. Other appeals simply derive from the hierarchic structure of bureaucracies. Some higher authorities will refuse to intervene, denying that they have jurisdiction (although the exercise of power is always tempting, so it is usually only the courts that show this kind of restraint: if you are running an organization, you do not want conflicts to fester at lower levels). But sometimes that refusal is intended to have a substantive impact, a way of attaining a desired result. A compound player with any degree of formal organization, remember, *is itself an arena* within which interaction occurs.

The idea that some arenas are more important than others helps explain a surprising choice made time after time in international affairs, when a smaller or weaker nation attacks a more powerful one. The Japanese attacked Russia in 1904 and the United States in 1941; China entered the Korean War in October 1950 against the combined United Nations and United States forces, which had nuclear weapons; Argentina seized the Malvinas from Britain in 1982. The key calculation in these situations seems to be that an arena is too small for the larger power to initiate a serious, all-out war over it. If the smaller power can win quickly, it will perhaps not be dislodged. The larger power may be occupied elsewhere, or it may simply calculate the cost of war to be greater than the benefits of regaining a small amount of territory. The greater power is often thousands of miles away, and few countries have the capacity or will to wage distant war. The initiator hopes that the larger power, facing the Engagement Dilemma, will see this as an optional game and decide against participating. And even if the larger power does respond militarily, most wars are limited and inconclusive. If the greater power decides to go beyond diplomacy, will it take the trouble to topple the government that started the war and take back all the territory? As Saddam Hussein found in 1991, it may do one but not the other. (Timing, culture, and psychology also play a role in decisions by small players to attack large ones, of course.)[14]

Other arenas are simply parallel, connected because the general conflict and the players are the same. A player does not appeal the decision in one arena to another, although events in one arena may have an informal *spillover effect* on morale in another, affecting that crucial sense of momentum discussed in chapter 3. But a victory in one arena can instead inspire a backlash in another: workers who lose an arbitration decision may redouble their shop-floor sabotage and slowdown. The effect of one battle on another depends on how it is cognitively and emotionally interpreted by and for the various players. Prominent public events provide opportunities for players in many arenas to make new demands.[15] In addition to having effects on morale, your success in one arena can impress other players—improving your general reputation (and the reverse in case of failure).

Election Year 2000 again provides a good example of how events in one arena can, at a key moment, influence, derail, or paralyze activities in another. The Miami-Dade County Canvassing Board was groping its way toward a procedure for recounting ballots when Republican protestors stormed the counting room. Several people were kicked, trampled, and punched before the police restored order. Intimidated, the board called off its recount, which was expected to yield additional votes for Gore. Disruption at the right moment has often given protestors what they wanted. At certain times, one arena can be vulnerable to events in another or activities imported from another (from the street to the counting room). The Canvassing Board was unprepared to deal with coercion.

Even if they are not formally related, some arenas can be ranked by their reputations. Like arguing before the U.S. Supreme Court, playing in the major leagues rather than the minors, or making a go of it in New York, success in certain arenas brings special prestige. If you come from an especially tough neighborhood, others think twice about messing with you. The spillover advantage in this case is less one of momentum than of reputation as a transferable asset. *Your arena's reputation affects your own.*

Many arenas have their own specialized language, which increases their autonomy. Law is perhaps the most formalized, although diplomacy, regulatory hearings, and even advertising have their special ways of talking and acting that are like languages. Modern legal jargon is bad enough, but five hundred years ago an English lawyer had to know French, a crude form of which ("Law French") was the language of certain pleadings, not to mention the Latin used in the realm of education and scholarship. The more specialized the language, the more likely it is that players will hire specialists to maneuver for them in those arenas.[16] In some cases natural languages form boundaries, especially in multilingual societies (just as they do for audiences, as we saw). After the British conquered India, for example, Hindus quickly learned English and monopolized appointments in the state bureaucracy, while Muslims refused to learn English and were excluded from what developed into an important arena.[17]

In large teams and alliances, subunits may find it efficient to specialize in different arenas. Political parties of both the Right and Left include not only politicians who concentrate on elections and legislation but also activists willing to take to the streets when necessary. (Like the Republican Party activists who flew to Miami to help shut down the Dade County recount while lawyers for both parties were battling each other in a baffling variety of law courts.) Indeed, the choice between institutional and irregular (or legal and illegal) channels is crucial for strategic players. The choice frequently slides into one between expected and unexpected, traditional and innovative, institutional and not, moderate and radical. The existence of different wings, operating in different arenas, proliferates strategic options, but it also means less centralized control of the team—and often results in two teams. Of course, the distinction is sometimes mostly a display, as with good and bad cops.

THE RADICALISM DILEMMA → In pushing ideas and actions to their extreme, radicals can gain publicity, recognition for a team, and often concessions. The moderate flank might then present itself as a reasonable compromise partner, so that other players give it power in order to undercut the radicals (although the moderates must distance themselves from the radicals to garner these benefits). But in its extremism, a radical wing will be less palatable to bystanders and authorities. In some cases, the radical wing undermines tolerance for the player as a whole, making it easier for its enemies to portray it as undesirable. Authorities may decide to repress the entire team or alliance, not just its radical wing. But if they do not, the chances of success are probably higher. A matter of risk, the Radicalism Dilemma is like the Basket Dilemma, with radicals polarizing the potential outcomes between extremely good and extremely bad.

Some arenas operate as *proxies* for broader or more important ones. They allow a *warmup* (providing practice), serve as a *substitute* (letting off emotional steam), or enable a *trial run* (yielding information) for the larger conflict. We used to hear about "proxy wars" between small countries backed by the United States and the Soviet Union. Many minor legislative votes (often over amendments) are seen as trial runs for more important votes to come. A young burglar may practice on family and neighbors before breaking into strangers' homes.

Actions on one front can often have unexpected results in another. In a classic study of working-class youths, Paul Willis noted that they rebelled against the discipline of schools, in the process guaranteeing that they would not gain the skills to do anything but manual labor the rest of their lives. Their strategy of resistance in one arena limited the options available to them in a subsequent arena. It is hardly surprising that choices made today limit your options tomorrow, but it is more surprising that the limitations may arise in a different institutional setting.[18]

SWITCHING ARENAS

One strategy, especially for those who are losing, is to switch to a different arena of decision making—in other words, to play another game. You will have different audiences for your words and actions, who may prove more sympathetic or helpful. You may prove to have capacities that are useful in the new arena. If you are likely to lose where you are, a new venue is frequently worth a try. Your opponents, if they see the odds as you do, will naturally try to block this shift. (You may also wish to get out of a strategic arena without getting into another, withdrawing from an engagement altogether.)

Switching is frequent because truly autonomous arenas are rare. Even in those that feature a single decision, all laws and decisions must be interpreted and implemented, meaning that there is usually another arena for further struggle. Constant vigilance and enforcement are necessary in these cases. You cannot relax after winning the main battle; follow-up operations may continue forever. This is why businesses have such an advantage in the ongoing implementation and interpretation of laws and regulations; they have the resources to watch and lobby constantly—that is part of their business—which their opponents may lack.[19]

A new arena is frequently appealing or appalling because it contains a strong player who can help or hurt you. Predictions about which it will do are only that—predictions. Corporate executives, for instance, may contemplate reorganization under bankruptcy laws, creating a new venue for strategic interaction with suppliers, labor unions, and creditors. But they can never know for sure what the bankruptcy judge, the new dominant player, will do.[20] As a result of the Extension Dilemma, uncertainty is present even when the new players are genuine allies.

As always, new arenas pose new risks as well as opportunities. You may be unsure of the value of your resources and competencies in a new arena. You may decide to go to court because your brother-in-law is a lawyer, but you do not know how good a lawyer he is. You have troops that look great on the parade ground but have never been tested in battle. (Machiavelli recommended putting troops of uncertain caliber or loyalty in front of the best troops, toward whom they would have to run if they retreated.) Each new arena reintroduces the Engagement Dilemma.

It is easy to misperceive unfamiliar arenas, especially the ease of entering or maneuvering within them. A young woman came to a neighborhood association meeting several years ago in the hope that, once we had solved our local problems, we would address New York City's problems more generally, in other words become something like a political party. I tried to inject some realism without dulling her enthusiasm. She had no clue what it would require to play in a citywide political arena—or how unlikely it was that we would ever "finish" with local problems.

Arena switches can change the nature of an interaction by changing the players involved. One way to cool down a conflict is to *privatize* it, shutting out certain audiences. Many players—especially those who benefit from existing routines—find it to their advantage to calm a conflict. When teachers have trouble with a student, they commonly remove him from class so that they can sort out their differences in a private setting where the student is not simultaneously playing to an audience of friends. Other teachers may change the setting for the whole class, taking them to the gym to play basketball when they get out of hand in the classroom.[21]

In contrast, you may wish to *publicize* an issue by adding new audiences, creating a new conflict. The whole point of most social movements is to transform a private issue into a public one, opening it to new audiences, struggle, and debate. Abortion is a classic example: opponents insist that it is a public, moral issue, not a private choice. Protestors may try regular politics first, only moving to the streets when they have failed to get attention (or results) through elected representatives, official hearings, or the courts. They frequently seek the attention of the news media, and through them a broader public. Sometimes they hope to pressure corporations or governments directly into changing policies by raising the cost of the status quo. But most social movements concentrate on multiple arenas, typically moving back and forth between individual persuasion, public action, and political lobbying within the system.

Strategic actors, often through trial and error, search for the arenas where they can be most effective. For antinuclear groups in the 1970s, this meant trying their hand at expert testimony in public hearings, blowing the whistle about design flaws to the news media, pressuring legislatures via public opinion, demanding that regulators live up to their stated standards of objectivity, and more. Different countries offered different venues: French antinuclear protestors had no access to expert hearings, but they could make international issues out of the placement of so many reactors near France's borders.[22] While some arenas, such as those determined by national political structures, may be unavoidable from the start, most players use trial and error to find those that provide advantages. Each arena offers different horizons of opportunity, but players still have room to maneuver within them.

Blockage in one arena strongly encourages switching. A whistleblower typically begins by complaining to superiors within her own organization. Only when they are unsympathetic (if not retaliatory) does she feel she must go outside her organization to get satisfaction: to regulators, the press, or politicians. This is a fateful switch of arena, from private to public, which usually sets the whistleblower on a different career trajectory (many are fired, and almost all face some form of retaliation). Part of the decision to go public derives from employees' outrage over their internal treatment. They start off assuming their bosses will be happy to know of problems that need to be addressed, but hostile responses make them think the problems are systemwide, endemic, unfixable. More drastic action is required and justified by the indignation they feel.[23]

Members of a group protesting a local hazard must choose how far to expand their arenas. Their most self-interested base consists of their neighbors, and their rhetoric may emphasize how they have been unfairly singled out for abuse, with the intent of getting the nuisance moved elsewhere.

They are highly focused and motivated, like a radical flank. This is the classic "not in my backyard" (NIMBY) group. But a neighborhood, unless it happens to be wealthy or to contain a powerful individual with access to relevant decision makers (or who is one), will probably not—by itself—be able to prevent or remove the nuisance. The group must link with organizations drawn from a larger geographic area: a regional environmental group, for instance, or a statewide political party, or a national historic preservation group. Preferably, it finds an organization that sees the local trouble as an example of a whole category of "bads" to which it is opposed. But as the local group becomes aligned with the nonlocal and enters new arenas, its specific goals may be diluted or transformed. Its ability to make alliances comes at the cost of its focus on the original grievances. It faces the Extension Dilemma, as new arenas and new allies frequently go together.[24]

More global rhetoric may help you win new audiences, but you risk losing the old. On the other hand, having a more general, less self-serving set of arguments may help you convince decision makers of the value of your argument. But with rhetoric that appeals to those in a larger arena, you may lose your neighbors. It is reasonable to expect different rhetoric to appeal to them. They may care about property values, not global warming. The leader of the local group may become an activist in a national group only to have the local group dissolve: she has jumped from one strategic game to another. It may be easier to stop an incinerator from being built in your neighborhood, pushing it off into a poor or rural site, than to stop the construction of all incinerators. (This is exactly what happened with nuclear reactors in the 1960s: a number of towns were able to block local plans, only to have the same reactors built elsewhere.)

Or take a couple who argue a lot. The man may feel that going to a counselor is a good idea, not just because she is an expert on these matters and may have practical suggestions, but also because he thinks he may do better with this new audience. His partner may not say outrageous things, or may appear overly narcissistic or demanding to an outsider. (Of course, in many cases each partner expects the therapist's support.) He hopes the new audience will become some sort of ally.

The example of the couple suggests another reason for switching arenas: to signal the seriousness of the interaction or conflict. Diane Vaughan suggests that this is a common reason for couples to seek outside help: one wants out, but cannot get her partner to take her complaints seriously. "How can the partner deny the seriousness of the situation if the couple seek the advice of an expert?"[25] Shifting to a new arena, especially when this introduces strangers as audiences, can get a person's attention. Abused spouses often complain to no avail until they call in the police, or in some cases until the abuser goes through the court and jail system.

Not all arena switches represent careful choices. Stalemate in one arena may inevitably push a conflict into another, or defeat in one may leave only the option of appealing to another arena. Your resources may be worth little in your current arena.[26] Indignation over how you were treated in one arena may propel you into the next. Or you may inadvertently open a new arena, for example by bringing people together for nonstrategic purposes who then take the initiative and act strategically. Romania's Nicolae Ceausescu lost his presidency—and his life—when a large crowd, rounded up to hear him speak, instead heckled him so badly as to shatter his legitimacy. No arenas are impermeable, unchangeable, and altogether controllable.

The very act of entering or exiting an arena can be an important move. Many politicians receive more attention for resigning than for anything they did in office. Every nonprofit that joins an ongoing consumer boycott calls a press conference to make the announcement. The timing of these moves must be right, and the words that accompany the action help to frame it. (This kind of publicity may have more of an effect than any drop in sales.)[27] Just as "being there" and being absent are important states in strategic engagements, as we saw in chapter 4, so movement between the two can have dramatic effects.

Sometimes you absent yourself intentionally—by storming out of a meeting or boycotting an election. In May 2003, fifty-five Democratic legislators left Texas to preclude a quorum at the statehouse, the only way they could deter the Republican majority from passing a sleazy redistricting plan. You reject the current interaction as illegitimate, presumably with a better alternative in mind and hopefully with the power to initiate it. But this effort to switch arenas has its risks: in an Engagement Dilemma, your absence from the current arena normally gives you less control over what happens there. Ideally, your very absence cripples or delegitimates it with the audiences you care most about.

Exits need not shut down an arena or switch the action to a new one in order to have an effect. When others depend on you, you can time your absence to maximize damage if you want to—for instance, if you are switching from ally to adversary. Sociologist Julia Wrigley notes that, if a child care worker quits in anger, she may well do so at just the worst time for the parents, exploiting her final chance for revenge.[28]

Because being there gives you more control over what happens, your opponents frequently wait until you are absent to advance their projects. Burglars look for empty homes, governing parties try to pass controversial legislation at night after the opposition has left. Michael Lipsky describes bureaucrats who, assigned to deal with complaints, made a point of calling complainants at times when they were unlikely to be home—if they got no answer after three calls, they could drop the case (this was before cell phones).[29]

Just as you may wish to exit an arena, you may intentionally or unintentionally push other players out of it. Normally, barring them from an arena includes barring them from resources and from certain moves that would advantage them. Even here there is some risk, since you cannot be sure who will replace them. In 1989 the Rainforest Action Network thought it had won an important victory when it pressured Scott Paper into withdrawing from an arrangement to cut down rain forests in West Papua. But the Indonesian government simply found another paper company, less vulnerable to public pressure because it does not sell directly to consumers, which cut down far more trees with fewer of the safeguards Scott had promised as part of its PR campaign. The "good guy"—relatively speaking—withdrew from this arena, only to be replaced by a less accommodating player beholden to fewer audiences.[30]

Sometimes a well-positioned player can veto the actions of others by shutting down an arena. In ancient Rome the College of Augurs—corruptible in a culture where everyone was for sale—could declare a day *nefastus*, meaning both "unlucky" and "unlawful." Many popular assemblies were prevented through this expedient. Claims of urgency can also preempt normal business. To stick with Roman examples, in 63 BCE a praetor managed to end a corrupt trial against Rabirius by taking down the flag on the top of Janiculan Hill—a traditional sign of enemy attack that ended all other business.

RULES AND CAPACITIES

Arenas are defined largely by their rules and by the capacities needed to compete in them. Players may have different relative positions in different arenas. A group with a lot of power in one may have little in another; that is why switching can be a sound move. A player may have an institutional or legal position in one arena or personal contacts there; it may have invested time and effort in cultivating the position and contacts; or it may have resources that are especially useful in one arena but not another.

In addition to relative advantages, relatively structured arenas have stark boundaries between insiders and outsiders, privileging all those inside. Fifty years ago, African Americans in the South were not allowed to vote, had few sympathetic legislators, could not get a fair hearing in the courts, and faced police repression. Institutional politics was simply not open to them. Environmentalists and animal protectionists had to fight hard to gain "standing" in American courts to bring lawsuits. Battles over the definition of citizenship have raged in advanced industrial countries. These are essentially conflicts over the definition of insider and outsider in national politics.

Resources influence what we can do in a given arena, while the arena determines their local value. We can get more of a resource, or we can try to invent new resources for the arena. New resources, though, change more than our strategic capacities; sometimes they shift the arenas of action. This is most obvious in war, as technologies create new subarenas. Once airplanes were invented, the front was no longer exclusively on the ground. Artillery that could shell positions twenty miles away and missiles that could cross oceans vastly extended the territories that were part of the arena of war. They also made industrial production a prime arena for competition. Communication technologies have also allowed us to expand fields of conflict enormously, coordinating actions across a continent and later around the globe. Corporations compete with one another worldwide thanks to transportation and communication technologies that allow global coordination and penetration. We can think of this as the enlargement of a single arena or the proliferation of subarenas, depending on how distinct the local rules are in different countries or localities (likewise how distinct and autonomous air and land battle are). How we define an arena depends on our purposes.

THE DILEMMA OF FORM AND CONTENT → As we saw in the opening vignette, a common strategic switch is from content to form. The content of the workfloor grievances no longer mattered— their sheer number did. One union gained clout by making them an issue in contract negotiations but gave up the ability to get individual grievances redressed. Generally, you can switch from fighting over the content of a decision (of your boss or of the government, say) to battling over the procedure by which it was made. *Procedural rhetoric* is a term I have used to describe arguments that focus on form rather than substance: proper rules were not followed, officials were corrupted, and so on.[31] But if the procedure turns out to have been correct, it may be hard to switch back to the content; it is usually easier to switch from content to form than the reverse. Questions of form may allow a broader structural critique, but this distracts from the immediate issues. It can be amusing to watch strategic actors trying to pursue their goals simultaneously at the substantive and formal levels. In November 2000, the world heard Bush and Gore each insist that the rule of law should prevail, but so should the will of the people—procedure and substance. Their rhetoric shifted, of course, as one or the other seemed to hold more promise for each of the candidates. (In some cases third parties, especially authorities, steer interactions from content to form as a way of defusing conflict, expecting agreement on form to be easier or at least distracting.)[32]

A classic case was the American South's efforts to prevent public debate over slavery in the 1830s by passing a "gag rule" against congressional debate in response to petitions against slavery in the District of Columbia. Naturally, argument shifted to the legality of gag rules and the right of the people to petition Congress.[33] In many cases players become engaged over formal issues but not substantive ones. Ethnographer Mitch Duneier presents a nice example of form and content used as rhetorical tropes in an argument between two street vendors over a prime sidewalk space in New York. One criticizes the other for coming late every day, expecting the space to be left empty all morning. The latter ignores the substance of the complaint and replies by invoking racial solidarity against that criticism, especially in light of the policeman walking toward them to end the contention. They shout past each other, neither accepting the other's terms of debate.[34]

Resting your case on an obscure rule can appear petty, as the letter of the law seems to subvert the spirit. If you win, such an appeal may be worth it—and usually quickly forgotten. But if you lose, you have probably damaged yourself with bystanders (at least). This happened to Massachusetts' Democrats when they tried to bar Mitt Romney from the governor's race on the grounds that he had not resided in the state for the seven consecutive years required by the Commonwealth's constitution. They lost the appeal and the election. In that case, sticking to content was the nice choice and switching to form the naughty one—and for the latter to work, the decision had to be quick and irreversible—not to mention successful!

Players differ in their taste for explicit rules. In chapter 4 we saw some effects of naïveté and paranoia, which also affect the kinds of rules players wish to establish in the arenas where they play. Paranoid players naturally want more rules and—expecting others to cheat—enforcement mechanisms for those rules.[35] Those contemplating the formulation of rules encounter a version of the Articulation Dilemma, applied in chapter 3 to goals: the new rules constrain as well as enable. Japan's Meiji restoration period saw debates between those who would elaborate the rights of the emperor in the new constitution and those who knew this would restrict his powers to those explicitly enumerated.[36]

Strategic actors often hide changes in content behind those in form. In addition it is often hard to distinguish form from substance. On November 5, 2000, for instance, Malawi's president fired his entire cabinet to demonstrate to foreign donors his opposition to corruption (suddenly stripped of their limousines, the surprised ministers had to find their own way home). But he used the new appointments to tighten his own grip on power, refusing to reappoint several ministers who had grown into rivals. American corporations also have many purposes behind formal changes. "The first action of most new CEOs," observes Robert Jackall, "is some form of organizational change. On the one hand, this prevents the inheritance of blame for past mistakes; on the other, it projects an image of bare-knuckled aggressiveness much appreciated on Wall Street. Perhaps most important, a shake-up rearranges the fealty structure of the corporation, placing in power those barons whose style and public image mesh well with that of the new CEO and whose principal loyalties belong to him."[37] The allocation of blame, redirection of loyalties, and creation of a sense of agency can all lurk behind formal moves.

An arena's rules never cover everything. For one thing, there are always exceptions. Most arenas of any complexity have rules to cover the applicability of the rules and what to do when they do not apply or are broken. Even children frequently interrupt their games with long debates over ambiguities, often hatching new rules to cover the exceptions.[38] In crises, the normal rules are insufficient—this is pretty much the definition of crisis. In ancient Rome the senate could declare an emergency and appoint a "dictator" to set things right in the face of foreign invasions, insurrections, and famines. The dictator's powers were unlimited, but circumscribed in time by the goal of restoring the system rather than changing it. There were rules for stepping outside the rules and then returning to them in order to protect the arena.[39]

In addition to exceptions, there is always room for interpretation and fudging of existing rules. In other words conflict continues over the application of the rules, which is to say over the arena itself—although battles over the application of the rules do not always result in permanent transformations of the arena, which, as we will see, are a crucial battleground too. With rules, we get into the issue of the formal versus informal dimensions of arenas. Sometimes a strategic actor finds one to his advantage, sometimes the other, facing Go-Sanjō's Dilemma (chapter 4).

THE RULES DILEMMA → Efforts to change an arena often end up following the rules of that same arena. Rather than ignoring it or using a different arena, an insurgent may end up embroiled in the arena's rules for changing the rules. If nothing else, the criticism legitimates the arena's existence and importance. Whether you are a sports player arguing with referees or a revolutionary trying to seize the state, it is often difficult to change or avoid the arenas you most dislike. One reason is that you often want simply to replace those in official positions with members of your own team; another is that you wish to retain the arena's powers for your own use (a form of the Sorcerer's Apprentice Dilemma).[40] More generally, players face choices over whether to follow rules or break them—a specific application of the Naughty or Nice? dilemma.

STRUCTURES

Some strategic games establish or shape the arenas themselves: for example, conflicts over constitutions and bylaws, over the legal recognition of groups such as professions or nonprofits, over what is allowed in market competition, over laws of inheritance or inequality. The effects of conflicts in these super-arenas are often profound: consider the Second Amendment to the U.S. Constitution, which has saddled Americans with a literally deadly "right" to bear arms that the majority of them oppose; the best efforts at gun control run up against these words on a piece of paper (or rather, the strategic efforts of the National Rifle Association are effective partly because of the Constitutional words they can utilize rhetorically). Structures like these are the bread and butter of sociology, but sociologists have often missed the extensive strategic struggles behind their development. Even historical sociologists often fall back into a functional vision that ignores the projects of individuals and groups in favor of examining the whole "society."

By definition, elites are those who control and benefit from a society's political, economic, and cultural structures. And to protect their positions, they usually hide their own efforts to create and maintain the structures from which they benefit. We have no choice but to bring on a recession, they say, as we must fight inflation. Or the rise of economic inequality, they say, is inevitable due to the globalization of markets. Economic growth simply requires the damming of the Yangtze River. Because they are not attuned to strategic action, social scientists often accept such rationalizations as explanations.

I studied just this process of the creation of "inevitable" structures in my book on nuclear energy. By comparing policymaking in France, Sweden, and the United States from 1950 to 1990, I was able to show how the nuclear industry and sympathetic government officials worked hard to establish uranium supplies, reactor designs, administrative structures, and even public opinion that would make nuclear commitments inevitable. They met opposition at every step, and only in France were they able to establish the economic and political structures they wanted. But in all three countries, options were continually narrowed through strategic interaction. In France, the very factors that elites had created became the "reasons" France needed a huge commitment to nuclear energy. They had created the arenas they wanted. In the other countries, different strategic outcomes created different "structures." In no country were elites driven by unavoidable market forces, as most of them claimed.[41]

Procedural rules are the central aspect of the structures crafted in these super-arenas. The legitimacy of an arena's rules establishes the legitimacy of that arena, so they are often jealously protected or venerated. "Contempt of court" and "resisting arrest" have to do with maintaining respect for procedures, however one may disagree substantively with decisions. As we saw with the Dilemma of Form and Content, both procedures and substance can be grounds for disagreement. Disputes over procedure often establish new precedents or even formal rules. Players may create a new battleground around the arenas themselves that have little to do with the original source of contention.

Players value their arenas for a variety of reasons beyond the games they can pursue there. Sometimes institutions take on a positive value of their own, becoming a norm in the manner suggested by situationalists. In his study of futures traders, Mitchel Abolafia found a number of "social mechanisms" that shaped market behavior, including "informal norms among traders, formal rules of trade, and organizational arrangements to coordinate collective action." Together, such mechanisms tempered short-term strategies in favor of the long-term strategies of keeping the exchange operating and autonomous from government intervention. Defense of such rules is often intended to reassure outside players such as regulators or customers.[42] (In the Today or Tomorrow? dilemma [chapter 3], different players may favor each option.)

The best way to arrange an arena in a way that sustains your advantages may be to exclude other groups from playing the game at all or from using certain kinds of moves. Max Weber used the term *closure* to refer to a group's success in this. He said that any group attribute could be used as the basis for closure: for example, language, race, religion, or blood lines. But these arbitrary traits are not the only ones that can form the boundary. Educational credentials allow M.D.'s to monopolize medicine and Ph.D.'s to monopolize academia. A society's rules of property may allow owners to monopolize decision making about their houses, land, or factories. Other rules may prevent certain people from owning such resources at all. Rules of citizenship may prevent certain categories of residents (for instance, those whose parents are not citizens) from voting. Preventing "outsiders" from being players in an arena is a powerful strategic objective.

Closure is not only the strategy of elites. White workers have worked hard to keep black workers out of trade unions throughout American history. Low castes often monopolize certain occupations—although admittedly not very desirable ones. Elites have greater resources to make their efforts at closure stick and to reinforce them continually, but many groups have succeeded in overcoming such opposition (especially with the right allies).

Success at establishing the rules of the game in this way is rarely permanent. Disadvantaged insiders may invent new rules or find new arenas. Outsiders must use other tools to gain access or play other games to get what they want. If they cannot vote for sympathetic political candidates, they may aim to disrupt economic profits instead, hoping that one group of insiders (profit makers) will be forced to take their side. This was one strategy of the civil rights movement in the United States as they organized boycotts of racist businesses. Or outsiders may find or create new arenas in which they can pursue their goals, just as early manufacturers avoided Europe's guild restrictions by setting up production outside of cities. As anthropologist Fredrik Barth commented, reflecting the difference between resources and strategic intelligence, "The unfortunate circumstance of a gross disadvantage of power does not mean that strategy is unavailing—indeed it may be all the more essential to the actor and all the more pervasive in shaping his behavior."[43]

To operate in an arena where the rules favor you seems to be a form of power—because those rules actually increase the value of the resources you control (see the discussion in chapter 4 equating power with resources). Arenas can also systematically advantage certain skills and knowledge. Other advantages—luck, for instance—do not seem to me to be usefully labeled as power. The advantage of closure is a kind of structural aspect of an arena that aids some players over others, allowing them more strategic room—but I would refrain from calling it power. I see it as an advantage rather like occupying a hill before a battle: a strategic accomplishment rather than a "thing" in itself (although the existence of the hill in the first place is an aspect of the arena).

An arena does not simply reflect one group's ability to impose rules that will benefit that group alone: it must accommodate other players to some degree. To gain the stability offered by an arena, even the most powerful groups are usually willing to set aside some of the weapons in their strategic arsenal. An English peasant procured the right to complain about his lord in a judicial hearing—even though the judge was usually his lord. But that was better than having his head lopped off for complaints. If a powerful player can *force* a weak one to play in an arena that altogether favors the former, then it probably does not need the arena at all (unless there is some even more powerful group it is trying to impress—the king, for example). All powerful groups *eventually* need some legitimacy and so cannot be transparently shameless in setting up rules in their own favor.

Sociologists have specialized in the effects of political, economic, and other structures, and occasionally in their origins. Oddly, and sometimes nonsensically, they have given structural explanations of the origins of structures, apparently lacking a vocabulary for describing the strategic action that in fact brings them into being and regularly reshapes them. (Without strategic action, structural changes can only be related to their functional contributions to some imagined social system.) Gamesters have taken a different approach, showing why certain structural arrangements are more stable over time (through many "rounds" of games) than others. But like the sociologists, they are more likely to explain survival than the (strategic) origins of institutions.

Do we gain anything with the term *structure*? Does it capture a reality not already available with the concepts of rules and arenas? In one of his discussions of "structuration," Giddens describes two types of "structural contradictions," as though to clinch the existence of structures. The first involves the kind of unintended consequences that are well described by game theory: if everyone does what makes sense to them as individuals, the consequences may not be what they had hoped for. This is merely a problem of aggregation, not structural properties in the usual sense. The second arises because organizations must do contradictory things, as in Claus Offe's example of the capitalist state that depends on economic growth but must encourage corporate power in order to achieve that growth, thereby eroding its own power. "The contradictory nature of the capitalist state is expressed in the push and pull between commodification, de-commodification, and recommodification."[44]

But it is easy to see the same "capitalist" state as reacting to strategic initiatives by a range of outsiders and insiders, especially big business on the one hand and normal citizens or workers on the other. The contradictions become dilemmas, a kind of balancing act among competing goals. Giddens seems to encourage this interpretation when he says that players can become aware of structural features: "The state is not just caught in the push and pull of primary contradiction; state agencies may seek to monitor the conditions of system reproduction in such a way as to minimize the conflicts that might otherwise tend to break out."[45] Dominant groups work hard to maintain their dominance; they are not given it automatically. Direct repression keeps many systems going.

At the more institutional end of structuration theory, Giddens says that researchers must specify the institutional orders at work and identify the bounds of knowledgeability. It remains hard to see what these are beyond resources and cultural meanings (rules partake of each). The point Giddens is trying to make has more to do with the reproduction of structures over time, through action. There is no structure outside action, he says; it is both "medium and outcome of the conduct it recursively organizes."[46] "Structure" is a poor simile, implying constraints like those of walls and buildings that physically constrain us. Most barriers come from other players trying to block us. Structures should be constraints (and aids) that operate independently of strategic intent—a rare condition. *Behind every "structure" is usually another player hard at work.*

Arenas can take on a structural *feel*, however, in that players take them for granted, playing by their rules. Players typically develop some interest in the arenas they inhabit, which help define them as players—sometimes legally. Yet it is always possible to challenge the rules, find new moves, re-shape the arenas themselves. We might think of such options as *structural strategies*, aimed at the arenas themselves by opening up new rule-making arenas "above" them. This is especially common in modern societies, where the state intervenes so actively in all other arenas, changing the rules of the game in markets, sports, workplaces, even interpersonal relations.

A great deal of strategic action is aimed at creating new arenas as well as transforming existing ones. Theda Skocpol makes this point about poli-cies: "According to this political-process approach, a policy is 'successful' if it enhances the kinds of state capacities that can promote its future develop-ment, and especially if it stimulates groups and political alliances to defend the policy's continuation and expansion."[47] A new policy becomes an arena, with its distinct set of players and their capacities, as well as a set of stakes.

FALSE ARENAS

If some arenas systematically advantage one set of players, at the extreme such players can establish them purely as a strategic move, only pretending to provide access or advantages to others. This is an extreme case of struc-tural bias. Critics of capitalism discuss this as the problem of co-optation, especially those who criticize trade unions as ineffective.[48] Political scien-tists also deal with it in discussing the agenda-setting function of "power," which can exclude certain issues from public discussion altogether.[49]

There are at least three kinds of false arenas. In one, decision making is moved to another arena just as a new group gains entry to the old, which formally remains the same but has less substantive impact than it used to. The real power now moves to the new arena. This is what happened to U.S. trade policy in 1994 with the creation of the World Trade Organization, which stripped Congress of much of its influence in this area.[50] If noth-ing else, decision makers can *claim* they no longer have power as a way of refusing unwelcome demands.

In other cases a player may create a false arena to allow the expression of discontent or provide a feeling of participation, though it never has much formal or informal influence. Blue-ribbon commissions and task forces are an example. As a political activist complains, "[T]ask forces sponsored by government officials are usually boondoggles, excellent weapons for slow-ing activist momentum. They can divert activists from their real goal and nearly always eat up a lot of time that could be better spent. Yet serving on a task force can be an attractive proposition for a grassroots organizer, who may get no other sign of recognition from the powers-that-be."[51] Often the player must give up so much in order to enter the arena that it loses ground overall, but sometimes it can take advantage of arenas in ways the gatekeepers did not anticipate. In Philip Selznick's original example of co-optation, concerning the Tennessee Valley Authority, both sides gained something: managers gave up some influence in exchange for outsiders' support. As Robert Freeland argues, "Once subordinates are formally incorporated into the planning process, there is always the risk that they will manage to use their representation in a way that will subvert or modify leadership's goals."[52] False arenas can sometimes be transformed into real ones.

In the third kind of false arena, a decision has already been made that deprives the arena of any power. Participation thus legitimates the decision already taken in your absence. For example, months into its invasion of Iraq, the administration of Bush II decided it needed UN support to please a number of audiences. It badgered Kofi Annan to sign on to Bush's transition plans. However, as a newspaper article stated, "People close to Mr. Annan say he has rarely been in a more uncomfortable position. For months, he has wanted the United Nations to oversee Iraq's transition to self-government. But he did not want it to be seen as merely giving in to an American plan worked out with the Iraqis chosen by Mr. Bremer."[53]

THE DILEMMA OF FALSE ARENAS → In many cases an arena is created only when—and because—you enter it. Knowing this, you may refuse to enter. You might then run the risk of looking foolish or deceptive (saying you want this power but refusing it when offered). If you enter, on the other hand, it is harder to make further demands for standing and participation because it looks as though you have already been granted what you claimed to want. You must demonstrate clearly to allies and bystanders that the arena is a trap—often a difficult thing to do.

Short of being intentionally false, an arena may simply prove a distraction from more important arenas. For instance, membership in the European Union allows poorer nations to apply for funds to improve infrastructure and training—but they must bear around half the cost themselves. Funds they might have used in other ways go to the regional development favored by the EU. This temptation—a willingness to be "bought"—lies at the intersection of two dilemmas: the Extension Dilemma and the Sorcerer's Apprentice Dilemma. Joining the EU alliance provides access to its extensive means, which may distract members from their own existing ends.[54]

If players gain entry to an arena that previously excluded them but cannot manage to influence its outcomes, it is not necessarily a false arena. They may not have the skills or information they need to maneuver well. Or the team's leaders may defect from their own team's goals as the price of being allowed to play in the new arena, pursuing their own games as individuals. Union leaders who golf with executives and enjoy other perks are an example. This kind of defection is not necessarily a function of the arena. (Such defections may occur because the individuals are persuaded by some of their opponents' ideas or because their own interests diverge more and more from those of the rest of their team.)

Whether it is a mistake to enter false arenas depends, as always, on the alternatives. You can enter one in the hope of turning it into a genuine source of decision making. Or you can satisfy yourself with the symbolic victory that entry represents. If you represent a constituency, that audience might be very pleased with the "symbolic politics" of this new participation.[55]

Even personal interactions can involve something like false arenas. For instance, we may be encouraged to vent our emotions without the possibility of affecting anyone else by doing so. On the other hand, emotional expression is often one of our goals, so the arena may not be entirely false. From the point of view of other players, though, engaging in such expression may distract us from actions that would affect them. Our displays may cost them little but give us considerable satisfaction.

✕

We have examined strategic arenas, the players who enter them, and the motives and goals, resources and competencies they bring with them. These appear to be the basic building blocks we need to describe strategic interactions in a more social way than the mathematics of game theory achieves. But these elements are only interesting in action as players make choices in the face of dozens of dilemmas and trade-offs. I conclude with a discussion of how we might use these dilemmas to explain social life.

CONCLUSION
THINKING THROUGH DILEMMAS

In strategic action there are few rules (as I try to show in the appendix) but many choices (as I hope the rest of the book has demonstrated). Lists of strategic principles never guarantee success, especially when other players have the same lists. At best, they offer problems to consider, mistakes to avoid. That is not bad, perhaps, given that so many interactions are determined by blunders. (But you must always probe to make sure the apparent mistakes of others are really mistakes rather than traps.)

From the Olympian heights of the analyst, we can see a number of dilemmas with which strategic players must grapple. And yet, most of the time, most of the choices are deep in the background. They do not feel like choices at all. Rules and routines tell us what to do. Or fads sweep organizations, disguising the choices we make so that they feel inevitable, the one right way of doing things. We must give the "situation" its due. This is what culture and habit and institutions do for us: they tell us what to do so that we do not have to think about all the possibilities from scratch. In many cases we can only recognize alternatives by looking at players in other settings, to see how they have done things differently (a good job for scholars).

What is more, not all dilemmas—even when we are conscious of them— are stark either/or alternatives. We must often find the right point along a continuum between two extremes, or at times we may have three or more discrete options. Sometimes, the costs of taking one path instead of another are obvious; at others the costs are probabilities that with luck we can avoid. In turn, those probabilities are sometimes known and sometimes not known. Further, we may be able to affect the likelihood of damage, addressing and alleviating the dilemma itself. The term *dilemma* may imply that we feel torn equally between two paths, recognizing the value of each, but much of the time nuances of the situation suggest one route rather than another. Alternate paths often seem to present dilemmas primarily from the analyst's perspective.

Some dilemmas allow or even encourage a cycling back and forth between their two horns. A successful strategic choice may lead opponents to react vigorously, so that, in retrospect, the choice appears to have been an error.[1] Extreme engagement frequently leads to burnout and extreme disengagement, which in turn may lead to an overcommitment in the future. The trick of a cycle, of course, is not simply that there is alternation, but that we can specify mechanisms that lead from one part of the cycle to the next.

Some dilemmas take the form of feedback loops that lead to unanticipated, perverse consequences. Many reflect trade-offs between short- and long-term costs and benefits: being naughty may achieve compliance now, but our victims may bide their time for later revenge. Even if we are unaware of dilemmas as choices to be made, they persist underground as trade-offs that will affect streams of action, our future abilities and chances to have an impact. Many dilemmas are hidden under layers of custom and institutional rules, only waiting for someone to realize that things can be done differently, that unexpected choices are possible. They generate innovations that are among the most effective strategic moves.

The point is that there is no single right answer for all times and places. The minutiae of circumstances differ, and so do the mentalities of the players. Both of these change so rapidly that we cannot lay them out in the kind of detail that a fully calculating player would require. Instead, intuition, trained by experience, is often crucial. Strategic interaction cannot be reduced to mathematical models.

And yet, we know people make choices. We can see them doing it. We watch a spouse struggle over what to do at work. We observe protest groups in their endless meetings debating tactics. We can read executive memos adopting one policy rather than another. Despite some limitations, in other words, I think my dilemmas capture many of the conscious choices with which strategists themselves grapple. They may make conscious decisions regarding a mere handful of the dilemmas I have presented, but these are frequently fateful choices. Certainly they are affected by cultures and structures, but they in turn remake these background circumstances. The point is that strategic actors make choices of many sorts.

We can group the dilemmas into rough categories reflecting existential conditions of being human. Many have to do with extension or *scope*, for example, including time and space and social groupings. How broadly do we reach out (the dilemmas of Extension, Universalism, and Janus)? Who should be at the negotiating table? How long a time frame do we adopt (Today or Tomorrow? and the Paradox of Education)? Whose goals get priority? How do we balance different audiences? Do we put all our eggs in one basket? Even the choice of being naughty or nice is, in some ways, an issue of pleasing some audiences while displeasing others.

A closely related set of dilemmas have to do with *hierarchy*. Do we reach up or down to get what we want? Do we establish vertical or horizontal teams to engage in strategic games? Do we jump on the bandwagons of the powerful or try to resist them? How do titans deal with their position? How do we treat underlings?

A third fundamental group has to do with *speed* and *change*. Do we adopt new moves, arguments, and images, or do we stick with familiar ones? Do we embark on new strategic interactions or let familiar routines channel our actions? How far can we push an audience rhetorically or push our own team tactically? The very question of strategic engagement might fall under this rubric: to what extent do we actively promote our projects?

Another cluster has to do with taking *risks*: the Risk, Home-Turf, Fodder, Basket, Scorched Earth, and Engagement dilemmas obviously fall into this category. At the same time, though, risk is an element in most of the other groupings as well. How far can we push the scope of our action without inviting failure? To what extent can we see or control the future? Is it worth transforming ourselves through education?

Some dilemmas reflect the nature of *social* life: we are both individuals and members of larger groups and networks. Whose Interests? shows that we can be torn over goals, while the dilemmas of Go-Sanjō, Players or Prizes, and Rules show that different means are available depending on whether we wish to use our individual or our connected qualities.

Finally, a surprising number of dilemmas have to do with *form and content*, or means and ends—which boils down to an issue of exactly what game to play. The Dilemma of Dirty Hands and those of the Sorcerer's Apprentice and Money's Curse pit means against ends. Naughty or Nice? is about different means. Others are about contrasting ends: Today or Tomorrow? Whose Goals? and Survival versus Success. The dilemmas of Form and Content, Rules, and False Arenas are about how to play the game itself, or perhaps which game to play.

Not every player faces the same dilemmas in the same way. Players have often made up their minds in advance through institutions, culture, emotional commitments, or personality. Moreover, different factions or positions in a compound player may argue in favor of one choice rather than another. Employers favor steeper pyramids, employees flatter ones; spies prefer stealth, and orators prefer public debate. In other words we can often interpret the dilemmas through the lens of role conflict or social conflict, linking strategy back to more structured aspects of arenas and resources. Some dilemmas may evolve or even be eliminated over time, in the face of social and physical inventions often meant to address a given trade-off. Future research will have to sort out these components.

Many of the dilemmas arise during confrontations between players, meaning that each side faces a dilemma at the same time. But they may not always face the same dilemma. You must decide whether to try to involve a bystander (Bystander's Dilemma), while the bystander faces the Engagement Dilemma. The Scorched-Earth Dilemma for one side may be the Home-Turf Dilemma for the other. In Go-Sanjō's Dilemma, you must decide whether to use personal or positional tactics, but others must decide which kind they will respond to. More often, interacting players face the same dilemmas: those of the Basket, Players or Prizes, Extension, and so on. Contrary to much game theory, adversaries rarely make their choices at precisely the same time, or even in strict alternation, because most decisions involve lengthy social processes. Rather than mere instants, they usually extend over days, weeks, even months, requiring several interactions within each team, and a number of tentative signals and trial runs.

✕

Many questions remain to be answered. I shall formulate them as questions that point to gaps to be filled, rather than as hypotheses, which imply that the author knows more than she does. As "choice points," I hope the dilemmas will focus future research at least as much as the general vocabulary I have provided will allow us to escape tired metaphors. How can researchers work with these dilemmas; what can they *do* with them? Each dilemma, I believe, is worthy of its own research project. I see four kinds of questions that we might ask about each. The first two groups take the dilemmas as things to be explained, the latter two as factors that help explain something else. Within each pair I further distinguish between explaining the dilemmas and explaining the choices made in facing them.

One family of questions asks why each *dilemma* exists, how broad its scope is, and how we can define its nature. This is the most structural set of questions. What is it about psychology, information, organizations, and so on that leads to this trade-off? And does the trade-off reflect a strict either/or situation? Or does a little more of one benefit lead to a little less of another? Is it possible ever to get the balance right, to solve the dilemma and get the benefits of both its horns? Does the dilemma arise because we are considering distinct audiences pleased by conflicting actions? Or does the dilemma reflect competing goals? Or tension between means and goals? Finally, what circumstances make the dilemma more urgent or more conscious?

A second set of questions aims to explain the *choices* made by real-life players facing a dilemma. What psychological or organizational or other factors lead to one choice rather than the other? What factors lead to biases in favor of one choice again and again, perhaps more often than an observer would judge to be optimal? At the extreme, a choice fades from conscious consideration into rule or routine. How and why does that happen? We need to explain non-choices as well as choices.

A third set of questions examines the *effects* of the existence of a given dilemma. What technologies, practices, organizational structures, and so on have been invented to resolve the dilemma, to clarify it, or to render it useful? What information is gathered, what alliances are formed, what promises made to deal with a dilemma? How have organizations structured themselves to avoid facing a controversial choice or to hide the choice made?

Finally, what are the *effects* of particular *choices*? Here, the choices become causal mechanisms that concatenate into concrete explanations. How is the player itself affected by the choice? How do other players react? Are arenas, players, symbols, or rules changed? Who is mobilized? Do resources or positions change hands? Who gets more of what they want? For the answers to such questions we would normally turn to strategic approaches, compiling a sequence of actions to explain outcomes of interest.

In recent years many social scientists have turned from general theory to explanation by mechanisms. I think that strategic dilemmas and choices are *useful causal mechanisms*. They frequently mediate between the micro and the macro level: micro choices have macro effects, and macro conditions shape the micro choices. We encounter the same dilemmas and choices across many different institutional settings, and so comparisons can get at the aspects of those institutions that influence outcomes. Best of all, choices are concrete and observable events, which can be defined with little controversy compared to most of the social phenomena we study and explain. Thus we can build on them to propose larger explanations, relatively unpolluted by the theories we hope to compare. Most often, in trying to explain institutional dynamics, we reach down to the level of individuals for our mechanisms.[2]

This advantage is crucial. As we try to build a general understanding of strategic interaction, we need to start modestly. If we build too much into our basic language and concepts, we will end up with an abstract but unrealistic edifice like that of game theory. We'll never be able to see things freshly. The danger is that we will dress up the same structural theories in new clothes. Attention to concrete choices and the underlying dilemmas may help us avoid this.

Even in the analysis of politics, that most strategic of settings, we have inadequate microfoundations for our institutional explanations. The most concerted efforts to work out these foundations—psychoanalysis and rational-choice theory—have simply not yielded reasonable starting points. One makes players appear pathological; the other, all too calculating— reflecting the poles in a very old debate over whether humans are rational. Other traditions, including the entirety of political sociology, pay no attention to microfoundations whatsoever, a vacuum into which rational-choice assumptions often creep unnoticed. Even when they are noticed and derided, political sociologists have little to offer in their place.[3]

There are no easy rules to follow in strategic interactions, despite thousands of books on self-help and business that promise answers. My aim has not been to provide lessons for practitioners. But I cannot resist one suggestion. When grappling with the many dilemmas I have outlined, you will make better choices if you are aware that you are making choices than if you are simply following custom or (as a recent book recommends) intuition. You can think about the hidden as well as obvious costs and risks, and you can work to deal with them as soon as possible. You can compensate for your main choice by doing damage repair on the other side of the dilemma. At least if you have time to think about what you are doing in a careful way (that is not always the case), awareness of your alternatives may help you think of new and effective actions. As Max Weber pointed out a century ago, the best that social scientists can do for others is to make them aware of the full consequences of their actions.

✂

I hope that you will have imagined several ways to apply the ideas in the preceding chapters to your own research and theory, but let me mention just a few fields that might benefit from a strategic approach. Some are obvious. Strategic action is at the heart of social movements, the state, electoral politics and parties, revolutions, and other patently contentious arenas. Claimsmaking over social problems is nothing if not strategic, as it employs rhetoric to persuade others to recognize and redress a problem. Often, a field of research has been inching toward a social approach to strategy without quite saying so, without recognizing it for what it is.[4]

In some cases, critiques of structural approaches have pushed research in the direction of a more strategic vision—or could if rightly understood. Electoral realignments are an example. Generations of American political scientists have examined turning points in party alignments, which for one hundred years came with surprising regularity—every thirty-six years (1860, 1896, 1932, and possibly 1968).[5] The approach relies on structural images of stable "party systems" that occasionally collapse and are replaced—for instance, as new issues arise or policies stagnate. In 2002 David Mayhew cast doubt on the whole tradition, questioning its empirical claims. Most interesting to us are three other factors he suggests for thinking about party competition. One is contingency: "A scandal, a fancy, a blunder, a depression, or a world war may come along and swerve voters." Chance events matter largely because parties take advantage of them in their short-term strategies—Mayhew's second factor. (I would suggest that long-term strategies, like Nixon's appeal to white southerners, matter just as much.) Third are valence issues, which "hinge chiefly on perceived government management," especially concerning war and the economy. It should be clear how easily these would fit into a strategic framework based on the obvious fact that parties and politicians pursue a number of goals in competition with others.[6]

Criminology has also been moving toward a strategic vision. A "routine-activity" approach emerged after 1979 with an emphasis on three entities: the potential offender, a suitable target, and a guardian capable of intervening.[7] When the target was a human victim, there were three players or potential players involved. When the target was property, the most likely guardian was that property's owner, again concentrating the model on three players. Crimes were more likely to occur in the absence of a guardian: police, of course, but also neighbors, bystanders, and property owners. Instead of moving in a strategic direction, however, this school adopted a behaviorist style that avoided motivations and placed crime in the context of large populations that could be studied with system metaphors.

Soon after, rational-choice theory was adapted to the study of crime, potentially filling some of the cognitive gaps of routine-activity theories.[8]

Criminologists usefully avoided some of the narrow models economists had applied to crime: the maximization of primarily or exclusively monetary rewards, the choice of crime as a distinct occupation, and a narrow, mathematical definition of rationality. With the recognition of how bounded rationality is came an expansive view in which rationality consisted of little more than this: criminals make a few decisions here and there, process some information about their environments, and must continually decide whether to continue, cease, or switch to other crimes. Rational-choice and routine-activity approaches both see criminals as having goals, acting in response to their situations (arenas), and anticipating and responding to other players. Both approaches focus on actions or events rather than on propensities—on crimes rather than "criminality."

Research on organizations, firms, and markets could also benefit from a more strategic perspective. Markets are arenas in which firms compete with each other, but other players include components of the state, organized groups of consumers, and other pressure groups (such as environmentalists). Foreign firms are often distinct players, sometimes backed by their own governments. Neil Fligstein has offered an explicitly strategic model of firms, but he posits only a single goal—stability—in an effort to counter the single goal of economic models—profit.[9] In my view, one of the benefits of a strategic approach should be to reveal recurrent clashes of goals, especially as individual executives defect from their teams (corporations) in pursuit of personal rewards. (Since the publication of his book, a lot of this behavior has been uncovered at firms like Enron, Tyco, Worldcom, and Parmalat.) I suspect that the most interesting strategic interaction occurs not between firms but within them.

Even public health is a field of social science that has shown signs of shifting to a strategic vision in recent years. Bruce Link and Jo Phelan, for example, have reexamined the McKeown thesis about the fundamental causes of disease, which suggests that the dramatic improvements in health and thus increases in population over the last two centuries "owe more to changes in broad economic and social conditions than to specific medical advances or public health initiatives." Instead, Link and Phelan find, people use new knowledge, interactions, and resources to actively pursue better health; there is no automatic process. Although most of what they do involves instrumental action, some of the work entails strategic interactions with others, especially health professionals. Those with more resources and skills deploy them to gain better health.[10]

Classic sociological and economic studies of individual mobility and earnings might also benefit from a more strategic orientation. The best of them, such as those by Christopher Jencks, have found large amounts of variance that could not be explained by ascriptive traits or structural factors.[11] Skills are important, but we know little about *which* skills matter. Test scores, for instance, thought to capture cognitive skills, contribute only mildly to success. I suspect that much of the unexplained variance is due to strategic capacities. Physical attractiveness, while irrelevant to job performance in the narrowest sense, may enhance interactive success—in both acquiring a job and doing well at it.[12] Charm, empathy, emotional intelligence, self-confidence, and other strategic capabilities must matter enormously. Goals probably do also: those who want to make money usually make more than those who do not care so much. Strategic skills matter for success at least as much as technical and cognitive ones.[13]

Similarly, strategic projects help reproduce hierarchies such as gender, race, and class. Most obviously, the groups favored by these hierarchies work hard, and sometimes concertedly, to maintain existing arenas and boundaries, to protect their resources and gain new skills. Elites busy themselves with maintaining their dominance.[14] But individuals, in addition, often reproduce these arrangements. Women, for instance, bargain less aggressively than men—and usually care more about fairness and other collective goals, reflecting Carol Gilligan's famous ethic of care.[15] African Americans, too, seem to value and pursue collective goals more than white Americans.[16] Collective identities and players must be created; they are never given by nature.

In my opinion no field of research cries out for a strategic rethinking more than the study of class. For a hundred and fifty years, scholars and activists have searched for structures lying beneath class loyalties, primarily in the hunt for reliable allies for the working class. Can those who work with their heads rather than their hands be trusted? What about those "unproductive" workers who do not, in Marx's model, generate surplus value and so are not exploited by others? Perhaps engineers are part of the working class if their work conditions are sufficiently miserable. Despite Sisyphean efforts, no structural factors have been found that regularly predict political sympathies and actions. The reason? *Class is a strategic construct*, a rhetorical accomplishment of those trying to organize political parties that speak in the name of oppressed segments of society. The "working class" proved, at least for part of the nineteenth and twentieth centuries, a resonant rallying cry and identity. Indeed, it worked well because it appealed to large segments of the middle class at least as much as to factory workers.

To the extent there has been a "working class" political agenda, it was due to the strategic construction of the working class as a player, not to economic structures that made "workers" the same. (I am not saying that the control of resources and positions does not matter—but "class" adds to this the idea that political solidarities tend to arise automatically from them. Class labels are strategic and rhetorical accomplishments.)

International relations, home of so much strategic insight already, is becoming even more strategic in many quarters, as the structural vision of traditional realism is split open to get at the interaction inside. Yale Ferguson and Richard Mansbach have called for researchers to pay greater attention to the subjective side of politics, to conduct research flexibly across different levels (arenas), especially domestic and international, and to recognize people's competing loyalties to different groups and institutions.[17] Their suggestion that we be empirical without being empiricist is one I have intended to follow in this book. I have turned to empirical studies to build a language of strategy without reifying any particular source of evidence into the ultimate clincher. I have tried to develop an approach that would be sensitive to historical context, that would be social rather than mathematical. This will be the greatest realism of all.

Sociologists need to shake off their structural and situational biases if they are to improve their explanations of the large areas of social life in which humans interact with purpose. They need to recognize strategy, not hide their heads in the sand and complain about the rationalists. Political scientists, economists, and many psychologists need to shake off the slumber of mathematical game theory, to recognize and incorporate arenas, culture, emotions, and other aspects of strategic action long ignored. Fortunately, there are signs of progress on both sides of this great divide. To meet in the middle requires a new, truly social, approach to strategy, a direction in which this book has only pointed.

APPENDIX
RULES OF STRATEGIC ACTION

A number of analysts of politics, war, protest, and business have tried to list the major rules of strategic choice. To be generally valid, these rules must be quite abstract, as in this list by the great twentieth-century community organizer Saul Alinsky:[1]

1. Power is not only what you have but what the enemy thinks you have.
2. Never go outside the experience of your people.
3. Wherever possible go outside the experience of the enemy.
4. Make the enemy live up to their own book of rules.
5. Ridicule is man's most potent weapon.
6. A good tactic is one that your people enjoy.
7. A tactic that drags on too long becomes a drag.
8. Keep the pressure on.
9. The threat is usually more terrifying than the thing itself.
10. The major premise for tactics is the development of operations that will maintain a constant pressure upon the opposition.
11. If you push a negative hard and deep enough it will break through into its counterside.
12. The price of a successful attack is a constructive alternative.
13. Pick the target, freeze it, personalize it, and polarize it.

These are familiar principles of managing attention and emotion, which good strategists know intuitively. They are simple because, if you push them further, you are smack in the middle of dilemmas (merely skirted in Alinsky's list) that have no easy or universal answers.

B. H. Liddell Hart, the great military strategist of twentieth-century Britain, compiled a similar list:[2]

1. Adjust your end to your means.
2. Keep your object always in mind, while adapting your plan to circumstances.
3. Choose the line (or course) of least expectation.
4. Exploit the line of least resistance—so long as it can lead you to any objective which would contribute to your underlying object.
5. Take a line of operation which offers alternative objectives.
6. Ensure that both plan and dispositions are flexible—adaptable to circumstances.
7. Do not throw your weight into a stroke whilst your opponent is on guard—whilst he is well placed to parry or evade it.
8. Do not renew an attack along the same line (or in the same form) after it has once failed.

Flexibility. A little surprise. Especially flexibility in pursuing an advantage, when your opponent has made poor choices. Again, though, much of Liddell Hart's adaptability consists of choices. His goal is to maximize the number of choices open to you.

A rather different list was given by one of Mao's revolutionary generals, P'eng The-huai, whom Edgar Snow interviewed in 1936.[3] His approach lies between Alinsky's, designed for those with few resources, and Liddell Hart's. It also reflects Sun Tsu's emphasis on stealth and surprise, crucial for a weaker player.

1. Partisans must not fight any losing battles.
2. Surprise is the main offensive tactic of the well-led partisan group.
3. A careful and detailed plan of attack, and especially of retreat, must be worked out before any engagement is offered or accepted.
4. The greatest attention must be paid to the *min-t'uan* [landlords' local militia, designed for putting down peasant uprisings], . . . which must be destroyed militarily, but must, if at all possible, be won over politically to the side of the masses.
5. In a regular engagement with enemy troops, the partisans must exceed the enemy in numbers. But if the enemy's regular troops are moving, resting, or poorly guarded, a swift, determined, surprise flank attack on an organically vital spot of the enemy's line can be made by a much smaller group.

6. In actual combat the partisan line must have the greatest elasticity. Once it becomes obvious that their calculation of enemy strength or preparedness or fighting power is in error, the partisans should be able to disengage and withdraw with the same speed as they began the attack.
7. The tactics of distraction, decoy, diversion, ambush, feint, and irritation must be mastered. In Chinese these tactics are called "the principle of pretending to attack the east while attacking the west."
8. Partisans must avoid engagements with the main force of the enemy, concentrating on the weakest link, or the most vital.
9. Every precaution must be taken to prevent the enemy from locating the partisans' main forces. . . . Secrecy in the movements of the partisans is absolutely essential to success.
10. Besides superior mobility, the partisans, being inseparable from the local masses, have the advantage of superior intelligence, and the greatest use must be made of this.

Surprise and flexibility again lead the list. Pretend to attack the east when you are actually attacking the west. Apparently, a speedy retreat was not considered a loss. This may reflect Eastern traditions in which deception was valued as an aid to the weak, whereas most Western military traditions have favored the massing of overwhelming strength.

Because many popular works on strategic choice are written for corporate managers, they focus on internal operations, the coordination of your team's actions. J. Edward Russo and Paul J. H. Schoemaker list the following rules for avoiding "decision traps":[4]

1. Don't plunge in before you have gathered information and thought about the situation.
2. Don't set out to solve the wrong problem because you have framed it badly in the beginning.
3. Try to frame the problem in more ways than one.
4. Don't be so confident in your own opinion that you fail to gather key information.
5. Avoid decision-making shortcuts that rely too heavily on information simply because it is easy to obtain.
6. Try to use your information systematically rather than shooting from the hip.

7. Group decision making must be managed; don't assume that the right choice will emerge automatically.
8. Make the most of past lessons, even if they are painful to your ego.
9. Keep systematic track of what has worked and what has failed in the past.
10. Monitor your own decision-making processes to avoid these mistakes.

These lessons add up to little more than this: rely on empirical evidence more than on your own hunches, which will always be biased in a variety of ways that you may not even be aware of.

Little lists like these might occasionally help a strategic player avoid a mistake or think freshly about a problem by stimulating a chain of thought. But no list can be more than suggestive. It cannot tell you much about what to do, as every context is complex and challenging in new ways. My approach, instead, has been to identify the choices you might encounter, setting them in cultural and institutional contexts. Only the players themselves can make the calls. Unlike game theory, a normative endeavor, my project is primarily explanatory or descriptive. Looking over my dilemmas will not tell players what to do, although it may trigger some new thoughts about overlooked options. Most of all, they will be more aware of the potential risks and benefits of their many options.

NOTES

INTRODUCTION → THE POLITICS OF SOCIAL LIFE

1. I will loosely, and probably not consistently, distinguish between groups (voluntary and usually face-to-face), organizations (formal and usually legally defined), and collectivities (categories and imagined communities, with or without legal boundaries). A compound player normally has (1) some sense of identity, (2) some control over resources, (3) some ability to discourage defections, (4) goals distinct from those of individual members, and (5) some capacity for internal coordination, control, and communication. For a related definition see Arthur Stinchcombe, "Monopolistic Competition as a Mechanism," in *Social Mechanisms*, ed. Peter Hedström and Richard Swedberg (Cambridge: Cambridge University Press, 1998), 287.

2. Economic models of social and political life are more common—indeed, ubiquitous. The most thorough by a sociologist is James Coleman's *Foundations of Social Theory* (Cambridge, MA: Harvard University Press, 1990). For detailed treatment of the many limits to economic metaphors (social interaction as exchange, human motivation as profit maximization), see Lars Udehn, *The Limits of Public Choice* (London: Routledge, 1996). Coleman's root metaphor of exchange works better in some areas of social life than others, just as my strategic model does. The difference is that mine is not meant as an exhaustive theory of social action, as his was. Interaction can be reduced to exchange only by reifying human satisfactions into "things" that can be transferred.

3. Erving Goffman pointed out a crucial difference between strategic interactions and interactions with physical nature. *You cannot cheat with nature*, but you almost always can in human games by switching the kind of game you are playing. You can deal cards from the bottom of the deck, bribe judges in trials, use your influence behind the scenes, and so on. The "loose games" of real life

are not pure; a number of games are always going on at once—suggesting that a game may not be a good metaphor for the complex strategic interactions of humans.

4. Considerable strategic action is aimed at getting people to believe certain things—but in preparation for future actions and statements, not usually for the sake of the belief itself, as is true for communicative action.

5. Georg Simmel, *Conflict and the Web of Group-Affiliations* (1923; repr., New York: Free Press, 1955), 14.

6. In *Politics and Markets* (New York: Basic Books, 1977), Charles Lindblom distinguishes three basic systems of social control: persuasion, exchange, and authority. (He mentions physical constraint, but oddly finds it of little consequence, perhaps because he is interested in normal political-economic organization rather than strategic action.) To me, authority is a provisional precipitate out of the other three, and depends on them (or the threat of their use) for its effectiveness. Authority can vanish instantly, for instance, when it is used illegitimately.

Ralph Turner and Lewis Killian, in *Collective Behavior* (Englewood Cliffs, NJ: Prentice-Hall, 1987), list persuasion, facilitation, bargaining, and coercion. Facilitation is often accomplished with the aid of payments, although it also suggests cooperative arrangements of other kinds. Bargaining, to me, consists of promises of coercion, persuasion, or money.

Raymond Aron, in *Peace and War* (1962; repr., New Brunswick, NJ: Transaction, 2003), gives payment, coercion, and persuasion an institutional grounding by speaking of three kinds of secular power or regime: economic, military, and political (299).

7. Rhetoric is a lost art for both practitioners and theorists. In the twentieth century scholars like I. A. Richards and Kenneth Burke broadened the term from the interaction between orator and audience to encompass meanings in all settings. This move "saved" rhetoric from modernist critics who saw it as "empty words," but left it vulnerable to other approaches to meaning, especially semiotic, text-based metaphors derived from French structuralism.

8. Ann Swidler described culture as a tool kit in "Culture in Action: Symbols and Strategies," *American Sociological Review* 51 (1986): 273–86. Although Swidler used "strategy" in too broad a sense, she suggested a way out of the semiotic model of culture based on the metaphor of language, which saw culture as highly constraining, outside our conscious awareness, slow to change, and relatively shared within national boundaries.

9. Thomas Cronin and Michael Genovese, *The Paradoxes of the American Presidency* (Oxford: Oxford University Press, 1998), vii.

10. One reason situationalists have avoided strategic interaction and gamesters have oversimplified it is that it involves extremely complex causal effects: not only is there immediate feedback, but each action is taken in anticipation of

that response. We can model these processes with precision only when the expectations reach some kind of equilibrium—the gamester's dream. Equilibria are uncommon outside the neat world of game theory's models. Karl Weick pointed out that we recognize one-way causal impacts ("causal arcs") more easily than two-way causation ("circuits"), but even the latter is simple relative to strategic expectations; see his "Middle Range Theories of Social Systems," *Behavioral Science* 19 (1974): 357–67.

CHAPTER 1 → STARTING POINTS

1. As critics of official statistics might guess, we did not report this robbery to the police—though we might have if they had gotten my hat.
2. Raymond Boudon, *La Logique du Social* (Paris: Librairie Hachette, 1979).
3. See Colin Camerer, George Loewenstein, and Matthew Rabin, eds., *Advances in Behavioral Economics* (New York: Russell Sage; Princeton, NJ: Princeton University Press, 2003) for a recent collection of relevant essays with a good introduction.
4. Anthony Giddens, *Modernity and Self-Identity* (Stanford, CA: Stanford University Press, 1991), 112, 114.
5. Erving Goffman, *Behavior in Public Places* (New York: Free Press, 1963).
6. Anthony Giddens, *The Consequences of Modernity* (Stanford, CA: Stanford University Press, 1990), 134–37. He cites Raymond Williams, who called politics in this accepting mode "Plan X."
7. As I have argued elsewhere, our moods typically persist from one setting to the next, unlike reflex emotions such as anger and fear. And our affective loyalties (love, hate, trust, respect) usually last even longer than our moods. The fourth type of emotion, in my view, comprises the moral emotions such as compassion, courage, or jealousy. See my "Motivation and Emotion," in the *Oxford Handbook of Contextual Political Analysis*, ed. Robert Goodin and Charles Tilly (Oxford: Oxford University Press, 2006).
8. According to game theorists, "A player will not move from an initial state if this move (i) leads to a less preferred final state (i.e., outcome); or (ii) returns play to the initial state (i.e., makes the initial state the outcome)"; Steven Brams, *Theory of Moves* (Cambridge: Cambridge University Press, 1994), 27. See also Marc Kilgour and Frank Zagare, "Holding Power in Sequential Games," *International Interactions* 13 (1987): 91–114.
9. Michel Foucault's work emphasized power as this ability to accomplish things, which requires all the various mobilizing and disciplinary techniques he describes.
10. For most people, anxiety increases when they do not feel in control of a situation; good leaders therefore try to make their teams feel that they *are* in control. Except for hegemonic players (those who are disproportionately more

powerful than others), however, strategic interaction is rarely under our control—and sometimes not even for hegemons.

11. On the personal costs of political strategy, see Ken Wiwa's memoir of his father, Ken Saro-Wiwa, a martyred rights campaigner in Nigeria: *In the Shadow of a Saint* (South Royalton, VT: Steerforth, 2001).

12. David Halberstam, in *War in a Time of Peace* (New York: Scribner, 2001), documents American commanders' reluctance to intervene in small, messy conflicts that pose little threat to the United States. Bush II showed no such reluctance.

13. The ability of one person to slow or derail everything is well known. In one academic version, I heard Charles Tilly refer to William Goode, who called this "the principle of the least moral member," thinking especially of committees. In *The Mystery of Courage* William Miller describes the failure of bodies in combat: "The body just goes its own way and the soldier looks on in dismay" (Cambridge, MA: Harvard University Press, 2000), 112.

14. Carl von Clausewitz, *On War* (1832; repr., Princeton, NJ: Princeton University Press, 1976).

15. Hannah Arendt, *The Human Condition* (Garden City, NY: Doubleday, 1959), 162.

16. Game theorists have discovered that the ability to choose interaction partners is an enormous advantage, as great as the choice of strategy: see Toshio Yamagishi, Nahoko Hayashi, and Nobuhito Jin, "Prisoner's Dilemma Networks: Selection Strategy versus Action Strategy," in *Social Dilemmas and Cooperation*, ed. Ulrich Schulz, Wulf Albers, and Ulrich Mueller (Berlin: Springer-Verlag, 1994). Game theorists have not yet modeled the entrances and exits of new players into a game.

17. Michael Burawoy quotes an operator: "I caught Eddie timing me with his back turned the other day. He was listening to the machine to see when I finished a piece. . . . You won't think he's watching you, but he'll be listening to your machine." *Manufacturing Consent* (Chicago: University of Chicago Press, 1979), 164.

18. Francesca Polletta has shown that the first students to engage in "sit-ins" in the civil rights movement insisted that their actions were spontaneous. This rhetoric served several functions, including a rejection of the labels "political" and "strategic." See "It Was Like a Fever . . .': Narrative and Identity in Social Protest," *Social Problems* 45 (1998): 137–59; and "Plotting Protest," in *Stories of Change*, by Joseph Davis (Albany: SUNY Press, 2002).

19. M. P. Baumgartner, *The Moral Order of a Suburb* (Oxford: Oxford University Press, 1988).

20. Diane Vaughan, *Uncoupling* (Oxford: Oxford University Press, 1986), 135.

21. Helmuth von Moltke recounted his experience of such a dilemma in Turkey. In the war between Constantinople and Cairo, he advised Hafiz Pasha to take up a strong defensive position, but Hafiz followed his other advisors, who urged

him to attack despite the risks. The result was a thorough rout. See Otto Friedrich, *Blood and Iron* (New York: HarperCollins, 1995), 74.

22. Early animal-rights efforts were also surprisingly successful: see James M. Jasper and Jane Poulsen, "Fighting Back: Vulnerabilities, Blunders, and Countermobilization by the Targets in Three Animal Rights Campaigns," *Sociological Forum* 8 (1993): 639–57.

23. Paul Farmer documents this asymmetry for Haitian voodoo in *AIDS and Accusation* (Berkeley and Los Angeles: University of California Press, 1993), 98.

24. Quoted in Robin Wagner-Pacifici, *Theorizing the Standoff* (Cambridge: Cambridge University Press, 2000), 99.

25. Robert Jervis points out this trade-off in *The Logic of Images in International Relations* (New York: Columbia University Press, 1989), 55.

26. Diane Vaughan documents this among couples who are breaking up (*Uncoupling*, 78). Even when one of the partners has decided to get out, both may collaborate in pretending this is not what is happening. "The initiator will not risk losing the relationship until he or she has created what seems to be a secure niche elsewhere." She gets at the underlying resistance to change: "It's hard to pose questions when we suspect the answers may cause us to rearrange our lives, even temporarily" (76).

27. See, for example, Kenneth Waltz, "The Stability of a Bipolar World," *Daedalus* 93 (1964): 881–909, versus Karl Deutsch and J. David Singer, "Multipolar Power Systems and International Stability," *World Politics* 16 (1964): 390–406, and Dale Copeland, "Neorealism and the Myth of Bipolar Stability," *Security Studies* 5 (1996): 29–89. Waltz's and Copeland's ideal-typical superpowers simply make different choices when confronting the Engagement Dilemma: Copeland's are willing to accept the risks of engagement, and Waltz's are not.

28. Thomas Christensen and Jack Snyder, "Chain Gangs and Passed Bucks: Predicting Alliance Patterns in Multipolarity," *International Organization* 44 (1990): 137–68.

29. John Keegan, *The Mask of Command* (New York: Penguin, 1987), 71.

30. Inga Clendinnen, *Ambivalent Conquests* (Cambridge: Cambridge University Press, 1987), 33.

31. *The Military Maxims of Napoleon* (New York: Da Capo, 1995), 78.

32. Miller, *Mystery of Courage*, 106.

33. Beth Roy describes a Hindu-Muslim conflict in a Bangladeshi village in which each side lined up in front of their homes to protect them, forming two long lines roughly facing each other. "The positions were overtly defensive, but they also had the character of an aggressive face-off. The main form of battle was sedentary"; see *Some Trouble with Cows* (Berkeley and Los Angeles: University of California Press, 1994), 80.

34. Barry Buzan, *People, States and Fear*, 2nd ed. (New York: Harvester Wheatsheaf, 1991), 297.

35. Stuart Bremer, "Dangerous Dyads: Conditions Affecting the Likelihood of Interstate War, 1816–1965," *Journal of Conflict Resolution* 36 (1992): 309–41.

36. Daniel Geller and J. David Singer, *Nations at War* (Cambridge: Cambridge University Press, 1998), 67.

37. Here is an example of how hard it is to predict the outcomes of complex strategic interactions. In 1994 the well-funded (by the CIA) State Failure Task Force set out to predict "state failure" in the world's nations, gathering a large set of mostly structural data (more than one thousand variables). How did they do? In a word, abysmally. For an evaluation, see Gary King and Langche Zeng, "Improving Forecasts of State Failure," *World Politics* 53 (2001): 623–58.

CHAPTER 2 → THREATS

1. Robert Jervis, *Perception and Misperception in International Politics* (Princeton, NJ: Princeton University Press, 1976). In *Fear* (Princeton, NJ: Princeton University Press, 2003), Corey Robin examines many uses of fear in politics, as well as social science's striking suppression of these dynamics in its models.

2. Anthony Giddens, *The Constitution of Society* (Berkeley and Los Angeles: University of California Press, 1984), 50. I have elaborated on this concept, and more generally on threat as a motivation, in *The Art of Moral Protest* (Chicago: University of Chicago Press, 1997), especially 122–26. Giddens draws on Husserl and Schutz and the concept of a taken-for-granted "lifeworld." For an oversocialized version of the latter, which sees it as dealing with the social rather than the physical world, see Jürgen Habermas, *The Theory of Communicative Action*, vol. 1, *Lifeworld and System* (Boston: Beacon, 1987).

3. See, for example, Theodor Adorno and Max Horkheimer, *The Dialectic of Enlightenment* (1944; repr., New York: Herder & Herder, 1972); Ernst Cassirer, *The Myth of the State* (New Haven, CT: Yale University Press, 1946); and Hans Blumenberg, *Work on Myth* (Cambridge, MA: MIT Press, 1989).

4. This was the gist of extensive research on attitudes toward nuclear energy and other risky technologies. The meaning of "fairly distributed" includes not affecting future generations, and "controllable" implies "voluntary." For a neat summary, see Paul Slovic, Baruch Fischhoff, and Sarah Lichtenstein, "Facts and Fears: Understanding Perceived Risk," in *Societal Risk Assessment: How Safe Is Safe Enough?* ed. Richard Schwing and Walter Albers Jr. (New York: Plenum, 1980). The antismoking movement would seem to be an exception, although much of its rhetorical force derives from the unfairness of second-hand smoke, out of its victims' control. Amusingly, in light of the subsequent rise of the antismoking movement, the field of risk-perception research was stimulated by the paradoxical contrast between widespread opposition to nuclear energy and complacency about tobacco use; see Chauncey Starr, "Social Benefit Versus Technological Risk," *Science* 165 (1969): 1232.

5. David Hume, *A Treatise of Human Nature* (1739–40; repr., New York: Penguin Books, 1969), 534.

6. Daniel Kahneman and Amos Tversky, "Prospect Theory: An Analysis of Decision under Risk," *Econometrica* 47 (1979): 263–91; George Quattrone and Amos Tversky, "Contrasting Rational and Political Analyses of Political Choice," *American Political Science Review* 82 (1988): 719–36. Later overviews include Richard Thaler, "Mental Accounting Matters," and Colin Camerer, "Prospect Theory in the Wild: Evidence from the Field," in *Advances in Behavioral Economics*, ed. Colin Camerer, George Loewenstein, and Matthew Rabin (New York: Russell Sage; Princeton, NJ: Princeton University Press, 2003). Michal Strahilevitz and George Loewenstein, in "The Effect of Ownership History on the Valuation of Objects" (*Journal of Consumer Research* 25 [1998]: 276–89), found that people value objects they own more highly than those they do not—but not as highly as those they had owned for a long time and recently lost! Alas, the vast field of behavioral economics has developed almost entirely through laboratory experiments that translate goals into money—brilliant work that misses most of the emotional and other complexities of strategic action.

7. Harry Stack Sullivan, *The Interpersonal Theory of Psychiatry* (New York: W. W. Norton, 1953).

8. "It is usually much easier for the average person to inspire another individual with distrust and suspicion toward a third, previously indifferent person than with confidence and sympathy"; see Georg Simmel, *Conflict and the Web of Group-Affiliations* (Glencoe, IL: Free Press, 1955), 30.

9. Tamar Levin, "Schools Across U.S. Await Ruling on Drug Tests," *New York Times*, 20 March 2002.

10. Georg Simmel, *Georg Simmel on Individuality and Social Forms*, ed. Donald N. Levine (Chicago: University of Chicago Press, 1971), 103.

11. Robert Wren, *Achebe's World* (Washington, DC: Three Continents, 1980), 132–33.

12. Robert Solomon, *Love* (Garden City, NY: Doubleday, 1981), 3–4.

13. John Skowronski and Donal Carlston, "Negativity and Extremity Biases in Impression Formation: A Review of Explanations," *Psychological Bulletin* 105 (1989): 131–42; Richard Lau, "Negativity in Political Perception," *Political Behavior* 4 (1982): 353–77; and Paul Martin, "Inside the Black Box of Negative Campaign Effects," *Political Psychology* 25 (2004): 545–62.

14. George Marcus and Michael MacKuen, "Anxiety, Enthusiasm, and the Vote," *American Political Science Review* 87 (1993): 672–85.

15. David Sears and Carolyn Funk, "Self-Interest in Americans' Political Opinions," in *Beyond Self-Interest*, ed. Jane Mansbridge (Chicago: University of Chicago Press, 1990), 160–61.

16. Robert Kennedy, *Thirteen Days: The Missile Crisis* (New York: Signet, 1969), 109.

17. James Richardson, *Crisis Diplomacy: the Great Powers since the Mid-Nineteenth Century* (Cambridge: Cambridge University Press, 1994), 26–30.

18. On the political advantages of aristocratic anger, see Stephen White, "The Politics of Anger"; and Richard Barton, "'Zealous Anger' and the Renegotiation of Aristocratic Relationships in Eleventh- and Twelfth-Century France," in *Anger's Past*, ed. Barbara Rosenwein (Ithaca, NY: Cornell University Press, 1998).

19. Nathan McCall's autobiography, *Makes Me Wanna Holler* (New York: Random House, 1994), finds a similar honor culture, otherwise unusual in modern societies, among young men of the inner city.

20. David Lloyd George, quoted in Ima Barlow, *The Agadir Crisis* (Chapel Hill: University of North Carolina Press, 1940), 298.

21. Diane Vaughan, *Uncoupling* (Oxford: Oxford University Press, 1986), 31.

22. Jon Elster comments, "The fact that the experience of shame is so overwhelmingly painful ensures that it will not enter into decision making merely as a cost." In extreme cases we altogether discount the future; see *Alchemies of the Mind* (Cambridge: Cambridge University Press, 1999), 156.

23. Thomas Scheff, *Bloody Revenge* (Boulder, CO: Westview, 1994), 32.

24. Eli Berman and David Laitin speak of the "hereafter term" and the "altruism term" in the equations by which Palestinians calculate whether to become martyrs; see "Rational Martyrs: Evidence from Data on Suicide Attacks," in *Suicide Bombing from an Interdisciplinary Perspective*, ed. Eva Meyersson Milgrom (Princeton, NJ: Princeton University Press, forthcoming). This is an example of a game approach that can incorporate anything; the emotional dynamics of revenge against people the martyrs hate seems a more straightforward mechanism. To reduce the acts of violence to a collective public good seems misguided, too, as they are also directly satisfying to the martyrs.

25. Max Heirich, *The Spiral of Conflict* (New York: Columbia University Press, 1971).

26. I used the term to help explain recruitment into protest movements (especially of individuals who themselves sought out groups) in *The Art of Moral Protest*.

27. The legendary screenwriting teacher Richard McKee uses this term, getting at a protagonist's new desire to act, to redress imbalances, to pursue her goals. The centrality of moral shocks to narratives suggests that we sometimes retrospectively reinterpret an event as a shock that we did not feel as one at the time.

28. Simmel, again, described many of these emotions; see *Conflict*, 46.

29. Vaughan, *Uncoupling*, 81–82.

30. Jack Katz, *How Emotions Work* (Chicago: University of Chicago Press, 1999), 280–81.

31. Clifford Geertz, *The Interpretation of Cultures* (New York: Basic Books, 1973), 100.

32. Erving Goffman, "On Cooling the Mark Out," *Psychiatry* 15 (1952): 451–63. Goffman "situationalizes" much of his strategic insight by emphasizing roles and identities as intervening variables.

33. Philosopher Peter Winch called these "limiting notions," where the social rubs against the biological and raises questions that all cultures must answer, as different as those answers tend to be; see "Understanding a Primitive Society," in *Rationality*, ed. Bryan Wilson (Oxford: Basil Blackwell, 1970).

34. The emotions needed to "bump" people into or out of strategic engagement are not easily digested by game theory and rational-choice models in which "[p]eople do not act unless it seems to them profitable to do so"; see Harry Bredemeier, "Exchange Theory," in *A History of Sociological Analysis*, ed. Tom Bottomore and Robert Nisbet (New York: Basic Books, 1978), 435. Such emotions are not really costs or benefits, although rationalists tend to treat them as very short-term versions of these. Many emotions are more like means, accompanying action and forming part of its satisfactions and pains.

35. Erving Goffman, *Frame Analysis* (New York: Harper and Row, 1974), 22.

36. I explored some aspects of god and nature as rhetorical referents in "The Politics of Abstractions: Instrumental and Moralist Rhetorics in Public Debate," *Social Research* 59 (1992): 315–44.

37. Daniel Dennett, *The Intentional Stance* (Cambridge, MA: MIT Press, 1987), 21.

38. Werner Güth, Rolf Schmittberger, and Bernd Schwarze, "An Experimental Analysis of Ultimatum Bargaining," *Journal of Economic Behavior and Organization* 3 (1982): 367–88.

39. Colin Camerer, *Behavioral Game Theory* (New York: Russell Sage Foundation, 2003), 467.

40. Alain Touraine, *Comment Sortir du Libéralisme* (Paris: Arthème Fayard, 1998).

41. William Freudenburg, "Risk and Recreancy: Weber, the Division of Labor, and the Rationality of Risk Perceptions," *Social Forces* 71 (1993): 913. See also Anthony Giddens, *The Consequences of Modernity* (Stanford, CA: Stanford University Press, 1990).

42. The malfeasance of executives consists not only of mistakes but also of defections: they might ransack their division to make themselves look better as individuals (for instance, avoiding costly investments with payoffs in the distant future). See Robert Jackall, *Moral Mazes* (Oxford: Oxford University Press, 1988).

43. William Gamson, *Talking Politics* (Cambridge: Cambridge University Press, 1992), 32.

44. Candace Clark, *Misery and Company* (Chicago: University of Chicago Press, 1997), chap. 6. As a situationalist, Clark describes the "sympathy margin" we have for each other, but that boils down to prior offenses, which can be read in a much more strategic way as experience and information.

45. V. Lee Hamilton and Joseph Sanders, *Everyday Justice* (New Haven, CT: Yale University Press, 1992).

46. Machiavelli, *The Prince* (New York: W. W. Norton, 1992), 24.

47. In gamesters' experiments, and contrary to many of their early predictions, people prove willing to pay a considerable amount to punish those they feel have acted unfairly—to others as well as to themselves.

48. Alan Wertheimer, *Coercion* (Princeton, NJ: Princeton University Press, 1987), 204.

49. Kent Greenawalt, "Criminal Coercion and Freedom of Speech," *Northwestern University Law Review* 78 (1983), 1081–1124. In distinguishing three and four, Greenawalt is trying to get at the difference between legal and illegal threats. In warning threats, I am about to exercise an accepted right; in manipulative threats, I am interposing myself between two other parties for my own gain.

50. Goffman, *Frame Analysis*, 110.

51. As Steven Brams points out, threat is a solution to the "prisoner's dilemma"; because threat involves communication, it substitutes for solutions that rely on trust. See his *Theory of Moves* (Cambridge: Cambridge University Press, 1994), 139–40.

52. As Robert Jervis puts it in *The Logic of Images in International Relations* (New York: Columbia University Press, 1989), "[T]o restrain yet not alienate its allies, a state may want to prevent them from being confident that it will fulfill its obligations" (87).

CHAPTER 3 → GOALS

1. See William Niskanen, *Bureaucracy and Representative Government* (Chicago: Aldine-Atherton, 1971). Here is his justification for his reduction of a range of satisfactions: "salary, perquisites of the office, public reputation, power, patronage, output of the bureau, ease of making changes and ease of managing. All of these variables except the last two, I contend, are a positive monotonic function of the total *budget* of the bureau during the bureaucrat's tenure in office" (38).

2. But not necessarily a straw lizard: the complexity of human desires is one reason the future of game theory lies not in social science but in evolutionary biology, where the observer can define the payoffs (especially number of offspring) independently of the players' own subjective goals. Lizards play simple games; humans do not.

3. Henry Hamburger, *Games as Models of Social Phenomena* (San Francisco: W. H. Freeman, 1979), 46–47.

4. Game theorists have found some evidence for all the principles. For one recent comparison, see Ernan Haruvy and Dale Stahl, "Empirical Tests of Equilibrium

Selection Based on Player Heterogeneity," University of Texas Working Paper, March 1999.

5. Herbert Simon, "The State of American Political Science: Professor Lowi's View of Our Discipline," *PS: Political Science and Politics* 26 (1993): 49–51. Also James March and Herbert Simon, *Organizations* (New York: Wiley, 1958).

6. Richard Rosecrance, *International Relations: Peace or War?* (New York: McGraw-Hill, 1973).

7. Neil Fligstein, in *The Architecture of Markets* (Princeton, NJ: Princeton University Press, 2001), replaces profitability with stability, for instance.

8. Research on relative deprivation has survived despite criticism. Tom Tyler and Heather Smith, in "Social Justice and Social Movements" (in Daniel Gilbert, Susan Fiske, and Gardner Lindzey, eds., *Handbook of Social Psychology* [Boston: McGraw-Hill, 1998]), claim that sociological approaches to relative deprivation have emphasized the intrapersonal comparisons, social-psychological approaches the interpersonal comparisons. W. G. Runciman has also suggested that one can feel personally deprived or feel that one's group is deprived; see *Relative Deprivation and Social Justice* (London: Routledge and Kegan Paul, 1966). John Urry, in *Reference Groups and the Theory of Revolution* (London: Routledge and Kegan Paul, 1973), relates reference-group comparisons to culture: "The concept of the reference group was developed to help account for the observation that the range of social objects to which an actor may relate is not necessarily coincidental with the groups of which he is a member. . . . It is because of man's ability through symbols, language and communication to take on the role of the other that he is able to orient himself to groups other than those with which he is directly and continuously implicated" (17, 18).

9. Max Weber, *Economy and Society* (Berkeley and Los Angeles: University of California Press, 1978), 55.

10. Raymond Aron distinguishes security, power, glory, and idea as the "essentially heterogeneous objectives" behind foreign policy; see *Peace and War: A Theory of International Relations* (1962; repr., New Brunswick, NJ: Transaction, 2003), 71–93.

11. Harry A. Scarr, *Patterns of Burglary* (Washington, DC: U.S. Government Printing Office, 1972).

12. Of course, Iago replies, "Reputation is an idle and most false imposition, oft got without merit and lost without deserving. You have lost no reputation at all, unless you repute yourself such a loser" (Act 2, scene 3). Shakespeare not only suggests that different individuals have different goals (although we are meant to be shocked by Iago's cynical opinion), but that one important effect of reputation involves one's own ability to act (ends and means).

13. On the sparse evidence for this "truth," see James Jasper and Michael Young, "The Tricks of Paradigms: the Structural Truths of Social Movement Research,"

Sociological Forum 21 (forthcoming). This is a "truth" derived surreptitiously from rational-choice theory.

14. Jon Elster, *Alchemies of the Mind: Rationality and the Emotions* (Cambridge: Cambridge University Press, 1999), 149. Along with Tom Scheff's extensive work, this is the best introduction to shame's effects on strategic interactions.

15. Randall Collins, "Social Movements and the Focus of Emotional Attention," in *Passionate Politics*, ed. Jeff Goodwin, James Jasper, and Francesca Polletta (Chicago: University of Chicago Press, 2001), 27. See also Randall Collins, *Interaction Ritual Chains* (Princeton, NJ: Princeton University Press, 2004).

16. Jon Elster, in *Strong Feelings* (Cambridge, MA: MIT Press, 1999), adds addictions. I compare urges with other feelings in "Motivation and Emotion," in *The Oxford Handbook of Contextual Political Studies*, ed Robert Goodin and Charles Tilly (Oxford: Oxford University Press, 2006).

17. Neil Smelser, *Theory of Collective Behavior* (New York: Free Press, 1962), 55.

18. Peter Kollock, "Social Dilemmas," *Annual Review of Sociology* 24 (1998): 183–214.

19. "States," says Arthur Klein in a good discussion of many scope dilemmas (*Why Nations Cooperate* [Ithaca, NY: Cornell University Press, 1990]), "can cooperate and pursue liberal economic policies that improve global welfare and efficiency. Yet in some cases a nation can improve its relative economic position by defecting and cheating on others. Each course of action makes sense" (21). Trade and other economic policies are rarely global but cover regions and other clusters of nations.

20. Amartya Sen, *Development as Freedom* (New York: Random House, 1999).

21. Heinz Kohut and Ernest Wolf, "The Disorders of the Self and Their Treatment: An Outline," *International Journal of Psychoanalysis* 59 (1978): 414.

22. Ellen Langer reports a number of experiments in *The Psychology of Control* (Beverly Hills, CA: Sage, 1983). See also Daniel Wegner, *The Illusion of Conscious Will* (Cambridge, MA: MIT Press, 2002).

23. See Burawoy, *Manufacturing Consent* (Chicago: University of Chicago Press, 1979) although he (following Donald Roy) conflates games against management with those against the clock. The latter are not usually strategic in the same sense as the former.

24. Edward Shils, "Privacy and Power," in *Center and Periphery* (Chicago: University of Chicago Press, 1975).

25. Richard Rumelt, "Evaluation of Strategy: Theory and Models," in *Strategic Management*, ed. Dan Schendel and Charles Hofer (Boston: Little, Brown, 1979), 197.

26. Carl von Clausewitz, *On War* (1832; repr., Princeton, NJ: Princeton University Press, 1976).

27. George Will, *Men at Work* (New York: Macmillan, 1990), 3.

28. At this extreme, when one's strategy is outrageously immoral, people may

engage in what Robert Jay Lifton has called "doubling": "the division of the self into two functioning wholes, so that a part-self acts as an entire self. . . . One part of the self 'disavows' another part. What is repudiated is not reality itself—the individual Nazi doctor was aware of what he was doing via the Auschwitz self—but the meaning of that reality"; see *The Nazi Doctors* (New York: Basic Books, 1986), 418, 422.

29. Tzvetan Todorov argues that morally impure effectiveness is better than morally pure self-righteousness in *The Fragility of Goodness: Why Bulgaria's Jews Survived the Holocaust* (Princeton, NJ: Princeton University Press, 2001). As usual, I instead see a trade-off between the two.

30. Michael Young, "A Revolution of the Soul: Transformative Experiences and Immediate Abolition," in Goodwin, Jasper, and Polletta, eds., *Passionate Politics*, 113.

31. On some complications of money, see Viviana Zelizer, *The Social Meaning of Money* (New York: Basic Books, 1994).

32. Michael Walzer, *Spheres of Justice* (New York: Basic Books, 1983). Walzer shows how money tends to pollute other institutional spheres.

33. Catherine Campbell, *"Letting Them Die": Why HIV/AIDS Programmes Fail* (Oxford: James Currey, 2003).

34. Michael Porter, *Competitive Strategy* (New York: Free Press, 1980), xxvii.

35. In rationalist terms, people can manipulate their own character, the information they receive, or the costs and benefits of various actions. See Jon Elster, *Ulysses and the Sirens* (Cambridge: Cambridge University Press, 1979), part 2.

36. Abigail Saguy, *What Is Sexual Harassment?* (Berkeley and Los Angeles: University of California Press, 2003).

37. John Dewey, *Human Nature and Conduct* (New York: Holt, 1922).

38. In "On Cooling the Mark Out," Erving Goffman comments, "A person may leave a role and at the same time leave behind him the standards by which such roles are judged. The new thing that he becomes may be so different from the things he was that criteria such as success or failure cannot be easily applied to the change which has occurred" (*Psychiatry* 15 [1952]: 453).

39. To want education is already to care about the long term. As Jon Elster puts it, "To want to be motivated by remote consequences of present behavior *is* to be motivated by remote consequences of present behavior" (*Strong Feelings*, 161).

40. Alexis de Tocqueville, *The Old Regime and the French Revolution* (New York: Anchor, 1955), 177.

41. Richard Scott, *Organizations*, 2nd ed. (Englewood Cliffs, NJ: Prentice-Hall, 1987), 21.

42. Brien Hallett, *The Lost Art of Declaring War* (Urbana: University of Illinois Press, 1998), xi.

43. Tom Ridge, *New York Times*, 21 April 2003.

44. James Fallows, *Breaking the News* (New York: Pantheon, 1996).

45. Jon Elster, "Introduction," in *Rational Choice*, ed. Jon Elster (Washington Square, NY: New York University Press, 1986), 21; see also C. C. von Weizsäcker, "Notes on Endogenous Change of Tastes," *Journal of Economic Theory* 3 (1971): 345–72.

46. Alasdair MacIntyre, *After Virtue* (Notre Dame, IN: Notre Dame University Press, 1981), 175.

47. James March and Herbert Simon, *Organizations* (New York: John Wiley, 1958), 185.

48. Roland Bénabou and Jean Tirole, "Willpower and Personal Rules," *Journal of Political Economy* 112 (2004): 848–86.

49. Elster, *Strong Feelings*.

50. "Desires are not always the same as intentions," comments Daniel Wegner, "because they are sometimes descriptive of future circumstances that cannot be fulfilled with this act alone. . . . Still, it doesn't make much sense to attribute agency for an action to a conscious mind that doesn't want *something*, and for this reason philosophers of action seem to agree that a mental representation of one's desire is a key feature of the conscious willing of action" (*The Illusion of Conscious Will*, 19).

51. Jean-Paul Sartre, *L'Etre et le Néant* (Paris: Gallimard, 1943), 493.

52. Anthony Giddens writes, "But it makes no more sense to claim that every act or gesture is motivated—meaning that a definite 'motive' can be attached to it—than it does to treat action as involving a string of intentions or reasons." *The Constitution of Society* (Berkeley and Los Angeles: University of California Press, 1984), 50.

53. Christian Smith, *Moral, Believing Animals: Human Personhood and Culture* (Oxford: Oxford University Press, 2003).

CHAPTER 4 → CAPACITIES

1. The best account is in Taylor Branch, *Parting the Waters* (New York: Simon and Schuster, 1988).

2. Steven Kelman, *Making Public Policy* (New York: Basic Books, 1987), 42.

3. If you'll forgive me a fanciful parallel, some scholars persuade through the brute accumulation of evidence, others through clever interpretation based more on intuition than facts (of course, scholars tend to overestimate their knack for the latter).

4. Nietzsche, quoted in Bent Flyvbjerg, *Rationality and Power* (Chicago: University of Chicago Press, 1998), 37.

5. Napoleon, *The Military Maxims of Napoleon*, 58–59.

6. Victor Davis Hanson, *The Western Way of War* (Berkeley and Los Angeles:

University of California Press, 1989), and *Carnage and Culture* (New York: Random House, 2001).

7. Arthur Stinchcombe, *When Formality Works* (Chicago: University of Chicago Press, 2001), 134.

8. Edward Luttwak, *Strategy: The Logic of War and Peace* (Cambridge, MA: Harvard University Press, 2002), chap. 3.

9. In the 1970s the "resource mobilization" school of social-movement theory developed from the idea that people utterly lacking in resources have a hard time organizing themselves without outside help. It may have overestimated the degree of formal organization necessary to engage in strategic action, missing the trade-off between resources and good choices. See John McCarthy and Mayer Zald, "Resource Mobilization and Social Movements: A Partial Theory," *American Journal of Sociology* 82 (1977): 1212–41.

10. Scott Boorman, *The Protracted Game* (Oxford: Oxford University Press, 1969), 12.

11. Max Weber, "Socialism," in *Weber: Selections in Translation*, ed. W. G. Runciman (Cambridge: Cambridge University Press, 1978), 258.

12. Kingsley Davis, "The Demographic Foundations of National Power," in *Freedom and Control in Modern Society*, ed. Morroe Berger, Theodore Abel, and Charles Page (New York: Van Nostrand, 1954).

13. Luttwak discusses the mass bombing of Japan and Germany after their air defenses had been eliminated: "That was still warfare, *but the logic of strategy no longer applied*, because the enemy's reaction—indeed his very existence as a conscious, living entity—could simply be disregarded" (*Strategy*, 13). I think he has it wrong. Normal citizens were not players, but the nations' leaders were, and mass bombing was intended to force *them* to surrender.

14. Beth Roy, *Some Trouble with Cows: Making Sense of Social Conflict* (Berkeley and Los Angeles: University of California Press, 1994), 84.

15. Trying to interpret the concept of structures, William Sewell Jr. suggests that they are combinations of physical resources with the ideas that give them shape or put them into use, although it is not clear to me what we gain through this conceptual combination. See his "A Theory of Structure: Duality, Agency, and Transformation," *American Journal of Sociology* 98 (1992): 1–29.

16. Anthony Giddens, *The Constitution of Society* (Berkeley and Los Angeles: University of California Press, 1984), 33. Like Talcott Parons and Michel Foucault, Giddens less usefully distinguishes "allocative" resources, command over material objects, from "authoritative" resources, or command over people. The latter seems better described in other terms, such as rules, legitimacy, and so on. In his terminology, any advantage is labeled a resource.

17. William McNeill, *Plagues and Peoples* (Garden City, NY: Doubleday, 1977), 72.

18. Don Sherman Grant II and Michael Wallace, "Why Do Strikes Turn Violent?" *American Journal of Sociology* 96 (1991), 1131, 1147.

19. None other than sociologist Talcott Parsons commented that "an object which is useful as a facility comes to be cathected directly so that its possession is also interpreted by the actor and by others as a reward." Means such as money and power become accepted "as symbols of achievement, whether actual or potential." Talcott Parsons and Edward Shils, eds., *Toward a General Theory of Action* (Cambridge, MA: Harvard University Press, 1951), 202.

20. Max Weber, ever aware of how our means crowd out our ends, wrote that "since the specialized knowledge of the expert became more and more the foundation for the power of the officeholder, an early concern of the ruler was how to exploit the specialized knowledge of experts without having to abdicate in their favor" (*Economy and Society*, 994). Raymond Aron made a similar point about the military: "[D]iplomacy risks becoming a prisoner, at the crucial moment, of military mechanisms which must be prepared in advance, which the government remains free to set off or not, but which it can no longer modify" (*Peace and War* [New Brunswick, NJ: Transaction, 2003], 43).

21. Buzan sees "two obvious ways in which defence and security can work against each other: because the cost of defence compromises other security objectives, or because the risks of defence appear to outweigh the threats that defence is designed to deter" (*People, States and Fear* [New York: Harvester Wheatsheaf, 1991], 272).

22. Robert Jackall, *Moral Mazes* (Oxford: Oxford University Press, 1988), 52.

23. Machiavelli, *The Prince* (New York: W. W. Norton, 1992), 11.

24. Erving Goffman, *Strategic Interaction* (Philadelphia: University of Pennsylvania Press, 1970).

25. I prefer the term *charm* to *charisma* because of the long situationalist tradition that has addressed charisma as "above all, a relationship, a mingling of the inner selves of leader and follower" (Charles Lindholm, *Charisma* [Cambridge, MA: Blackwell, 1990], 7). At the extreme, situationalists act as though there is nothing unusual about charismatic leaders at all, as though they were entirely created by circumstances. This is always assumed, never demonstrated.

26. Baldassare Castiglione, quoted in Jorge Arditi, *A Genealogy of Manners* (Chicago: University of Chicago Press, 1998), 102. Arditi emphasizes the bodily aspects of the courtier's "je ne sais quoi": "Elegance, parsimony of movement, decorum, moderation, sociability, and courtesy in general, are unquestionably attributes of courtiership. But the concern with virility, strength, physical fitness, agility, and the exercises associated with the education of the good warrior are equally central" (107). These two tendencies are hardly alien to contemporary images of masculine charm.

27. Erving Goffman, *Interaction Ritual* (Garden City, NY: Doubleday, 1967), 9.

28. As Sei Shonagon observed in tenth-century Japan, "A preacher ought to be good-looking. For, if we are properly to understand his worthy sentiments, we must keep our eyes on him while he speaks; should we look away, we may

forget to listen." See *The Pillow Book of Sei Shonagon*, ed. and trans. Ivan Morris (Oxford: Oxford University Press, 1967), 33.

29. Dale Carnegie, *How to Win Friends and Influence People* (New York: Simon and Schuster, 1937), 146.

30. Rationalist Dennis Chong has shown that a good reputation helps maximize long-run gain, but he notes that it is easier to actually be a good person than to make everyone think you are when you are not. Many phenomena can be *made* compatible with a rationalist language in this cumbersome way. But the fact that things like a reputation are both a means and an end in themselves ultimately stymies this form of description. See Dennis Chong, *Collective Action and the Civil Rights Movement* (Chicago: University of Chicago Press, 1991).

31. Douglas C. Mitchell, "The Editorial Character," *Bookmark* (University of Chicago Press newsletter, summer 2004), 3.

32. James Dowd describes how U.S. army generals deal with the Charm Dilemma by distinguishing good ambition (oriented toward group goals) from bad (aimed at individual promotion and recognition); see his "Hard Jobs and Good Ambition: U.S. Army Generals and the Rhetoric of Modesty," *Symbolic Interaction* 23 (2000): 183–205.

33. Bjørn Lomborg, "Nucleus and Shield: The Evolution of Social Structure in the Iterated Prisoner's Dilemma," *American Sociological Review* 61 (1996): 278–307.

34. Candace Clark comments, "[S]ympathy giving begins with cognitive, emotional, or physical empathy, that is, in one way or another taking the role of the other" (*Misery and Company* [Chicago: University of Chicago Press, 1997], 78).

35. The American Psychiatric Association gives the following criteria for diagnosing antisocial personality disorder: "failure to conform to social norms with respect to lawful behaviors as indicated by repeatedly performing acts that are grounds for arrest; deceitfulness, as indicated by repeated lying, use of aliases, or conning others for personal profit or pleasure; impulsivity or failure to plan ahead; irritability and aggressiveness, as indicated by repeated fights or assaults; reckless disregard for safety of self or others; consistent irresponsibility, as indicated by repeated failure to sustain consistent work behavior or honor financial obligations; lack of remorse, as indicated by being indifferent to or rationalizing having hurt, mistreated, or stolen from another" (*Quick Reference to the Diagnostic Criteria from DSM-IV* [Washington, DC: American Psychiatric Association, 1994], 279–80). This could describe most of the great conquerors of history.

36. Psychologists have found a parallel in shows of intelligence, in which people undermine the tests used on them, knowing that they will no longer be accurate assessments of their intelligence. Because this leads to worse performance, it has been called "self-handicapping"; see Raymond L. Higgins, C. R. Snyder, and Steven Berglas, *Self-Handicapping* (New York: Plenum, 1990).

37. In *The Punic Wars* (London: Cassell, 2001), Adrian Goldsworthy makes Rome's

unwavering determination central to his explanation of its eventual triumph over Carthage.

38. When ibn Saud, founder of the Arabian dynasty, was wounded in battle—and rumored to have been "unmanned"—he immediately summoned a local sheikh to find a virgin, whom he married that night. He consummated the event in his tent in the middle of camp, insisting that everyone celebrate. Similarly, Wellington went out of his way to sleep with at least two of Napoleon's mistresses. Times have changed, somewhat, but physical prowess (in various areas) remains a key component of male charisma.

39. Walter Mischel, *Personality and Assessment* (New York: Wiley, 1968).

40. John Roemer calls it the "psychology of tyranny": subjects fear but hate you. See "Rationalizing Revolutionary Ideology," *Econometrica* 53 (1985): 85–108.

41. Stephen Skowronek, *The Politics Presidents Make* (Cambridge, MA: Harvard University Press, 1993), 17.

42. John Keegan, in *The Mask of Command* (New York: Penguin, 1987), describes a disagreement between Alexander the Great and his aged advisor Parmenio. The latter wanted to fight a naval battle against the larger Persian fleet, on the grounds that a defeat would not be very serious. Perhaps not in practical terms, but a defeat could devastate their army's morale. Alexander saw that it was important to feed success with success: "He could not risk sacrificing the skill and courage of the Macedonians; should they lose the engagement it would be a serious blow to their warlike prestige." This was also a short-run versus long-run trade-off, as "[t]he old general's thoughts were of immediate advantage in a local campaign, Alexander's of ultimate victory on the stage of the world" (42).

43. See Martin E. P. Seligman, *Helplessness* (San Francisco: W. H. Freeman, 1975), and *Learned Optimism* (New York: Knopf, 1991).

44. Marc Myers analyzes luck as a creation in *How to Make Luck* (Los Angeles: Renaissance, 1999). His suggestions? Make life look easy, but don't rub it in; make yourself appealing to other people; be curious; improve the lives of others; let power brokers own a piece of you; don't burn your bridges behind you.

45. Erik Erikson, *Childhood and Society*, 2nd ed. (New York: Norton, 1963), 247. This confidence rests on trust, according to Erikson.

46. In baseball, unequal resources (payrolls) generally overwhelm strategic choices, but there are exceptions, such as the Oakland Athletics' general manager Billy Beane, described by Michael Lewis in *Moneyball: The Art of Winning an Unfair Game* (New York: Norton, 2003).

47. Jon Elster, *Strong Feelings* (Cambridge, MA: MIT Press, 1999), 64.

48. Edward Gonzalez, *Cuba under Castro* (Boston: Houghton Mifflin, 1974).

49. The (distorting) influence of leaders' rhetoric on rank-and-file perceptions of their own efficacy is a problem for most game theories, which generally adopt rational-choice models of people's calculations. "Morale" is a widespread and

intentional solution to the so-called free-rider problem. Donald Green and Ian Shapiro address this scathingly in *Pathologies of Rational Choice* (New Haven, CT: Yale University Press, 1994), 85–88.

50. See, for instance, Ronald Toby, *State and Diplomacy in Early Modern Japan* (Princeton, NJ: Princeton University Press, 1984), chap. 3; and Charles Korr, *Cromwell and the New Model Foreign Policy* (Berkeley and Los Angeles: University of California Press, 1975).

51. On experts' overconfidence in their own predictions, see Sarah Lichtenstein and Baruch Fischoff, "Do Those Who Know More also Know More about How Much They Know?" *Organizational Behavior and Human Performance* 20 (1977): 159–83. On sources of expert bias, see Lee Clarke, *Mission Improbable* (Chicago: University of Chicago Press, 1999), 162–66. Dominic Johnson views overconfidence—or "positive illusions"—as a former evolutionary advantage, even while showing how it can lead nations into disastrous wars; see his *Overconfidence and Wars* (Cambridge, MA: Harvard University Press, 2004). Once again, absolute prescriptions fail, as overconfidence has both benefits and costs.

52. Robert Keohane observed that "the United States contracted a disease of the strong: refusal to adjust to change," in *After Hegemony* (Princeton, NJ: Princeton University Press, 1984), 179.

53. "With victory, all of the army's habits, procedures, structures, tactics, and methods will indiscriminately be confirmed as valid or even brilliant— including those that could benefit from improvement or even drastic reform" (Luttwak, *Strategy*, 19).

54. Lauren Alloy and Lyn Abramson, "Judgment of Contingency in Depressed and Nondepressed Students: Sadder but Wiser?" *Journal of Experimental Psychology: General* 108 (1979): 441–85; Lauren Alloy, ed., *Cognitive Processes in Depression* (New York: Guilford, 1988).

55. For a good discussion of the strategic capacities of organizations, see Marshall Ganz, "Resources and Resourcefulness: Strategic Capacity in the Unionization of California Agriculture, 1959–1966," *American Journal of Sociology* 105 (2000): 1003–62.

56. G. Cameron Hurst, *Insei* (New York: Columbia University Press, 1976).

57. See Flyvbjerg, *Rationality and Power*, especially chap. 10, for good examples of this infiltration and domination of committees by special parties. On EdF, see my *Nuclear Politics* (Princeton, NJ: Princeton University Press, 1990).

58. F. G. Bailey, *Humbuggery and Manipulation: The Art of Leadership* (Ithaca, NY: Cornell University Press, 1988), 14.

59. Erving Goffman, *Encounters* (Indianapolis, IN: Bobbs-Merrill, 1961), 55–61.

60. Nancy Whittier's *Feminist Generations* (Philadelphia, PA: Temple University Press, 1995) offers good examples and discussion of generational differences. I discussed tastes in tactics in *The Art of Moral Protest* (Chicago: University of Chicago Press, 1997), chap. 10.

1. Bert Klandermans notes, for example, that protest groups devote attention to authorities, to internal maintenance of the organization, to interactions with opponents, and to attracting new participants and resources. But the existing scholarly literature deals almost exclusively with the first interaction; see *The Social Psychology of Protest* (Oxford: Blackwell, 1997), 130–31. If analysts of protest overemphasize state players, business analysts underemphasize them. Michael Porter points to the multiple players a business faces, usefully moving beyond a simple focus on direct industry competitors to include buyers, suppliers, producers of substitute products, and potential entrants—but not regulators and other state agencies; see his *Competitive Strategy* (New York: Free Press, 1980).

2. Elisabeth Bumiller, "Behind Bush's Speech at U.N. Today, a White House on Edge," *New York Times*, 23 September 2003.

3. Audience metaphors are usually associated with formal theaters, with backstage and front, curtains, and a strong contrast between active players and passive audience. Perhaps a better image is the interaction at a bar or around a campfire, with different people taking turns at performing (although not necessarily equal turns).

4. On presidents, for example, see Samuel Kernell, *Going Public* (Washington, DC: Congressional Quarterly Books, 1986); on lobbyists, see Ken Kollman, *Outside Lobbying* (Princeton, NJ: Princeton University Press, 1998).

5. Edward Luttwak, *Strategy* (Cambridge, MA: Harvard University Press, 2002), 57–68.

6. For example, Weber wrote, "In Protestantism the external and internal conflict of the two structural principles—of the 'church' as a compulsory association for the administration of grace, and of the 'sect' as a voluntary association of religiously qualified persons—runs through the centuries from Zwingli to Kuyper and Stöcker"; see *From Max Weber* (Oxford: Oxford University Press, 1946), 314.

7. Jane Mansbridge argues that this is what happened to many of the groups fighting for the ERA in *Why We Lost the ERA* (Chicago: University of Chicago Press, 1986). Mary Douglas and Aaron Wildavsky make a similar argument for voluntary groups in *Risk and Culture* (Berkeley and Los Angeles: University of California Press, 1982).

8. Political scientists have elaborated on the Janus Dilemma to understand the relationship between foreign and domestic strategies. Michael Mastanduno, David Lake, and G. John Ikenberry use the term in "Toward a Realist Theory of State Action," *International Studies Quarterly* 33 (1989): 457–74. See also Robert Putnam, "Diplomacy and Domestic Politics," *International Organization* 42 (1988): 427–60; and Peter Evans, Harold Jacobson, and Robert Putnam, eds.,

Double-Edged Diplomacy (Berkeley and Los Angeles: University of California Press, 1993).

In another arena entirely, Francie Ostrower comments about elite board members of arts organizations: "Faced with heightened organizational need for funds, affluent trustees exhibit a receptivity to organizational accessibility and change that is surprisingly at odds with traditional images of elite exclusivity" (*Trustees of Culture* [Chicago: University of Chicago Press, 2002], 35). In other words they turn outward.

9. For one effort to read dilemmas as structural variability (that is, to see organizations as making the choices they have to, which of course leaves them no choice at all), see Walter Powell, "Expanding the Scope of Institutional Analysis," in *The New Institutionalism in Organizational Analysis*, ed. Walter Powell and Paul DiMaggio (Chicago: University of Chicago Press, 1991).

10. See Calvin Morrill, *The Executive Way* (Chicago: University of Chicago Press, 1995), 23.

11. Finding patrons is one of the main "solutions" to the challenges of collective action in rational-choice theory; see Mark Lichbach, *The Rebel's Dilemma* (Ann Arbor: University of Michigan Press, 1998), 177–93. He also recognizes the downside of patrons: external control.

12. See Georg Simmel, *The Sociology of Georg Simmel* (Glencoe, IL: Free Press, 1950), 148–49; also Theodore Caplow, *Two Against One: Coalitions in Triads* (Englewood Cliffs, NJ: Prentice-Hall, 1968).

13. Stephen Wilson, *Feuding, Conflict, and Banditry in Nineteenth-Century Corsica* (Cambridge: Cambridge University Press, 1988), 190.

14. Roger Gould, *Insurgent Identities* (Chicago: University of Chicago Press, 1995), 19–20.

15. See, for instance, Erik Ringmar, *Identity, Interest and Action: A Cultural Explanation of Sweden's Intervention in the Thirty Years War* (Cambridge: Cambridge University Press, 1996).

16. Azar Gat recounts French debates over this dilemma in the 1890s: "More exhaustive conscription for a shorter term of active service implied that, while the size of the regular army was slightly reduced, France was going to have many more trained men in case of war. It also followed that the regular army was now regarded less as a professional fighting force of seasoned soldiers and more as a training-school for the reserves" (*A History of Military Thought* [Oxford: Oxford University Press, 2001], 417). In an earlier case of over-extension, Darius lost to Alexander, despite having a much larger army, partly because he "had over-insured by including too many contingents of inferior or negligible worth, who in action would merely get in the way of the serious warriors"; see Keegan, *The Mask of Command* (New York: Viking 1987), 85.

17. Even nations face the Extension Dilemma, as Alberto Alesina and Enrico Spolaore show in *The Size of Nations* (Cambridge, MA: MIT Press, 2003).

18. T. M. S. Evens analyzes such a case in *Two Kinds of Rationality* (Minneapolis: University of Minnesota Press, 1995): a kibbutz expanded gradually to the point of considerable internal specialization, which was not recognized as a case of the Extension Dilemma but seen as generational strife.

19. Georg Simmel, *Conflict and the Web of Group Affiliations* (Glencoe, IL: Free Press, 1955), 101. Simmel also suggests that a group's unity is greater if there is a continual external threat than if hostilities actually occur (104).

20. "Despite Birth Bonuses, Zoroastrians in India Fade," *New York Times*, 23 April 2003.

21. Kenneth Lapides, ed., *Marx and Engels on the Trade Unions* (New York: Praeger, 1987), 141–42.

22. Eiko Ikegami, *The Taming of the Samurai* (Cambridge, MA: Harvard University Press, 1995), 27.

23. David Meyer, *A Winter of Discontent* (New York: Praeger, 1990), 224–25.

24. Todd Gitlin describes how many New Left leaders were unable to negotiate the Janus Dilemma, eventually abdicating as leaders altogether, in *The Whole World Is Watching* (Berkeley and Los Angeles: University of California Press, 1980).

25. Martin Ruef, Howard Aldrich, and Nancy Carter, "Don't Go to Strangers: Homophily, Strong Ties, and Isolation in the Formation of Organizational Founding Teams," paper presented at the 2002 meeting of the American Sociological Association (Chicago).

26. John Skrentny, *The Minority Rights Revolution* (Cambridge, MA: Harvard University Press, 2002), chap. 2.

27. One critic of strategic studies comments, "What escapes critical analysis in this tradition is the question of how states capable of conducting warfare emerge in the first place. . . . War as organized violence requires more than the marshaling of material resources. It requires human resources and forms of political identity" (Bradley Klein, *Strategic Studies and World Order* [Cambridge: Cambridge University Press, 1994], 37). In other words, there is a sociology behind the strategy. But situationalists make the opposite error, portraying allies as structural conditions. Thus Don Grant and Michael Wallace, in "Why Do Strikes Turn Violent?" include having "the pro-labor party in power" among the "political-institutional factors" affecting strike violence (*American Journal of Sociology* 96 [1991]: 1126). Fair enough, but this hides the effects of allies behind a structural curtain.

28. Erving Goffman, *The Presentation of Self in Everyday Life* (Harmondsworth: Penguin, 1959), 141–43.

29. Thomas Edsall and Mary Edsall discuss racial coding in American politics in *Chain Reaction* (New York: W. W. Norton, 1991).

30. Gary Alan Fine refers to audience segregation, hidden messages, and role distancing as three ways to deal with the problem of reaching diverse audiences with the same words (and actions, I would add); see *Difficult*

Reputations (Chicago: University of Chicago Press, 2001), 170. He notes that Goffman also recognized the audience-segregation dilemma, seeing it as a matter of role confusion. To me this adds an extra conceptual layer without adding to our understanding.

31. Michael Beschloss, *The Crisis Years* (New York: HarperCollins, 1991), 201.

32. Realists such as Kenneth Waltz, in their enthusiasm for deterministic models, once again hide the underlying dilemma.

33. Arjun Appadurai notes, in speaking of debates over globalization, "For polities of smaller scale, there is always a fear of cultural absorption by polities of larger scale, especially those that are near by. One man's imagined community is another man's political prison"; see "Disjuncture and Difference in the Global Cultural Economy," *Theory, Culture, and Society* 7 (1990): 295.

34. On Scandinavia, see Gösta Esping-Anderson, *Three Worlds of Welfare Capitalism* (Princeton, NJ: Princeton University Press, 1990); on Britain, the United States, and Canada, see Ann Orloff, *The Politics of Pensions* (Madison: University of Wisconsin Press, 1993); on Britain, and especially the United States, see Edwin Amenta, *Bold Relief* (Princeton, NJ: Princeton University Press, 1998).

35. I addressed this ideological distortion especially in "Three Nuclear Energy Controversies," in *Controversy*, ed. Dorothy Nelkin, 3rd ed. (Newbury Park, CA: Sage, 1992).

36. See James Jasper and Scott Sanders, "Big Institutions in Local Politics," *Social Science Information* 34 (1996): 491–509.

37. Robert Jervis, "Cooperation under the Security Dilemma," *World Politics* 30 (1978), 169. The original formulation comes from John Herz, *Political Realism and Political Idealism* (Chicago: University of Chicago Press, 1951).

CHAPTER 6 → ARENAS

1. Although Bourdieu uses the term *field* to emphasize the conflict beneath much social life, he makes the field implicit rather than explicit (I think it can be either): "In the social fields, which are the products of a long, slow process of autonomization, . . . one does not embark on the game by a conscious act, one is born into the game, with the game" (*The Logic of Practice* [Stanford, CA: Stanford University Press, 1990], 67). Bourdieu's structuralist aim is primarily to emphasize the relationships among elements in a field, which can exist independently of interaction.

2. F. G. Bailey calls arenas "structures" because, as a situationalist, he sees rules as things more than as variables. See *Stratagems and Spoils* (Boulder, CO: Westview, 2001). Political structures, he says, define what the prize will be, who is eligible to compete, the composition of teams, fair and unfair tactics, as well as—interestingly—rules to follow when rules have been broken.

Institutions are a similar concept, acknowledging patterned constraints and expectations. Ronald Jepperson contrasts institutionalized behaviors with actions: "The point is a general one: one enacts institutions; one takes action by departing from them, not by participating in them." See "Institutions, Institutional Effects, and Institutionalism," in *The New Institutionalism in Organizational Analysis*, ed. Walter Powell and Paul DiMaggio (Chicago: University of Chicago Press, 1991), 149. The tacit, taken-for-granted nature of institutions explains their appeal to situationalists, and arenas too must demonstrate some limits to strategic action. But arenas can be changed through action, whereas institutions must be—by Jepperson's definition—something else if actors set out to change them.

3. Erving Goffman, *Encounters* (Indianapolis, IN: Bobbs-Merrill, 1961), 65.

4. As Graham Allison and Philip Zelikow put it, "Increasing the number of participants in a decision process beyond a single mind helps a decision maker dodge many pitfalls. He or she will be less likely to misconceive the issue, neglect relevant interests in settling on one objective rather than another, or misestimate consequences, among other dangers. But these benefits have a price: namely, the inclusion of additional, autonomous interests" (*Essence of Decision* [New York: Longman, 1999], 271).

5. Joseph Persico, *Roosevelt's Secret War* (New York: Random House, 2001). The Japanese used the same codes through the end of the war, apparently having missed American newspaper headlines after the Battle of Midway that attributed the U.S. victory to advance knowledge (obtainable only by breaking the messages).

6. In the Napoleonic wars, Azar Gat observes, "Austria was totally dependent on her standing army, which was large, but expensive and difficult to replace. Safeguarding this army and ensuring that it was not rushed into major battle under less than favorable conditions were thus paramount considerations for both Daun and Charles, even to the point of letting many potentially decisive opportunities slip away" (*A History of Military Thought* [Oxford: Oxford University Press, 2001], 99). Alexander the Great preferred to build confidence through a series of smaller victories, refusing to risk a defeat, but Napoleon thought big victories built confidence best.

7. Edward Luttwak, *Strategy* (Cambridge, MA: Harvard University Press, 2001), 39–40.

8. Adam Heinrich Dietrich von Bülow developed a geometric approach to military strategy, much of which depended on the arcs describing how far an army could march from its supply base or into hostile territory. Too narrow an arc left them vulnerable to being cut off—a rather obvious point for which Bülow's elaborate geometry was unnecessary. It all depends on what you gain with your decisive salient—leading back to the Basket Dilemma. See *The Spirit of the Modern System of War* (London: Egerton, 1806). See also R. R. Palmer,

"Frederick the Great, Guibert, Bülow: From Dynastic to National War," in *Makers of Modern Strategy*, ed. Peter Paret (Princeton, NJ: Princeton University Press, 1986).

9. Ruth Benedict, *The Chrysanthemum and the Sword* (Boston: Houghton Mifflin, 1946), 30–31, 41.

10. For example, see Simmel, *Conflict and the Web of Group-Affiliations* (Glencoe, IL: Free Press, 1955).

11. Realists have distinguished relative and absolute gains, presenting the former as a distinctive component of their approach (e.g., see John Mearsheimer, "Back to the Future," *International Security* 15 [1990]: 5–56). If a player gets enough power *relative to you*, the theory goes, he will clobber you. But in many cases, the relative power is used to pursue other, absolute goals. In a truly player-based conflict, your goal is the defeat (or destruction or humiliation) of the other player.

12. On universities as big, bad players in local politics, see James Jasper and Scott Sanders, "Big Institutions in Local Politics," *Social Science Information* 34 (1996): 491–509.

13. See, for example, Niklas Luhmann, *Social Systems* (Stanford, CA: Stanford University Press, 1995).

14. T. V. Paul, *Asymmetric Conflicts* (Cambridge: Cambridge University Press, 1994).

15. As Steven Kelman puts it, after "precipitating events, . . . [a]dvocates work to attach preexisting solutions to newly perceived problems" (*Making Public Policy*, 39).

16. At the extreme, the systems theory of Luhmann and others sees arenas (restricted to legally defined institutional arenas) as so mutually autonomous that each is only part of the broader "environment" for the others. Such approaches ignore how conflicts spill across arenas as players enter new ones. This functionalism assumes a mutual incomprehensibility of arenas' languages, ignoring the translation possible on the basis of everyday or "natural" language. Jürgen Habermas mentions these weaknesses of systems theory in *Between Facts and Norms* (Cambridge, MA: MIT Press, 1996).

17. Beth Roy, *Some Trouble with Cows* (Berkeley and Los Angeles: University of California Press, 1996), 28.

18. Paul Willis, *Learning to Labor* (New York: Columbia University Press, 1981).

19. Jeffrey Pressman and Aaron Wildavsky, *Implementation* (Berkeley and Los Angeles: University of California Press, 1973).

20. On the strategic uses of bankruptcy, see Kevin Delaney, *Strategic Bankruptcy* (Berkeley and Los Angeles: University of California Press, 1992).

21. Both classroom examples come from Daniel McFarland, "Resistance as a Social Drama: A Study of Change-Oriented Encounters," *American Journal of Sociology* 109 (2004): 1249–1318.

22. See Herbert Kitschelt, "Political Opportunity Structures and Political Protest," *British Journal of Political Science* 16 (1986): 57–85. Kitschelt's emphasis is on fixed national political structures, which predetermine what strategies can be used. He ignores the possibility of change in those systems as well as the strategic maneuvering within these horizons of opportunity.

23. Mary Bernstein and James Jasper, "Interests and Credibility: Whistleblowers in Technological Conflicts," *Social Science Information* 35 (1996): 565–89.

24. Cynthia Gordon and James Jasper, "Overcoming the 'NIMBY' Label: Rhetorical and Organizational Links for Local Protestors," *Research in Social Movements, Conflicts and Change* 19 (1996): 153–75.

25. Diane Vaughan, *Uncoupling* (Oxford: Oxford University Press, 1986), 120.

26. Bourdieu makes this point about science and politics, remarking that scientists who are "least eminent on scientific criteria tend to appeal to external powers to enhance their strength, and even sometimes to triumph in their scientific struggles" (*Science of Science and Reflexivity* [Chicago: University of Chicago Press, 2004], 58).

27. James Jasper, *The Art of Moral Protest* (Chicago: University of Chicago Press, 1997), chap. 11.

28. Julia Wrigley, *Other People's Children* (New York: Basic Books, 1995).

29. Michael Lipsky, *Street-Level Bureaucracy* (New York: Russell Sage Foundation, 1980), 101.

30. Alissa Stern, "How They Won the Battle and Lost the Rain Forest," *Washington Post*, 1 June 2003.

31. See Gordon and Jasper, "Overcoming the 'NIMBY' Label."

32. Form and content are not necessarily in conflict but merely provide different arenas for struggle. In some cases forms are established to conceal a different content, established in a different arena, as revealed by writers such as Murray Edelman (*The Symbolic Uses of Politics* [Urbana: University of Illinois Press, 1964]) and Theodore Lowi (*The End of Liberalism* [New York: W. W. Norton, 1979]). But a player can also switch to formal arenas in order to redress particular outcomes, in order to change the initial arena's rules, or simply to extend or refine the initial arena. Arthur Stinchcombe, in *When Formality Works* (Chicago: University of Chicago Press, 2001), criticizes the tradition, derived from Weber, that sees form and content as necessarily in conflict.

33. William Miller, *Arguing about Slavery* (New York: Knopf, 1996). In the field of social problems, Malcolm Spector and John Kitsuse showed how procedural issues may become new grievances in *Constructing Social Problems* (New York: Aldine de Gruyter, 1987). See also E. E. Schattschneider, *The Semisovereign People* (New York: Holt, Rinehart, and Winston, 1960).

34. Mitch Duneier, *Sidewalk* (New York: Farrar, Straus and Giroux, 1999), 242.

35. Toshio Yamagichi, "The Provision of a Sanctioning System as a Public Good," *Journal of Personality and Social Psychology* 51 (1986): 110–16, and "Group Size and the Provision of a Sanctioning System in a Social Dilemma," in *Social*

Dilemmas, ed. Wim Liebrand, David Messick, and Henk Wilke (Oxford: Pergamon, 1992).

36. Tachiro Mitani, "The Establishment of Party Cabinets, 1898–1932," in *The Cambridge History of Japan*, vol. 6, ed. Peter Duus (Cambridge: Cambridge University Press, 1988), 55–59.

37. Robert Jackall, *Moral Mazes* (New York: Oxford University Press, 1988), 25.

38. According to Carol Gilligan, boys devote more time to rule-making than girls do; girls simply move on to other games when disputes arise. See *In a Different Voice* (Cambridge, MA: Harvard University Press, 1982), which cites Janet Lever, "Sex Differences in the Games Children Play," *Social Problems* 23 (1976): 478–87.

39. Carl Schmitt, who later sided with the Nazis, was the great theorist of the exception and the dictator. In *Die Diktatur* (Munich: Duncker and Humblot, 1921), he embraced the Roman ideal of the limited dictator: "Dictatorship hence suspends that by which it is justified, the state of law, and imposes instead the rule of procedure interested exclusively in bringing about a concrete success . . . [a return to] the state of law" (quoted in John McCormick, *Carl Schmitt's Critique of Liberalism* [Cambridge: Cambridge University Press, 1997], 124). Within a year, Schmitt took a more expansive (and dangerous) view of the dictator as a charismatic leader who brought about change rather than restoration. See also George Schwab, *The Challenge of the Exception* (New York: Greenwood, 1989).

40. "When an antisystemic movement organizes to overthrow or replace existing authorities in a state," observes Immanuel Wallerstein, "it provides itself with a very strong political weapon designed to change the world in specific ways. But, by so organizing, it simultaneously integrates itself and its militants into the very system it is opposing" ("The National and the Universal," in *Culture, Globalization and the World-System*, ed. Anthony King [Minneapolis: University of Minnesota Press, 1997], 100).

41. James Jasper, *Nuclear Politics* (Princeton, NJ: Princeton University Press, 1990). On the French case, see my "Rational Reconstructions of Energy Choices in France," in *Organizations, Uncertainties, and Risk*, ed. James Short Jr. and Lee Clarke (Boulder, CO: Westview, 1992).

42. Mitchel Abolafia, *Making Markets* (Cambridge, MA: Harvard University Press, 1996), 41. I challenge his tendency to view strategic action intended to protect arenas as a form of structure, and he and Frank Dobbin respond, in "Structure and Strategy on the Exchanges: A Critique and Conversation about *Making Markets*," *Sociological Forum* 20 (2005): 473–86.

43. Fredrik Barth, *Process and Form in Social Life* (London: Routledge and Kegan Paul, 1981), 89.

44. Anthony Giddens, *The Constitution of Society* (Berkeley and Los Angeles: University of California Press, 1984), 315.

45. Ibid., 318.

46. Ibid., 374.

47. Theda Skocpol, *Protecting Soldiers and Mothers* (Cambridge, MA: Harvard University Press, 1992), 59.

48. For example see John Witte, *Democracy, Authority, and Alienation in Work* (Chicago: University of Chicago Press, 1980).

49. "Non-choices" can be due to the intervention of powerful players or to hidden structural forces that keep certain issues *off* the table. For a discussion of the former, see Peter Bachrach and Morton Baratz, *Power and Poverty* (Oxford: Oxford University Press, 1970); for the latter, see Steven Lukes, *Power* (London: Macmillan, 1974). Most of this work shares the problem of all research on "false consciousness": the more successful the powerful players, the less evidence there is of their activity. The only way we can show that issues are being suppressed is to find times when they were openly discussed, only to be suppressed later. The debate may occur behind closed doors rather than in public, but *someone* is usually thinking about the potential choices. By identifying general choices available to players, whether they explicitly face them or not, my approach should actually allow us to uncover the suppression more clearly. Why was a certain dilemma never discussed? Did no one think of it, due to cultural or psychological reasons? Or did powerful players within the team make the decision for everyone else? Did one team manage actively to set the agenda for others?

50. Nitsan Chorev, "Trading in the State: U.S. International Trade Policy and the Rise of Globalization," PhD diss., Dept. of Sociology, New York University, 2003. Chorev also shows how trade policy was moved from Congress to the president in 1974, as a way of bypassing the influence of protectionist industries in Congress. What she fails to show is how Congress allowed this to happen.

51. Randy Shaw, *The Activist's Handbook* (Berkeley and Los Angeles: University of California Press, 1996), 56–57.

52. Robert Freeland, *The Struggle for Control of the Modern Corporation* (Cambridge: Cambridge University Press, 2001), 32.

53. "U.S. Joins Iraqis to Seek U.N. Role in Interim Rule," *New York Times*, 16 January 2004.

54. Karen Midelfart-Knarvik and Henry Overman express skepticism about EU regional aid in "Delocation and European Integration—Is Structural Spending Justified?" *Economic Policy* 35 (2002): 322–59.

55. Murray Edelman, in *The Symbolic Uses of Politics*, observes that "organized" interests usually receive material resources from government policies, while the broader population must make do with symbolic reassurances. All strategic engagements have their symbolic side, which is not, as Edelman implies, simply fraudulent.

CONCLUSION → THINKING THROUGH DILEMMAS

1. Edward Luttwak mystifies this somewhat in referring to "paradoxical action," but provides many useful examples, in *Strategy* (Cambridge, MA: Harvard University Press, 2002).

2. For a useful introduction to mechanism theory, see Peter Hedström and Richard Swedberg, eds., *Social Mechanisms* (Cambridge: Cambridge University Press, 1998).

3. I have tried to describe the impact of inadequate microfoundations in the study of social movements in the forthcoming *Passion and Purpose*.

4. I have addressed one of these fields in "A Strategic Approach to Collective Action: Looking for Agency in Social-Movement Choices," *Mobilization* 9 (2004): 1–16.

5. There are more regularities: in each thirty-six-year cycle, the minority party won two of nine presidential elections; four years before the realignment, an election is a harbinger of it. The 1968 election is a problem for the theory, in that Democrats retained control of Congress and most state capitals. On the other hand, the defection of many white southerners and urban Democrats that year would eventually prove crucial to an emerging conservative coalition, as Kevin Phillips saw immediately (see *The Emerging Republican Majority* [New Rochelle, NY: Arlington House, 1969]). Perhaps the realignment was simply delayed, although Walter Dean Burnham plausibly argued that party alignments would be weaker in the future because voters' party identification had relaxed; see *Critical Elections and the Mainsprings of American Politics* (New York: W. W. Norton, 1971).

6. David Mayhew, *Electoral Realignments* (New Haven, CT: Yale University Press, 2002), 148, 150. Along with this strategic interpretation, he also provides a historical interpretation relating elections to bellicosity, race, and economic growth—but these also fit neatly into a strategic approach to parties and elections.

7. Lawrence Cohen and Marcus Felson, "Social Change and Crime Rate Trends: A Routine Activity Approach," *American Sociological Review* 44 (1979): 588–608.

8. Ronald Clarke and Derek Cornish, "Modeling Offenders' Decisions: A Framework for Research and Policy," in *Crime and Justice*, vol. 6, ed. Michael Tonry and Norval Morris (Chicago: University of Chicago Press, 1985).

9. Neil Fligstein, *The Architecture of Markets* (Princeton, NJ: Princeton University Press, 2001).

10. Bruce Link and Jo Phelan, "McKeown and the Idea that Social Conditions Are Fundamental Causes of Disease," *American Journal of Public Health* 92 (2002): 730; and "Social Conditions as Fundamental Causes of Disease," *Journal of Health and Social Behavior* special issue (1995): 80–94; and "Understanding

Sociodemographic Differences in Health," *American Journal of Public Health* 86 (1996): 471–73.

11. Christopher Jencks et al., *Inequality* (New York: Basic Books, 1972); and Christopher Jencks, *Who Gets Ahead?* (New York: Basic Books, 1979).

12. Daniel Hamermesh and Jeff Biddle found that better-looking men made 14 percent more than the average: see "Beauty and the Labor Market," *American Economic Review* 84 (1994): 1174–94.

13. Samuel Bowles, Herbert Gintis, and Melissa Osborne take their fellow economists to task for their "presumption that anything rewarded in a competitive labor market must be a skill." What they mean is that it is not necessarily a technical skill that contributes to efficient production—it may well be strategic skill. See "The Determinants of Earnings: A Behavioral Approach," *Journal of Economic Literature* 39 (January 2001): 1142–76.

14. Pierre Bourdieu and Jean-Claude Passeron most famously showed how elites pass on their status to offspring by getting them the right cultural skills in *Les Héritiers* (Paris: Minuit, 1964) and *La Reproduction* (Paris: Minuit, 1970). Ezra Suleiman has described how French economic elites watch for new opportunities in *Elites in French Society* (Princeton, NJ: Princeton University Press, 1978).

15. See Carol Gilligan, *In a Different Voice* (Cambridge, MA: Harvard University Press, 1982).

16. Behavioral economists have observed gender and race effects in their experiments. For example, women punish unfairness more than men; see Catherine Eckel and Philip Grossman, "The Relative Price of Fairness: Gender Differences in a Punishment Game," *Journal of Economic Behavior and Organization* 30 (1996): 143–58. The same authors found that in ultimatum games, black students made more generous offers and rejected unfair ones more often: "Chivalry and Solidarity in Ultimatum Games," *Economic Inquiry* 39 (2001): 171–88.

17. Yale Ferguson and Richard Mansbach, "Between Celebration and Despair: Constructive Suggestions for Future International Theory," *International Studies Quarterly* 35 (1991): 363–86.

APPENDIX → RULES OF STRATEGIC ACTION

1. Saul Alinsky, *Rules for Radicals* (New York: Random House, 1971), 127–130.
2. B. H. Liddell Hart, *Strategy* (New York: Praeger, 1967), 348–49.
3. Edgar Snow, *Red Star over China*, rev. ed. (New York: Grove Press, 1968), 275–76.
4. J. Edward Russo and Paul J. H. Schoemaker, *Decision Traps* (New York: Simon and Schuster, 1989), xvi–xvii.

INDEX

elites, 164, 165, 179, 214n14

Elster, Jon, 64, 74, 81, 110, 192n22, 196n16, 197n39

emotions: bonds of obligation created by, 104; calculation of outcomes overpowered by, 20; information filtered by, 112–13, 138; initiating interaction and, 23; mastery of, 99, 100; moral, 187n7; moral shocks arousing, 45, 48; negative, 38; as pervasive in strategic action, 3, 12; and sense of urgency, 37; threats of harm arousing, 43; "venting," 124, 170; victims of attack arousing, 24. *See also* affection; fear

empathy, 98, 103–4

ends. *See* means and ends

energy, 111

engagement, as element of charm, 100

Engagement Dilemma, 26–27; and blackmailers' dilemma, 54; and Bystander Dilemma, 123, 174; and charm, 101, 102; for new arenas, 155, 158; and resources, 93, 94; in response to others' actions, 52; risk involved in, 173; weaker nation initiating war, 151–52

engagements: accidental, 31–32; decisive, 146–49. *See also* Engagement Dilemma

Engels, Friedrich, 128–29

enmity, common, 38

entrances and exits: for arenas, 158–59; timely, 21, 158

entry costs, 20

envy, 64

Erikson, Erik, 110

escalation: social and psychological, 126; of threats, 39

European Union, 169–70

Evens, T. M. S., 206n18

executives: actions presented as response to natural forces, 49; bankruptcy as new arena for, 155; defections by, 193n42; labor accused of stirring up conflict by, 21; as moving on before their mistakes surface, 51; nothing ventured, nothing lost for, 106; organizational changes by new CEOs, 162; popular works on strategy for, 183–84; strategic initiative launched by, 16; success versus survival for, 61

exits. *See* entrances and exits

experts, 51, 97, 98, 125, 145, 200n20

Extension Dilemma, 127–28, 130, 136, 155, 157, 170, 173, 174

faculty, competition over, 17–18

fads, 171

failure, 47

Fallows, James, 81

false arenas, 168–70

False Arenas, Dilemma of, 169–70, 173

false consciousness, 212n49

fame, 62

family feuds, 36, 127

fatalism, 108, 117

fateful moments, 19, 48

fatigue, 105, 111

fear: as driving force in human action, 37; in Naughty or Nice? dilemma, 106–7; as paralyzing, 43–44

Ferguson, Yale, 180

feudalism, 129

field, as metaphor, 142, 207n1

fighting words, 41

fight or flight response, 43

filibusters, 20

Fine, Gary Alan, 206n30

first impressions, 22

of rules, 163; sending messages
requiring further, 132–33
inventors, 16
Iraq: Saddam Hussein, 25, 95, 152;
invasion of, 25, 30, 77, 78, 122, 136,
169
"iron triangle" pattern, 116
Israel, 43

Jackall, Robert, 99, 162
Jackson, Andrew, 31
Jackson, Jesse, 67
Janus Dilemma, 118, 124–25, 128, 129,
173, 204n8
Japan: attacking stronger nations,
151; daimyos, 79; diplomatic code
broken, 146, 208n5; Go-Sanjō,
114–15; Meiji restoration, 162;
samurai, 129; World War II, 112,
148–49, 151
Jencks, Christopher, 179
Jepperson, Ronald, 208n2
Jervis, Robert, 138, 194n52
jihad, 102
Job, 48
Johnson, Dominic, 203n51
Julius Caesar, 111, 116

Katz, Jack, 46
Keegan, John, 202n42
Kelman, Steven, 89, 209n15
Kennedy, John, 134
Kennedy, Robert, 39
Kennedy, Ted, 129
Keohane, Robert, 203n51
Kerry, John, 116, 148, 149
Khrushchev, Nikita, 134
Killian, Lewis, 186n6
King, Martin Luther, Jr., 88, 98, 104
Kitschelt, Herbert, 210n22
Kitsuse, John, 210n33

Klandermans, Bert, 204n1
Klein, Arthur, 196n19
Klein, Bradley, 206n27
knights, medieval, 40–41
knowledge: curiosity contrasted with,
85; formalizing know-how, 113; as
goal, 63, 69; transferability of, 90
Kohut, Heinz, 68
Korean War, 89, 151
Kublai Khan, 83–84
Kuwait, 25

labor movement: agency sought by,
44; blacks kept out of unions,
165; economic threats as cause of
labor insurgency, 49; executives
accuse of stirring up conflict, 21;
and Extension Dilemma, 128–29;
grievance procedures, 140–41, 160;
in New Deal, 136; strikes as wars of
attrition, 96
Laitin, David, 192n24
law: costs of entry to practice, 20;
specialized languages in, 152–53
least interest, principle of, 117
Liddell Hart, H., 182
Lifton, Robert J., 196n28
Lindblom, Charles, 186n6
Link, Bruce, 178
Lipsky, Michael, 159
Lloyd George, David, 41
lobbyists, 11, 130, 136
Loewenstein, George, 191n6
love: bonds of obligation created by,
104; in Naughty or Nice? dilemma,
106–7; and sensual pleasure, 66–67.
See also loved ones
Love Canal, 34–35
loved ones: adversaries using, 79–80;
providing for, as goal, 58; threats to,
43

initiating interaction affecting, 23; spillover effect on, 152

moral principles, appeals to, 10–11

moral shocks, 45–48, 58

motivation: backfiring, 104; language of, 84–85; power as, 81

mugging, 15, 22, 33, 44

multiple players, 121–25

Myers, Marc, 202n44

Nader, Ralph, 80

Napoleon, 30, 89, 202n38, 208n6

national pride, 41, 63

nature, 48, 49, 51

Naughty or Nice? dilemma, 106–7, 132, 163, 173

needs: deprivation of, 43; hierarchy of, 59–60

negative, power of the, 38–39

New Deal, 136

Nietzsche, Friedrich, 89

9/11, 23, 71, 78

Niskanen, William, 194n1

Nixon, Richard, 103, 115, 177

non-choices, 175, 212n49

nonhuman species, interaction with, 7

norms of behavior, 144

"not in my backyard" (NIMBY) groups, 157

nuclear energy, 164. *See also* antinuclear protestors

objectives, 69–73. *See also* goals

obligation, bonds of, 104

odds, 109

Odin and Thor, 89

Odysseus and Achilles, 89, 99

Offe, Claus, 167

offense: attempting to define actions as, 25; balance of power with defense as shifting, 28; and defense as interrelated, 30–31; military theorists flip-flopping between defense and, 27; personal traits associated with, 30; sense of agency strengthened by, 23, 32–33

onion model, 60, 76

ontological security, 36

organizational capacities, 113–15

Osborne, Melissa, 214n13

Ostrower, Francie, 205n8

Othello (Shakespeare), 63, 195n12

outsiders: arenas distinguishing between insiders and, 160; in audiences, 124–25; external threats heightening boundaries between insiders and, 39; and Janus Dilemma, 125; new arenas created by, 165–66; and segregating audiences, 131

overconfidence: in defenses, 28–29; as leading to reckless actions, 111–12, 203n51; as risk of initiating interaction, 26

pain, 43, 65

Palestinians, 43, 192n24

Paradox of Education dilemma, 76, 173

Paranoid Dilemma, 103

paranoids, 52, 103, 162

parenting styles, 130

Parks, Rosa, 87, 88

Parsons, Talcott, 21, 86, 199n16, 200n19

Passeron, Jean-Claude, 214n14

passive-aggressive individuals, 102

payment: as means of action, 10, 11, 88, 186n6; resources involved in, 88, 91

peacekeeping forces, 123

Pearl Harbor, 95, 146

pecking orders, 145

P'eng The-huai, 182–83

public players: advantages and disadvantages of initiating amplified by, 27; celebrities as allies for, 129; defined, 12; private players becoming, 121, 156; size of bystander audience of, 135; threat perceptions manipulated by, 38

public relations, 107–8

race, strategic projects reproducing hierarchies of, 179. *See also* African Americans

Radicalism Dilemma, 153–54

Rainforest Action Network, 159

ransom, 53, 79, 96

rational-choice models: and act/consequences problems, 81, 82; calculating image of humans in, 3–4; in criminology, 177–78; and distorting effects of leaders' rhetoric, 202n49; and emotions, 3, 193n34; as inadequate microfoundation for understanding politics, 176; as never determinate, xiv

rationality: calculating definition of, 20; as power of the weak, 89; utility maximization for defining, 59. *See also* rational-choice models

rationalizations, 75, 164

Reagan, Ronald, 132

real estate, 17, 122

realist view of international relations, 136, 138, 180, 207n32, 209n11

reflexivity, 68

religious groups: and Extension Dilemma, 128; and Janus Dilemma, 124–25, 204n6

reputation, 105–8; of arenas, 152; as audience-dependent, 107; bullies seeking, 145; collective, 41;

confidence and, 108; engagement putting on the line, 26–27; failure to honor commitments affecting, 54; fragility of, 106; as goal, 62, 63–65; as goal for compound players, 61; good versus bad, 106; insult to, 40–43; long-term gain maximized by good, 201n30; as result of strategic actions, 105–6; as variable, 65

resistance, 5, 154

resourcefulness, 98

resources, 91–98; arenas and strategies restricted by, 93, 160; arenas as open-ended bundles of rules and, 141; coercion and payment involving, 88; cultural meanings in use of, 93; decreasing those of your opponent, 95–96; different arenas requiring different, 144–45; distribution changing during course of action, 90; existing prior versus acquired during action, 90; gathering right, 95; general versus specific, 90; humans as, 92; intelligence compared with, 89–91; intelligence required for inventing new, 93; as interaction specific, 94; opponents attempt to exploit lacks in, 90–91; of organizations, 113; physical traits of players as, 94; potential versus actual use of, 94; as property, 94; and rules, 94; for show, 93; size of, 94; as symbols, 93; in wars of attrition, 96

respect, 63, 104

responsibility, 50–51

revelations, 41

revenge: as goal, 58; for humiliation, 43, 192n24; threats and, 54

Revenge Dilemma, 52–53